Practical Handbooks in Archaeology No 14

ROMANO-BRITISH GLASS VESSELS: A HANDBOOK

Jennifer Price and Sally Cottam

Drawings by Yvonne Beadnell

1998
Council for British Archaeology

Copyright © 1998 Authors
and Council for British Archaeology

Published 1998 by the Council for British Archaeology
Bowes Morrell House, 111 Walmgate, York YO1 9WA

British Library Cataloguing in Publication Data

A catalogue card for this book is available from the British Library.

ISBN 1 872414 96 6

Typeset by Archetype Information Technology Ltd
Printing by Pennine Printing Services Ltd

Front cover: Dark blue pillar-moulded bowl with spirals, and yellow/brown conical jug with vertical ribs, from Flavian cremation burial at Radnage. Photo: Michael Holford Photographs.

Back cover: Biconical jug, cylindrical bottle, mould-blown cylindrical bottle with corrugated body and hemispherical cup from Butt Road cemetery, Colchester. Photo: University of Leeds.

Contents

Preface

This handbook has been written as an introductory guide to the glass vessel forms of Roman Britain. The major types which an archaeologist might expect to encounter have been included, as well as some of the more unusual forms. The material has been collected from published and unpublished excavation reports, and from the archive notes of the Romano-British Glass Project. The need for a handbook has long been recognised by people working in Roman material culture, as much of the available information on Romano-British glass is restricted to site-specific reports. Continental publications, in particular *Roman Glass from Dated Finds* (Isings 1957), are often consulted for the identification of glass found in this country, but these books do not provide sufficient up-to-date information on the glass of Roman Britain and it has become clear that patterns of use and deposition in Britain do not always correspond with those in other Roman provinces in western Europe.

We hope that this handbook will be used as a first point of reference for those wishing to become more familiar with Romano-British glass vessels. Roman window glass has not been discussed, nor does the book contain information on beads, bangles or other glass objects. It is hoped that these may be considered in a future publication.

Acknowledgements

This handbook could not have been produced without the help of many people and organisations and we are very grateful to all of them. The work is largely based on the glass reports from excavated sites in England, prepared for publication by the Romano-British Glass Project since 1983, together with other published and unpublished material from archaeological sites in Britain. None of this would have been possible without the support of English Heritage who funded the work of the Romano-British Glass Project from 1983 until 1994 and who have also funded the production of the handbook.

We particularly wish to acknowledge the contribution made by Hilary Cool, who worked with Jennifer Price when the Romano-British Glass Project was based in the University of Leeds (1983–1990). Material from many of the unpublished reports produced during this time has been incorporated throughout the handbook. In addition, Lindsay Allason-Jones (University of Newcastle-on-Tyne), Denise Allen (Andover), the late George Boon (National Museum of Wales, Cardiff), Brenda Compton (Bignor), Hilary Cool (Nottingham), Ian Freestone (British Museum), Pan Garrard (Canterbury Archaeological Unit), Chris Going (Cambridge), Yael Gorin-Rosen (Department of Antiquities, Israel), Vivienne Holbrook (Verulamium Museum), Christine Howard-Davis (Lancaster Archaeological Unit), Dominic Ingemark (University of Lund), Christine Jones (then in Museum of London), Georgina Plowright (Corbridge Museum), Eddie Price (Frocester Court, Gloucestershire), John Shepherd (Museum of London), Mark Taylor and David Hill (Andover) and Rachel Tyson (Calne, Wiltshire) have provided unpublished information. Justine Bayley (Ancient Monuments Laboratory, English Heritage), Susan Hardman (University of York), Catherine Johns (Department of Prehistoric and Romano-British Antiquities, British Museum) and Sally Worrell (Department of Archaeology, University of Durham) have read drafts of the book and have given advice and constructive comments, and Pam Irving and Jan Summerfield have provided support in their role as the English Heritage monitors of the Romano-British Glass Project and of the handbook. All the drawings and the map are by Yvonne Beadnell.

Jennifer Price and Sally Cottam
Department of Archaeology, University of Durham
November 1997 (References revised August 1998)

PART 1: ROMAN GLASS:
ARCHAEOLOGY AND TECHNOLOGY

How to use this handbook

Part 1 of the handbook serves as a general introduction to Romano-British glass, briefly discussing aspects of supply, deposition and manufacture and highlighting some of the most important published groups of excavated glass. It covers topics common to all vessels, and provides more detailed descriptions of types of rims, handles, bases and styles of decoration than is possible in Part 2.

Part 2 of the handbook comprises individual descriptions of the common Romano-British vessel forms. Each is illustrated by one or more complete or nearly complete profiles, and as well as a guide to the form of the vessel, there is information on the date, a discussion of the variants, a selection of similar finds from Britain and references for further research. It is not the purpose of the handbook to discuss the vessels in detail, and the coverage of forms is not intended to be comprehensive. New forms will be identified and variations within some forms will require further subdivisions in the future. The date ranges suggested for each type are general, and are also under continuous review. Many forms are very common, so to keep the book concise, only a selection of examples is included.

Part 2 is principally a typological guide, and identification of individual vessels often relies on comparison with the illustrated forms. Nevertheless, since most of the vessels from Romano-British sites are represented by small single fragments, it is important to take account of other features such as colour, the quality, thickness and feel of the glass, and the surface weathering, as sources of additional clues to identification.

As with all categories of artefact, familiarity with Roman glass can best be achieved by handling large quantities of material. No book can be a substitute for direct contact with glass itself, but the references and illustrations given here will allow those investigating their own assemblages to get some idea of the range and date of their material, and will provide a starting point for research for those with a more general interest in the subject.

Recognising Roman fragments

A site assemblage usually includes glass fragments from many periods of activity, possibly ranging from Roman times to last week's picnic. In Britain, more glass from the first four centuries AD survives in the archaeological record than from any other period until the 17th century. Much smaller quantities of glass of Anglo-Saxon and medieval date are known.

Roman glass vessels are found on all types of settlements, from the most prosperous towns and villas to small rural farms and native settlements, and from legionary fortresses to signal stations. They were also deposited in burials. The glass generally survives in very good condition in archaeological deposits, which sometimes leads to mis-identification between Roman and modern glass in the preliminary sorting of an assemblage. This is because Roman glass was produced from a set of basic ingredients similar to those used for many modern vessels and windows.

A little surface weathering is visible on most Roman fragments. This usually consists of a slight cloudiness on the surfaces of the vessel. A greater degree of weathering occurs when the surfaces acquire an iridescent deposit or sheen, which sometimes comes away in flaking layers. Little can be done to reverse this condition, but in Britain it is only rarely severe enough to damage the vessel. At worst, strain cracks appear in the vessel wall, which can make the vessel crumble into tiny chips. This condition occurs most frequently on colourless vessels, and may be encouraged by the addition of decolorising agents to the original glass mixture.

In Britain, Roman glass is readily distinguished from medieval glass. From the 9th–10th centuries onwards, the alkali used in most vessel and window glass in north west Europe was potash rather than soda, although a few high quality vessels were made in soda glass or in high-lead glass. Potash glass suffers badly in the ground and generally has pitted, devitrified surfaces with opaque weathering deposits. It is often only preserved in small fragments and quite frequently disintegrates entirely into grainy chips or brown powder.

Although most modern glass is very distinctive, particularly when features such as screw tops, mould-seams or lettering are preserved, some fragments can be quite deceptive. Thin modern window glass fragments can sometimes be mistaken for Roman bottle or window glass, and pieces of dark yellow/green or yellow/brown wine and beer bottles are occasionally quite similar to the thicker walled jugs of the later 1st–mid 2nd centuries.

Modern window glass is usually absolutely flat. The most recent panes are entirely colourless and very distinct from Roman window glass, but 17th–19th century window fragments are often thin and have a greenish or bluish tinge. These can be distinguished from Roman bottles or late Roman window glass by their flatness, the near absence of bubbles, and the very smooth texture of both surfaces.

Glass supply

A little evidence for glass vessels in Britain before the conquest of AD 43 has been found in settlement and burial sites in the south and east such as Camulodunum, Puckeridge/Skeleton Green, Hertford Heath and elsewhere (Price 1996a). These vessels came from the Mediterranean world, probably from Syria/Palestine or from Italy. In the second and third quarters of the 1st century AD, a large number of the high quality tablewares were probably imported into Britain from Italy and southern Gaul, while from the later 1st century onwards, the majority of the imported vessels came from the Rhineland and elsewhere in the north-western provinces. Certain types of vessels, particularly those with 'snake thread' and wheel-cut figured decoration are found in large numbers in burials in Bonn, Cologne, Strasbourg, Trier and other Rhineland sites. They are assumed to have been produced in the region, but the precise origin of most vessels is very hard to determine.

Glass vessels were also produced in Britain. Evidence for production from the second half of the 1st century onwards has come from London (Shepherd and Heyworth 1991, and information from John Shepherd). Furnaces, crucibles and glass waste have been found at several sites, but tools for glass working have not yet been recognised from Britain. The types of vessels produced in Romano-British workshops have rarely been recognised, although glass waste found at Mancetter in Warwickshire suggested that jars with collar rims were being made. For a review of evidence for Roman glass production in Britain, see Price and Cool 1991. Broken vessel glass was frequently recycled in the Roman world. Large quantities of broken vessels found at furnace sites in Britain and elsewhere are often interpreted as cullet gathered for remelting. Pits filled with broken vessel glass and glass waste at Guildhall Yard in London (information from John Shepherd) and in the *canabae legionis* at Nijmegen (Isings 1980) indicate that the use of cullet played an important part in glass production in the north-western provinces.

The deposition of glass

Numerous reports have been published on glass from Romano-British settlements and burials, particularly in the last twenty years. The references given for each of the forms in Part 2 of this handbook are the best way of finding further information on individual vessel types, but the following list is a guide to some useful publications for general reading.

SITE	REFERENCE	SUBJECT
Brougham, Cumbria	Cool 1990	Cups from 3rd century cremation cemetery; discussion of drinking cups.
Burgh Castle, Norfolk	Harden 1983	Pit deposit in Saxon Shore fort, containing late 4th–early 5th century vessels.
Caerleon, Gwent	Allen 1986	Glass from legionary bath-house, closely dated late 1st–3rd century deposits.
Caister-on-Sea, Norfolk	Price and Cool 1993	Large assemblage, predominantly 3rd–4th century military occupation.
Canterbury, Marlowe Car Park and other sites, Kent	Shepherd 1995, Charlesworth and Price 1987	Large assemblages from urban occupation, 1st–early 5th century vessels.
Carlisle, Blackfriars St and Castle St, Cumbria	Price 1990a, Cool and Price 1991	Glass from military and urban occupation; predominantly 1st–3rd century, few 4th century vessels.
Colchester, Essex	Cool and Price 1995	Glass from various military and urban contexts, including late Roman cemetery at Butt Road. Wide range of 1st–late 4th century forms.
Colchester, Sheepen, Essex	Harden 1947, Charlesworth 1985a	Mid 1st century glass at Camulodunum.
Dorchester, Greyhound Yard, Dorset	Cool and Price 1993	Glass from 1st–late 4th century urban occupation; emphasis on late Roman period.
Exeter, Devon	Charlesworth 1979a, Allen 1991	Glass from military and urban occupation; emphasis on 1st–2nd century.
Fishbourne palace, West Sussex	Harden and Price 1971, Price and Cottam 1996a	Glass from 1st–3rd century occupation of prestigious rural site; many high quality 1st–2nd century vessels.
Frocester Court villa, Gloucestershire	Price 1979	Glass from 1st–late 4th century occupation of rural site; emphasis on late Roman period.

SITE	REFERENCE	SUBJECT
Gloucester, Kingsholm	Price and Cool 1985	Glass from Neronian military contexts.
Harlow, Felmongers, Essex	Price 1987a	Tablewares and containers in pit deposit dated c AD 160–170.
London, 15–23 Southwark St and Leadenhall Court	Shepherd 1995b, 1996	Glass from urban occupation; large assemblages, emphasis on 1st–2nd centuries, some late Roman material.
Lullingstone villa, Kent	Cool and Price 1987a	Glass from 1st–4th century occupation of rural site, information on 4th century wheel-cut figured bowls.
Towcester, Park St and Alchester Road, Northants	Price 1980a, Price and Cool 1983	Glass from small town; tablewares and containers in pit deposit dated c AD 155–65, and predominantly 4th century assemblage.
Usk, Gwent	Price 1995a	Large assemblage from Neronian–early Flavian legionary fortress.
Verulamium (St Albans), Herts	Charlesworth 1972, 1984a	Glass from 1st–late 4th century urban occupation; some closely dated deposits.
Winchester, Lankhills, Hants	Harden 1979a	Glass from burials in closely dated 4th century cemetery.
York – general, Blake Street, Minster	Harden 1962, Cool 1995a, Price 1995b	Overview of glass in Roman city, including vessels from cemeteries; 1st–late 4th century occupation in legionary fortress.

Occupation sites

In most contexts it is unusual to find more than a few fragments of any individual glass vessel, and often a single fragment may be all that has survived. Even when more than one fragment can be assumed to come from the same vessel, so much is usually missing that the chances of them joining are low.

Incomplete excavation may be one reason why so few glass vessels from occupation sites can be reconstructed, but the active collection of broken fragments for recycling is often likely to be an additional factor. If systematic collection took place on a site, only the smallest pieces would be likely to escape the attention of the collectors. Systems of collection may often have been more thorough in towns than at rural sites, and the collection and recycling of Roman glass is likely to have continued during the Anglo-Saxon and early medieval periods in some towns. This may explain why glass fragments are often noticeably smaller on urban sites where intense occupation continued throughout and beyond the Roman period, such as Lincoln, London, Winchester and York, than they are on sites which were abandoned after the Roman period. Excavations at the fort at Ribchester in Lancashire, for example, have produced a large quantity of 1st century bottles in substantial fragments, suggesting that little or no collection of fragments for cullet had taken place either during the life of the settlement, or at a later time.

However, large fragments and reconstructable vessels tend to survive in some contexts on occupation sites, such as ditches, drains, pits and wells. The pits already mentioned containing glass collected for remelting (cullet) include large pieces, and other deposits sometimes have reconstructable glass vessels. These vessels may have been deposited without recycling for several reasons. Accidental loss may account for some of the finds in drains and wells, and on some occasions, as when a military site was vacated and demolished or a building was emptied, clearing the site may have been a more urgent priority. Moreover, if there was no glassworking in the vicinity, a system of collection for recycling may not have been organised.

A number of pits and other closed deposits with glass vessels in the list above also contained groups of items in other materials. These often provide useful information about dating because of associated pottery or coins, and can sometimes help to identify the functions and social context of the material.

Burials

Complete glass vessels were placed in some burials in Roman Britain. Some large jars were probably made specifically to contain cremations (Figures 59–60). In the 1st and 2nd centuries large glass storage vessels such as wide-necked cylindrical, square and hexagonal bottles (Figures 88–90) and other large jars were sometimes reused as containers for ashes. Small unguent bottles were placed in both cremation and inhumation burials in the 1st–3rd centuries (Figures 75, 77, 80). These vessels contained scented oils, pastes and powders which played a part in the ritual of burial, either accompanying the deceased as a gift into the afterlife or being sprinkled onto the corpse. In cremations, these vessels have sometimes been distorted by the heat of the fire and a few are entirely melted.

Other forms of glass vessels accompanied burials in Britain throughout the Roman period. Cups, bowls, jugs, flasks and jars are all known in funerary contexts. These rarely occur in large numbers in any burial, although ten or more have sometimes been recorded. Comparison of burial finds from Britain with the large numbers of vessels from cemeteries elsewhere in the north-western provinces, for example at Bonn, Cologne, Strasbourg and Trier, reveals a number of differences in the types of vessels deposited, particularly in the later Roman period. For example, 2nd–3rd century vessels decorated with serpentiform scored trails ('snake-thread' – Figure 4.10) and 4th century vessels with figured cutting, such as hemispherical and segmental bowls and conical beakers (Figures 6.8–10, 49, 51a), have not been noted in burials in Britain, although their presence as fragments on occupation sites indicates that they were in quite widespread use.

Residuality

Glass fragments often occur in residual contexts, particularly on urban sites where post-Roman phases of occupation have mixed material of different periods. In cities such as Lincoln, London, Winchester and York, Roman glass is frequently found in medieval and more recent contexts.

Another factor affecting residuality is the retention of valued vessels as heirlooms, and interesting fragments as keepsakes, which means that they enter the archaeological record long after their normal period of circulation. This practice is often difficult to recognise, though heirlooms are sometimes visible in burials. For example, a claw beaker produced in the late 4th or early 5th century was found in a burial dating from the early 6th century or later at Mucking, Essex (Harden *et al* 1987, 257–9 no 146).

Reuse and wear patterns

Vessel fragments were sometimes retained after the vessel was broken, and many of these were reshaped for secondary use. The broken edges of the fragments were usually carefully chipped and flaked (grozed) to produce more even and less sharp surfaces. Decorative features such as mask medallions from jugs (see Figure 4.4), were often reworked in this way, presumably to serve as keepsakes. On base fragments, particularly tubular pushed-in base rings (see Figure 3.7), the broken edge at the junction with the lower body was grozed, leaving a glass disc which could be used for a variety of purposes, such as a counter or small lid. The broken necks on jugs were occasionally grozed and then smoothed; an example of this practice can be seen on a thin-walled convex jug from Usk (Figure 65). Some flat fragments, particularly from blue/green bottles and window panes, were grozed to form small circular or sub-circular discs, perhaps for use as counters or gaming pieces. Other methods of reshaping bottle fragments have occasionally been recognised. For example, some were flaked to create sharp edges for re-use as blades; these have been discussed in connection with finds at Prestatyn, Clwyd (Allen 1989,120–1).

Patterns of wear can be helpful in deciding which part of the vessel is represented by a particular fragment. Base rings, for example, are often heavily worn, having tiny scratches and rough patches from contact with a hard surface. Rim edges are usually less severely worn, but the inside and outside edges often show tiny scratches. The intensity of wear on a vessel may be an aid to establishing how long it was in use.

Specific patterns of wear can provide information on other aspects of vessel use. Blue/green cylindrical and prismatic bottles, for example, almost always have numerous vertical scratches on the body, which result from lifting these vessels in and out of tightly fitting wood or wicker-work cases. Similarly, horizontal scratches around the neck of bottles and flasks may indicate that a stopper or covering was attached by a cord or thong.

Broken vessel fragments sometimes show patterns of wear arising from secondary use. Wear marks on the inside surface of a base fragment, for example, are likely to fall into this category. Some fragments from thick-walled prismatic bottles have evidence of very heavy wear on the inside and outside surfaces, and on one or more broken edges, suggesting that they may have been used as smoothing tools.

Manufacture

Ingredients

As a manufactured material, glass has three principal constituents: a former, a flux and a stabiliser. In antiquity, silica, in the form of sand, acted as the former. The flux generally used was soda. This ingredient was added to reduce the melting temperature of the batch; it was obtained either from naturally occurring minerals (natron) or from saline plants (salicornia). One source of natron has been located in Egypt, in Wadi Natrun. Calcium, in the form of lime, was used as a stabiliser. This made the glass more durable and less soluble in water. It was readily available in very many parts of the Roman world and may have become part of the glass batch mixed with either the former or the flux, rather than as a separate ingredient.

Coloured and colourless glass were formed by the addition of various ingredients to this basic glass mixture. Different quantities of these colouring agents and the manipulation of furnace temperatures produced a very wide range of translucent and opaque colours (see discussion in Biek and Bayley 1979; Henderson 1985). The addition of copper, for example, produced a range of blues, greens and reds, depending upon furnace conditions. Cobalt produced dark blue, iron was used for yellow/brown colours, manganese for purple and yellow glass, and antimony for opaque white and yellow. Manganese and antimony were also used in the production of colourless vessels. These ingredients have distinctive chemical compositions, but recycling tends to mix the constituents in many different vessels which hampers attempts to identify the sources of the ingredients by scientific analysis.

Production

It has generally been assumed that the ingredients were initially heated together to a temperature of about 600°C to remove the volatile impurities, and that the material produced from this process, frit, was then broken up and heated in a crucible to 1100°C or more to form glass. However, it has recently been shown that glass in the Roman world was often produced from the ingredients as a single process, and that lumps of glass were re-heated to form vessels (information from Ian Freestone and Yael Gorin-Rosen). Another source of glass for forming vessels was cullet, which had already been processed at least once and so was comparatively free of impurities, which reduced the melting temperature. When the glass in the crucible was heated to a very high temperature, the bubbles and impurities rose to the surface and could be skimmed off, leaving a much clearer glass to be worked, whereas heating to a lower temperature produced a glass full of tiny bubbles and impurities.

Comparatively little is known about the form of the furnaces in use in Britain in the Roman period, although the ground plans of excavated examples indicate that they were very small structures (Price and Cool 1991). Fragments of crucibles containing glass have also been recorded. These appear to have been either coarse pottery jars available locally or rectangular tanks formed from tiles.

Processes of manufacture

The three principal processes used to manufacture Roman glass vessels were casting, mould-blowing and free-blowing (see Cummings 1980 and Gudenrath 1991 for modern experiments in these processes, and Price 1976a for general discussion). Blowing was invented, probably in Syria/Palestine around the mid 1st century BC, and by the time of the Roman invasion of Britain in the reign of the emperor Claudius in AD 43, most glass vessels in the Roman world were produced by this method. Cast forms were still produced in the mid–later 1st century. These were in widespread use in the early years of the Roman province, but became rare towards the end of the 1st century and occur only occasionally thereafter (see Figures 7–13). Mould-blown tablewares were also most common in the early years of the Roman province, particularly during the second and third quarters of the 1st century (see Figures 14–17), while mould-blown storage bottles were produced in very large numbers in the 1st and 2nd centuries (see Figures 57, 88–90). Mould-blown tablewares and storage vessels also occur in smaller numbers in the 4th century (see Figures 48c, 50b, 95, 96).

Casting

Casting is a very general term given to methods of vessel manufacture which do not involve blowing at any stage. The exact processes involved in the production of most cast vessels are difficult to establish, as various methods using different tools and temperatures can achieve similar results. Cast vessels are recognised by the fine horizontal polishing marks on the interior and sometimes on the exterior surfaces. Polychrome, strongly coloured monochrome, blue/green and colourless cast vessels are known in Britain.

The most common and distinctive cast vessel found in Roman Britain is the pillar-moulded bowl (Figure 7, Plate 3.1). The name 'pillar-moulded bowl' has been adopted from 19th century glassworking terminology and has no relevance to the process by which these bowls were formed, which itself is still a matter of debate (the argument is outlined in Price 1995a, 140–41). A convincing explanation which compares well with the excavated evidence is that they were produced by impressing a hot glass disc with a slotted tool to form the ribs, before sagging the disc over a convex former (Cummings 1980, 26–29, figs 20–24; Gudenrath 1991, 222, figs 59–64). Exposure to the heat left the exterior surface shiny. When cold, the bowl was finished by grinding and polishing the inside surface which had been in contact with the mould, and the outside surface at the top of the ribs. This produced a distinctive combination of surfaces which allows even very small fragments of these bowls to be recognised. The sagging process was probably also used to produce other forms of hemispherical cast bowls.

Polychrome cast vessels were formed either from lengths of twisted or layered canes or from sections of composite canes. The following types are known from Roman Britain:

Strip and Lace Mosaic Both types are rare in Britain, and are usually found on sites occupied in the early–mid 1st century. Strip mosaic vessels were produced from lengths of multicoloured cane placed side by side and fused together. Occasionally strips of gold leaf were encased in colourless glass and incorporated into strip mosaic designs (Plate 1.1). Lace mosaic bowls were formed from lengths of narrow cane with single or double twisted threads in a colourless ground which were fused together by heat. On both types, a single twisted cane often in blue and opaque white formed the rim of the bowl.

Floral Mosaic Sections of composite canes of two or more colours were fused together before the shape of the vessel was formed. Sometimes these appear as distinct floral patterns (see Figure 9a and Plate 1.2–3), having a coloured centre surrounded by petals in a translucent ground. The most common ground colours for these complex canes are purple, dark blue, dark green and dark yellow/brown with flowers formed in combinations of opaque yellow, opaque pale blue, opaque white and translucent green. Sometimes rods or roundels of a single colour (see Figure 7b and Plate 1.4) are grouped together in a translucent ground. Spiral motifs (see Figure 8a and Plate 1.5) were formed by cutting sections from a cane made of layers of contrasting colours rolled lengthways (Gudenrath 1991, figs 40–45). A few vessels were formed from square-sectioned rods in various colours (Plate 1.6).

Mould-blowing

The inflation of a gather of glass on a blowing iron within a multi-piece mould produced a fixed shape for the vessel and for the decoration on the vessel. Moulds rarely survive but were probably made in stone, metal and clay. They consisted of more than one piece, so they could be removed from around the vessel once it was fully inflated. These moulds were therefore re-usable, and it is often possible to recognise several vessels as products of the same mould or series of moulds (see discussion in Price 1991b, 56–8). The decoration on the inside surface of the mould was reproduced in relief on the exterior of the vessel. The inside surface of a mould-blown vessel follows the contours of the outside surface and this characteristic, as well as the presence of vertical seams where the parts of the mould joined, are the most distinctive features of vessels formed in a multi-piece mould (see Figures 14–17 and Plate 2.3).

Some late Roman vessels were blown into one-piece moulds, so mould-seams are absent. Sometimes the mould-blown decoration on the exterior surface also occurs in relief on the interior surface, rather than following the exterior decoration at an even thickness. This effect appears to have been produced by inflation of the vessel into a plain mould or against a flat surface after it was blown into the decorated mould, thus partly transferring the design back into the interior of the vessel

When a vessel was removed from the mould it was finished in the same manner as a free-blown vessel. The rims of cups and bowls were usually cracked-off after the vessel was annealed, and jugs and flasks with mould-blown bodies often have folded rims, tooled necks and handles.

Mould-blown Bottles
The most common forms to be produced by the mould-blowing technique were the blue/green prismatic storage bottles of the 1st and 2nd centuries (see Figures 89–91 Plate 3.2 and 4–5). Prismatic bottles were blown into multi-piece body moulds with a separate base piece. In the western provinces, stone body and base moulds for bottles have been found at Augst, Switzerland (Rütti 1991, 163–4 abb 103 taf 218.05–06) and Saintes, south-western France (Hochuli-Gysel 1993, 87 figs 5–7), and base moulds are known from Lyons and Köln (Foy and Sennequier 1989, 100–1 nos 30–1) and elsewhere. The design was cut into the base-piece of the mould and appeared in relief on the underside of the vessel. This frequently consisted of concentric circles or some other form of geometrical design, which may have served to strengthen and stabilise the vessel. More rarely lettering and pictorial motifs were employed. A faint impression of

the same or a different base design sometimes appears below the raised moulding, indicating the movement of the mould during the blowing process or a mistake in the original engraving of the mould which was later filled in or smoothed. Light diagonal lines are also sometimes noted on bottle bases. These may be guide lines cut into the mould to allow the base design to be correctly aligned. Cylindrical bottles (see Figure 88) are identical to prismatic bottles in the form of their rims, necks, handles and shoulders, but they have concave bases without designs, which indicates that they were either free-blown or formed in cylindrical body moulds without base pieces.

Optic-Blowing
A mould (or a decorated ring through which the gather was blown) could also be used to transfer ribs or other designs onto the body of a vessel in the initial stage of the blowing process, before further inflation and manipulation took place. This method, often called 'optic-blowing', produced expanded designs in low relief, and was used on jugs, jars, bowls and other vessels at different times within the Roman period (see Figures 55, 72, 95, Back cover).

Free-blowing

Free-blowing was the dominant method of manufacture throughout the Roman period; the majority of the vessels in this handbook were produced in this manner. Hot glass was gathered onto the end of a blowing iron and inflated whilst being shaped by rolling across a flat stone or metal surface (marver block) and by manipulation with metal and wooden tools. Most of the vessel was shaped whilst it was on the blowing iron; bases and handles were applied to the body, and hot decoration, such as trails and blobs, was added at this time. The vessel was removed from the blowing iron by shearing, or by tooling a constriction between the vessel and the blowing iron, and tapping this sharply to separate the vessel from the iron (see Gudenrath 1991, 223–5 figs 65–87 for descriptions and illustrations of these processes). The rim was formed by one of the techniques described below.

Pontil Marks

Blown vessels were often held by a long solid iron rod (pontil rod) attached to the underside of the base, to allow the rim to be worked or a handle to be attached. A distinctive rough scar or circle was left by the pontil rod when it was detached. Sometimes an additional disc of glass was applied to the centre of the base, to reduce the risk of breakage when the pontil was removed (for examples of pontil marks, see Figures 54, 95 Plate 5.2). The presence of a pontil mark on a base fragment provides clues about the way the rim of the vessel was finished, indicating that it was fire-rounded or folded, rather than cracked-off when cold finished. It may also suggest that a handle was attached to the rim.

Terminology

Forms

The forms described in the handbook have been grouped into five sections. These sections are based on the terms commonly adopted by people working with Roman glass, although there is not always full agreement about their use, and some vessels are known by several different names. The first and largest section deals with cups and bowls. This is followed by sections on jars, jugs, flasks, unguent bottles and bath-flasks, and bottles. There are inevitably some overlaps and inconsistencies in these divisions. The numerical ordering of the forms has been avoided, in the knowledge that the book contains only a selection of the vessel types rather than a complete corpus of Roman glass vessel forms in Britain. The sections are therefore loosely defined, being based upon shape, size, perceived function, and the presence of certain characteristic features. Within each section, the vessels are ordered in a loose chronological progression, and the first section (cups and bowls) has three sub-divisions, based on the methods of manufacture.

New Romano-British glass vessel forms are being identified continually and many variations occur within a single basic form. Simple changes in manipulation during manufacture, particularly in the case of free-blown vessels, may alter their shape, size or decoration considerably. Some forms fall into certain clearly defined categories, whereas others are more ambiguous. The decision, for example, as to whether a particular vessel is best described as a cup, bowl or beaker, or as a bottle or flask, is based as much as possible on definable features, but there is often room for a different interpretation.

The question of function is particularly open to debate. Although glass vessels are occasionally shown in Roman wall paintings (Naumann-Steckner 1991), in mosaics and on funerary monuments, no direct evidence of this kind has been recorded in Britain. Furthermore, pictorial representations may not reflect the complete range of uses of vessels of any particular form. Bowls may have been used for drinking, eating or serving foods and liquids, or have functioned as lamps. Flasks and jars could be used for serving at table, or for storage, or for medical or other purposes. It is often assumed that smaller decorated pieces were tablewares, whereas larger, plain items, such as blue/green bottles, were used for general storage purposes, but this may not always have been the case.

Colour

Describing the colours used to make Roman glass is very difficult. Colours can appear as different shades depending on the light in which they are viewed, and they change in intensity with the thickness of the vessel. The terms used to describe colours often mean different things to different people, although those used in this handbook have become current in many glass reports.

Strong colours (Plates 1–2)

In the 1st and early 2nd centuries, some polychrome and monochrome tablewares were produced in a range of bright colours. Strong translucent colours, such as dark blue, yellow/brown (Plate 2.1), yellow/green (Plate 2.2), dark green (Plate 2.3) and purple, and opaque colours, such as pale blue or turquoise, orange/red, green and white are known. Polychrome and strongly coloured translucent and opaque vessels appear most frequently on sites occupied from the Claudian conquest to the early Flavian period. Most colours are unusual after this time, although yellow/brown and yellow/green vessels continued to be produced throughout the later 1st and early 2nd century, and sometimes occur in dated deposits until the third quarter of the 2nd century, as at Alcester, Warwickshire (Price and Cottam 1994), Felmongers, Harlow, Essex (Price 1987a), Stonea, Camrbidgeshire (Price 1996b) and Park Street, Towcester, Northamptonshire (Price 1980a). Very few vessels were made entirely from strongly coloured glass in the 3rd and 4th centuries.

Translucent and opaque glass was used as decoration on some vessels at many periods in the 1st–4th centuries. In the 1st century, opaque white marvered and unmarvered trails and blobs occur on a range of cups and other vessels (for example, see Figures 4.1 & 5, 18, 19 and Plate 2.4). Opaque white, yellow and blue trails occur on late 2nd and early 3rd century vessels (see Figures 4.10, 40a and Plate 2.5), and the discussion of 'snake thread' trails below). In the 4th century, strongly coloured translucent dark blue, dark green and yellow/brown trails and blobs are found on cups and beakers (for example, see Figure 4.2). Enamelled decoration is sometimes found on drinking vessels (Plate 2.6).

Some vessels were produced in coloured glass of such intensity that they appear to be black. This effect was achieved by using very dark yellow/brown, yellow/green, green, blue or purple glass. 'Black' cups , bowls, jugs and other forms were produced in small quantities in the 1st and 2nd centuries.

Blue/green glass (Plate 3)

Blue/green has been used to describe a wide and variable range of shades of blue and green. Blue/green is the most common colour used to produce glass vessels in the 1st–3rd centuries, and also occurs quite frequently in the 4th century. Bottles and household containers of the 1st–2nd centuries were almost always made in blue/green glass (Plate 3.4), but higher quality blue/green tablewares were also common (Plate 3.5). Blue/green tints were not brought about by the intentional addition of colouring agents to the mixture, but by the presence of iron oxide as a naturally occurring impurity in the sand used to make the glass. The different shades within the range of pale blues and greens depend on the impurities in the sand, and on other factors, particularly variations in the temperature and working conditions of the furnace. The term blue/green therefore indicates that the colour of the glass is natural, not created by the deliberate addition or removal of colouring agents.

Colourless glass (Plate 4)

Colourless glass began to be produced in quantity in the third quarter of the 1st century

AD (see Price 1995a, 145, 152–3, 158–9, for a discussion of the introduction of colourless glass in connection with finds from Usk). During the 2nd and 3rd centuries, colourless glass was used extensively for good quality tablewares. Colourless glass is rarely water-clear, as it often has a greenish or yellowish tinge. In the later 3rd–4th centuries, colourless glass was still used for some good quality vessels, such as cups and bowls with figured or facet-cutting, but it was less common, generally being replaced by bubbly greenish glass for ordinary tablewares.

Late Roman colours (Plate 5)

By the end of the 3rd century there was a marked change in the quality and colour of ordinary glass vessels. Vessels in the 3rd century were generally made in good quality colourless and blue/green glass, but these colours became scarcer and a series of pale greenish, greenish colourless and yellow/green shades came into use in the 4th century. Late Roman tablewares are often noticeably thin-walled and the glass is full of tiny bubbles and dark specks. These features help to distinguish 4th century glass from similarly coloured vessels of the 1st–3rd centuries. Strong shades of yellow/green occur among the glass vessels of the later 4th century.

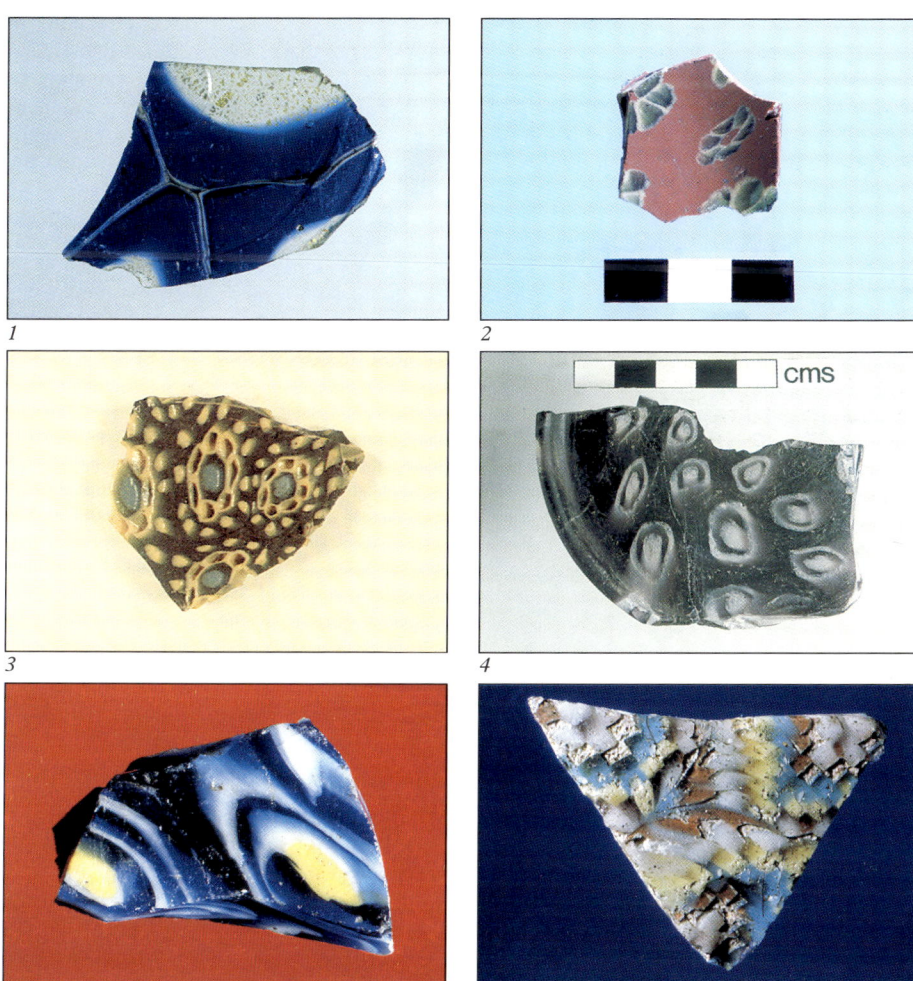

Plate 1 Polychrome glass

1) Fragment of dark blue, purple and opaque white strip mosaic glass with gold leaf in colourless glass, from Castleford. (Photo: Univ of Leeds)
2) Fragment of opaque red bowl with opaque yellow and translucent green floral motifs, from Llandovery. (Photo: Univ of Wales at Cardiff)
3) Fragment of dark green bowl with opaque turquoise and yellow floral motifs, from Lodge Farm, Falfield, Glos (the glass of the petals has disappeared). (Photo: Univ of Leeds)
4) Fragment of purple plate with opaque white roundels, from Piercebridge. (Photo: Univ of Wales at Cardiff)
5) Fragment of dark blue pillar-moulded bowl with opaque white and yellow spiral motifs, from Usk (Photo: Univ of Durham)
6) Fragment of bowl composed of opaque turquoise, yellow, red and white, and translucent purple square-sectioned rods, from Wroxeter. (Photo Univ of Durham)

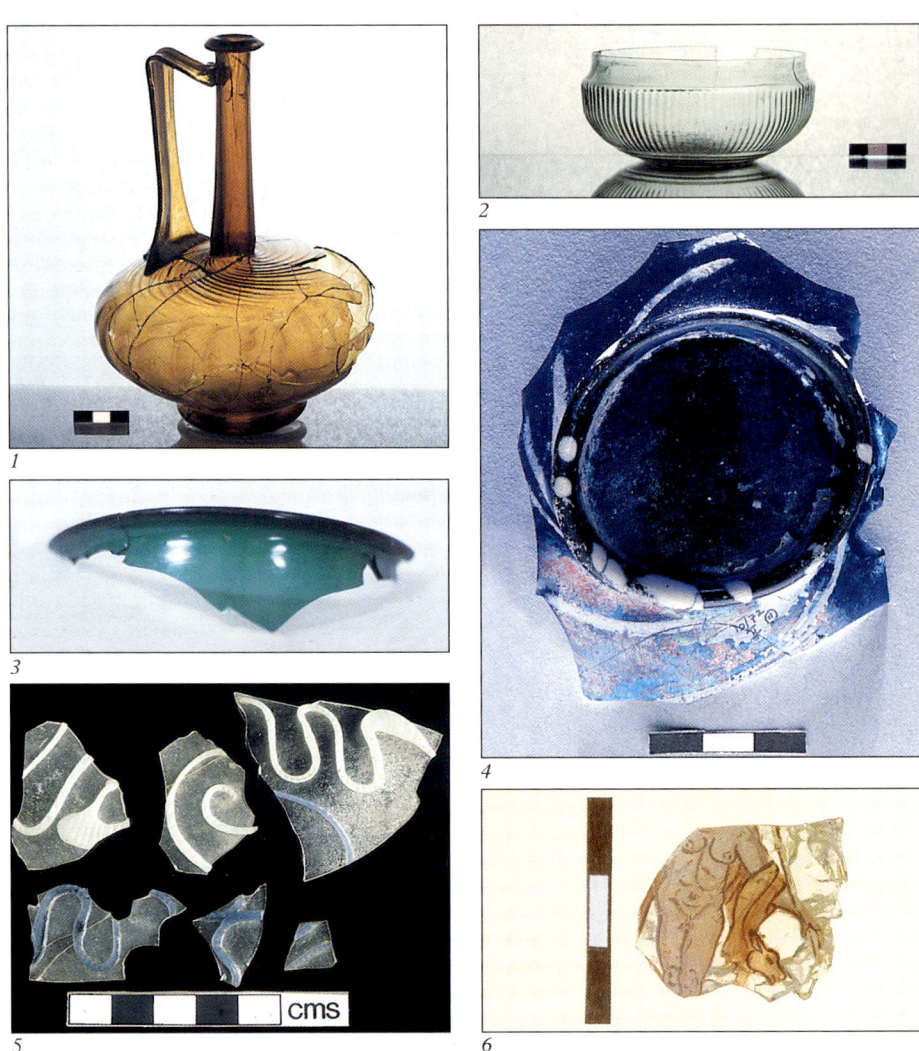

Plate 2 Strong colours and glass with blobbed, trailed and enamelled decoration

1) *Yellow/brown discoid jug with diagonal and vertical ribs, from Enfield, London. (Photo: Univ of Wales at Cardiff)*
2) *Pale green mould-blown hemispherical ribbed bowl, from Usk. (Photo: Univ of Wales at Cardiff)*
3) *Fragment of dark green bowl, from Usk. (Photo: Univ of Wales at Cardiff)*
4) *Fragment of dark blue bowl with marvered opaque white blobs and streaks, from Kingsholm (Photo: Univ of Leeds)*
5) *Body fragments of colourless cylindrical beaker with blue and opaque white `snake-thread' trails, from Whitton. (Photo: Univ of Wales at Cardiff)*
6) *Body fragment of cylindrical cup with enamelled decoration, showing figure of Bacchus, from Catterick. (Photo: Univ of Leads)*

Plate 3 Blue/green vessels

1) *Pillar-moulded bowl, from Stansted. (Photo: Univ of Durham)*
2) *Square bottle, unguent bottle and flask, from Usk. (Photo: Univ of Wales at Cardiff)*
3) *Bath-flask, from London. (Photo: Museum of London)*
4) *Square bottle from Godmanchester and cylindrical bottle from Stansted. (Photo: Univ of Durham)*
5) *Discoid unguent bottles, indented flask and small square bottle, from Felmongers, Harlow. (Photo: Univ of Wales at Cardiff)*
6) *Bowl from Butt Rd cemetery, Colchester. (Photo: Univ of Leeds)*

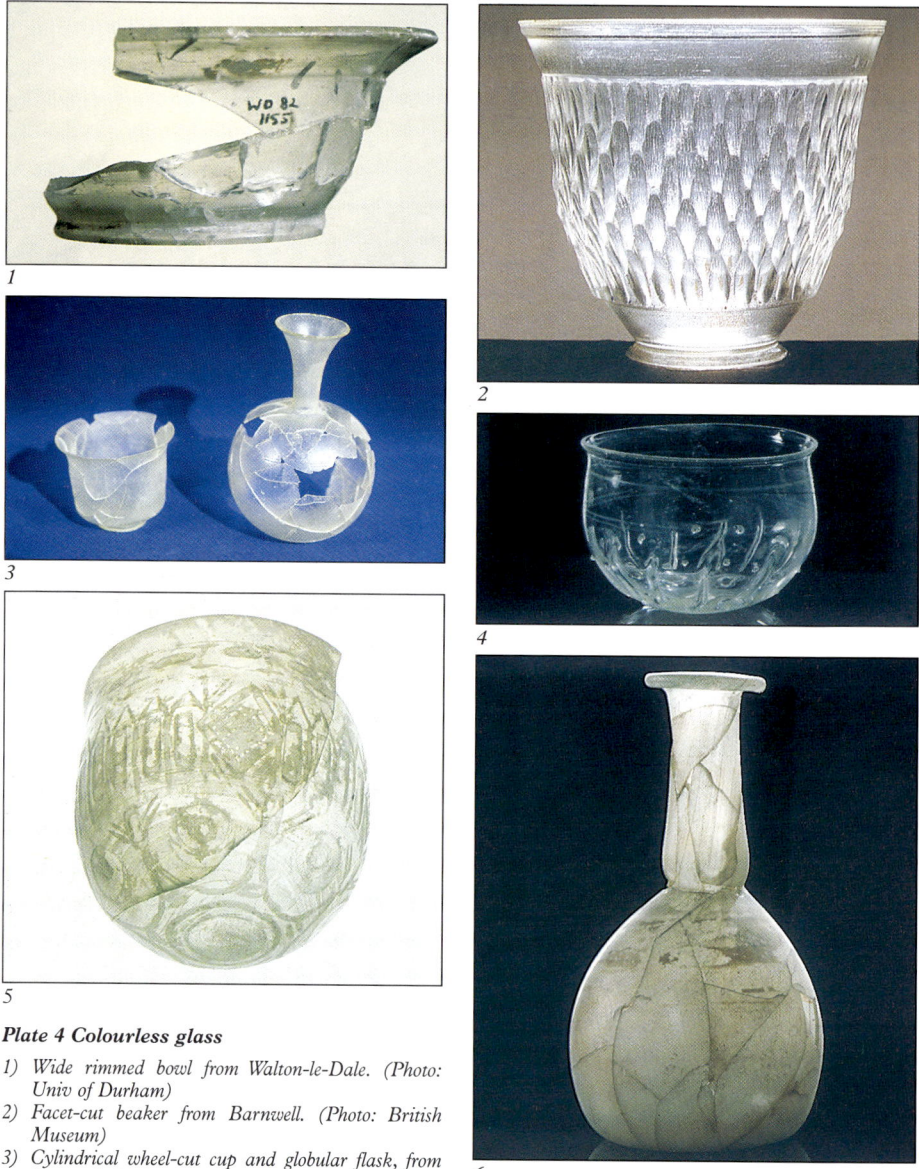

Plate 4 Colourless glass

1) *Wide rimmed bowl from Walton-le-Dale. (Photo: Univ of Durham)*
2) *Facet-cut beaker from Barnwell. (Photo: British Museum)*
3) *Cylindrical wheel-cut cup and globular flask, from Stansted. (Univ of Durham)*
4) *Convex cup with tooled ribs and points, from Brougham. (Photo: Univ of Leeds)*
5) *Deep convex bowl with facet cutting, from King William St, London. (Photo: Museum of London)*
6) *Ovoid flask from Maldon Rd cemetery, Colchester. (Photo: Univ of Leads)*

1

2

3

4

5

6

Plate 5 Late Roman colours

1) Pale green globular jug with two handles, from Bourne Park, Canterbury. (Photo: J Price)
2) Pale yellow/green base with FRO (retrograde), from mould-blown cylindrical bottle with corrugated body from Butt Rd cemetery, Colchester. (Photo: Univ of Leads)
3) Two convex cups from Burgh Castle (Photo: British Museum. Objects in private ownership on loan to British Museum)
4) Two cylindrical beakers with fire-rounded rims and tubular base ring, from Burgh Castle. (Photo: British Museum, as 3 above)
5) Two Bowls with tubular rims, from Burgh Castle. (Photo: British Museum, as 3 above)
6) Two small globular jugs, from Burgh Castle. (Photo: British Museum, as 3 above)

Characteristics

Many of the characteristic features of Roman glass vessels in Britain, such as the methods of finishing rims and bases, or certain styles of decoration, occur on a wide range of forms. The common techniques of style and decoration have therefore been described in this introductory section, to avoid repeating the descriptions of these details whenever they are mentioned in relation to the forms included in this handbook.

Parts of the vessel

Rims (Figure 1)

Rims of cast vessels were finished by grinding on all surfaces. Pillar-moulded bowls, for instance, generally have ground vertical or sloping rims with rounded edges (Figure 1.1). Many cast vessels have vertical or small out-turned rims, but some plates and bowls have wide, almost horizontal rims, often with an overhanging edge (Figure 1.2).

A greater variety of rim finishes occurs on mould-blown and blown vessels. Sheared rims were produced by separating the vessel from the unwanted part of the gather on the blowing iron with shears. This was usually the first process in the formation of a wide range of rims described below, but occasionally, particularly on 1st century unguent bottles, no further manipulation of the rim took place (Figure 1.3). Sheared rims are often uneven, and have a rounded edge without the thickening characteristic of fire-rounded rims (see Figure 1.8 below).

Folded rims, noted in particular on 1st–2nd century jugs and bottles, were produced by bending the sheared edge of the vessel out, up and in to form a horizontal or diagonal rim (Figure 1.4). The top surface was flattened.

Rolled-in rims are found on jars, beakers and unguent bottles of the 1st–2nd centuries, and are also on later vessels, such as some 4th century cups. A small part of the sheared edge was folded inwards and sometimes flattened (Figure 1.5). Rolled-in rims have a smooth edge, similar to that on a fire-rounded rim. A shallow horizontal groove on the inside surface just below the rim edge may indicate that a vessel has a rolled-in rather than a fire-rounded rim.

Tubular rims, common on 1st–2nd century bowls and jars, and found on other forms throughout the Roman period, were produced by turning the sheared edge of the vessel outwards and downwards (Figure 1.6). By first rolling the edge inwards, a rim with a double fold was produced (Figure 1.7). Tubular rims are often slightly flared or horizontal. Tall vertical tubular rims, sometimes found on 1st–2nd century globular jars, are often known as 'collar' rims.

Fire rounding was one of the most common means of finishing rims. It was used on some vessels in the 1st and 4th centuries, but was particularly common from the mid 2nd century to mid 3rd century. The sheared edge was heated to produce a rounded, slightly thickened rim (Figure 1.8).

Pouring spouts with either rolled-in or fire-rounded edges are most common in the 2nd and 3rd centuries, though they are occasionally found on 1st and 4th century jugs.

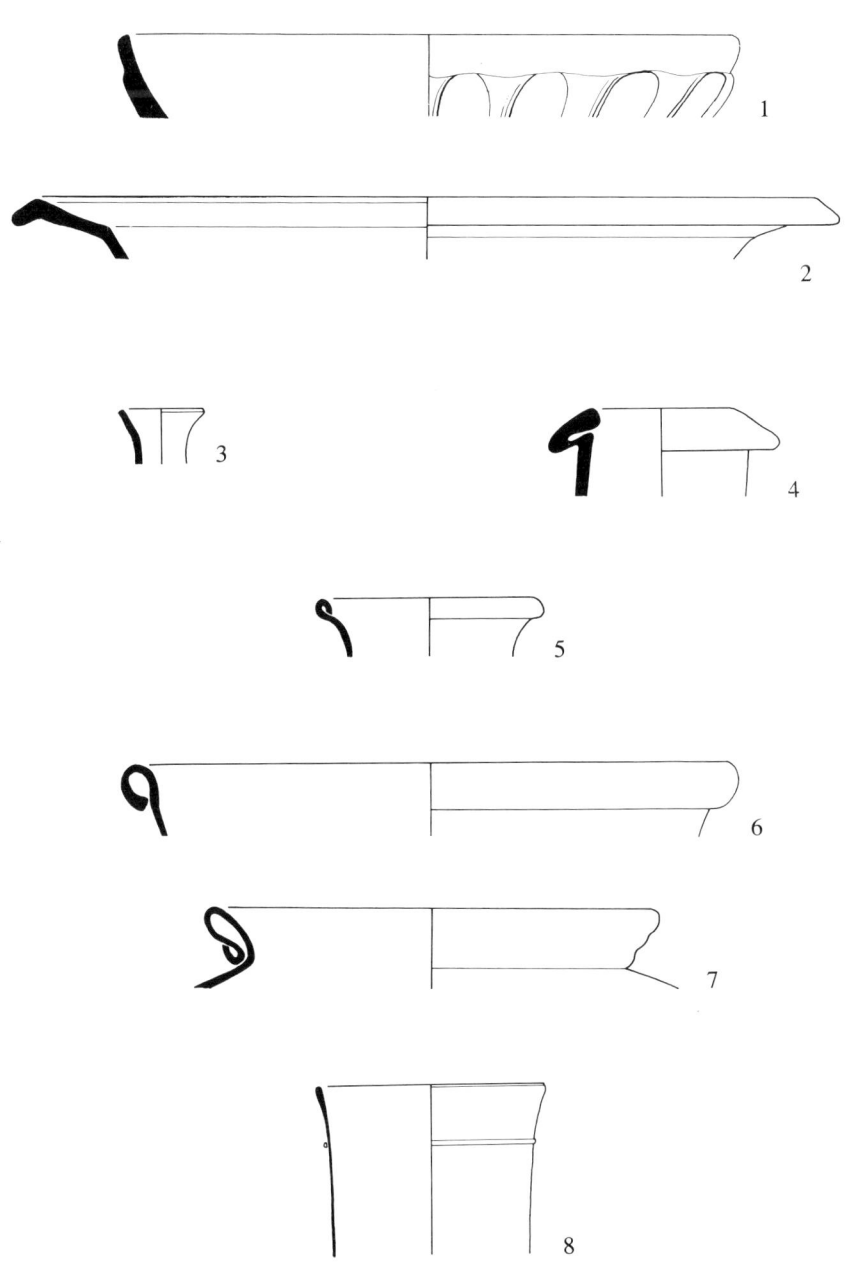

Fig 1.1–8   Scale 1:2

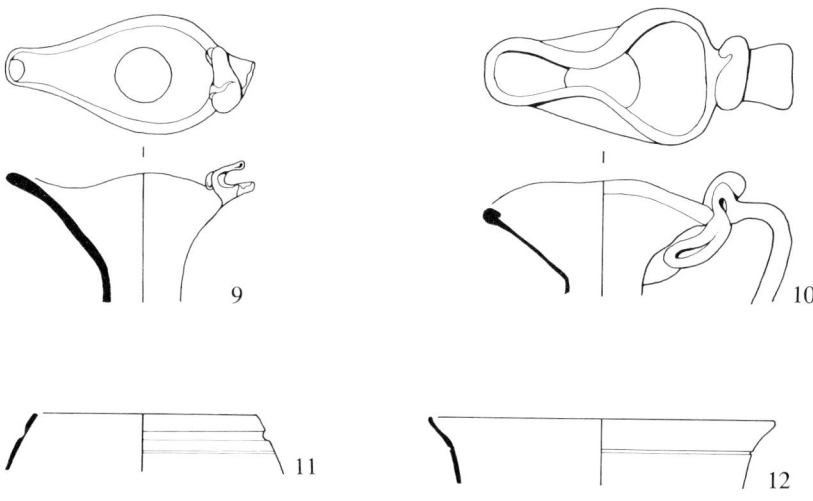

Fig 1.9–12 Scale 1:2

There were two principal methods of forming spouts. The first involved grasping one part of the edge of the rim with pincers and pulling it out and up to form an oval mouth with a pointed, beak like, spout (Figure 1.9). A tooling mark is present at the end of this kind of spout. The second involved applying inward pressure at two opposing points on the outside of the rim, forcing the mouth into a 'trefoil' shape (Figure 1.10).

Cracked-off rims were produced after the vessel had been removed from the blowing iron, annealed and allowed to cool. The superfluous glass above the desired rim position was removed. This may have been achieved by applying a thin horizontal trail of hot glass at the position of the rim edge. The stresses created by the sudden application of heat causes the glass immediately underneath the trail to crack (Gudenrath 1991, 226–7 figs 93–7). Alternatively, a horizontal line may have been scored by a flint at the position of the rim edge, and the superfluous glass tapped and removed. The resulting edge was sharp and often uneven. A smooth finish was produced by grinding and polishing the rim edge (Figure 1.11–12), although on many 4th century vessels, the rim edge was left unworked or only lightly smoothed.

Necks

The necks of flasks, jugs and bottles are almost always circular in section. Tall narrow cylindrical necks are often found on 1st–2nd century jugs. Bottles and later jugs usually have shorter necks. Sometimes the junction with the shoulder or body is defined by tooling marks, or by a constriction. The neck may be uniform in diameter, or expand out to join the shoulder, or taper in from a funnel-shaped mouth.

The internal diameter of a neck may help to indicate the function of the vessel. Most jugs have narrow necks which could only allow the passage of liquids, while bottles have necks in a range of widths which suggests that they contained a variety of substances. Bottles with very wide necks may have contained semi liquid substances, such as honey, or even small solid items, such as dried or pickled fruits and vegetables.

Handles (Figure 2)

Handles were usually applied to the shoulder or upper body of the vessel and drawn up and attached at or just below the rim edge. Huge variety exists in the form and decoration of handles, and only a few basic types are illustrated here.

Ribbon handles, the most common type, consisted of a flattened strip of glass, often with vertical ribs. The handle was either curved (Figure 2.1), or bent through a sharp angle to join the neck (Figure 2.2–3). A looped attachment was a feature of some handles, as on Figure 2.1, and this was sometimes pinched and tooled to form a thumb rest. On some 1st and 2nd century angular ribbon handles, the central rib was drawn down onto the body of the vessel as an extended trail, which was often pinched into projections at intervals (Figure 2.3). Rod handles, also common, had circular or D-shaped sections (Figure 2.4).

Short, wide angular ribbon handles occur on bottles. They are applied to the edge of the shoulder and attached to the neck below the rim. On 1st and 2nd century bottles, handles are nearly always finished with fine vertical ribs (reeding), pulled into points onto the shoulder and upper body (Figure 2.5).

Chain handles occur on blue/green and colourless ovoid, globular and discoid jugs of the later 2nd–3rd centuries. Two rods of glass were applied to the body and attached to the neck of the jug. These were pinched together at intervals to form the links of the chain (Figure 2.6). Small fragments often preserve part of a junction between the two strands of the handle.

Looped (dolphin-shaped) handles are found on several forms of flasks from the 1st–4th centuries. They are a diagnostic feature of 1st–3rd century globular bath flasks (Figures 2.7, 87a-c), and larger versions are known on late Roman bottles (Figures 94–95). Dolphin-shaped handles were applied in several different ways to the neck and shoulder (for examples, see Figures 87, 94–95) and were manipulated round a circular-sectioned tool.

Bases (Figure 3)

Cast vessels have bases ground from the blank, and these have horizontal polishing marks on all surfaces. Some cast bowls and plates with wide rims have high vertical base rings, while others have vertical or diagonal base rings in low relief (Figure 3.1; see also Figures 9c, 11, 12a-e, 13a-d). Some blown vessels, particularly facet-cut beakers, also have diagonal base rings ground from the blank (Figure 3.2; see also Figure 26a-d).

On the majority of blown vessels, the bases and base rings were formed while the glass was hot and often while the vessel was still on the blowing iron. Concave bases occur on a wide range of vessels. Most concave bases are shallow, and some are scarcely more than flattened (Figure 3.3; see also Figures 21a, 35–36, 45, 48–52, 60, 62–3, 65, 67, 70a, 73, 75–79, 82–4, 88). A few vessels, including some 1st century cups, 2nd–3rd century flasks and 4th century beakers, have more pronounced concave bases sometimes with a central pointed 'kick' (Figure 3.4; see also Figures 21b, 28b, 54a, 85).

Open base rings have a constriction just above the base edge and a concave base (Figure 3.5). This base ring type is found on a number of vessel forms, particularly jugs and jars of the 1st and 2nd centuries (for example, Figures 58, 65b–66, 68).

Tubular bases are constricted in the same way as open base rings, but they have a closed tubular base edge and concave base (Figure 3.6–7). Tubular bases occur on a wide variety of vessels from the 1st–4th centuries (for example, Figures 23, 29, 41, 72, 74). Diagonal tubular base rings with high central kicks (Figure 3.8) occur throughout

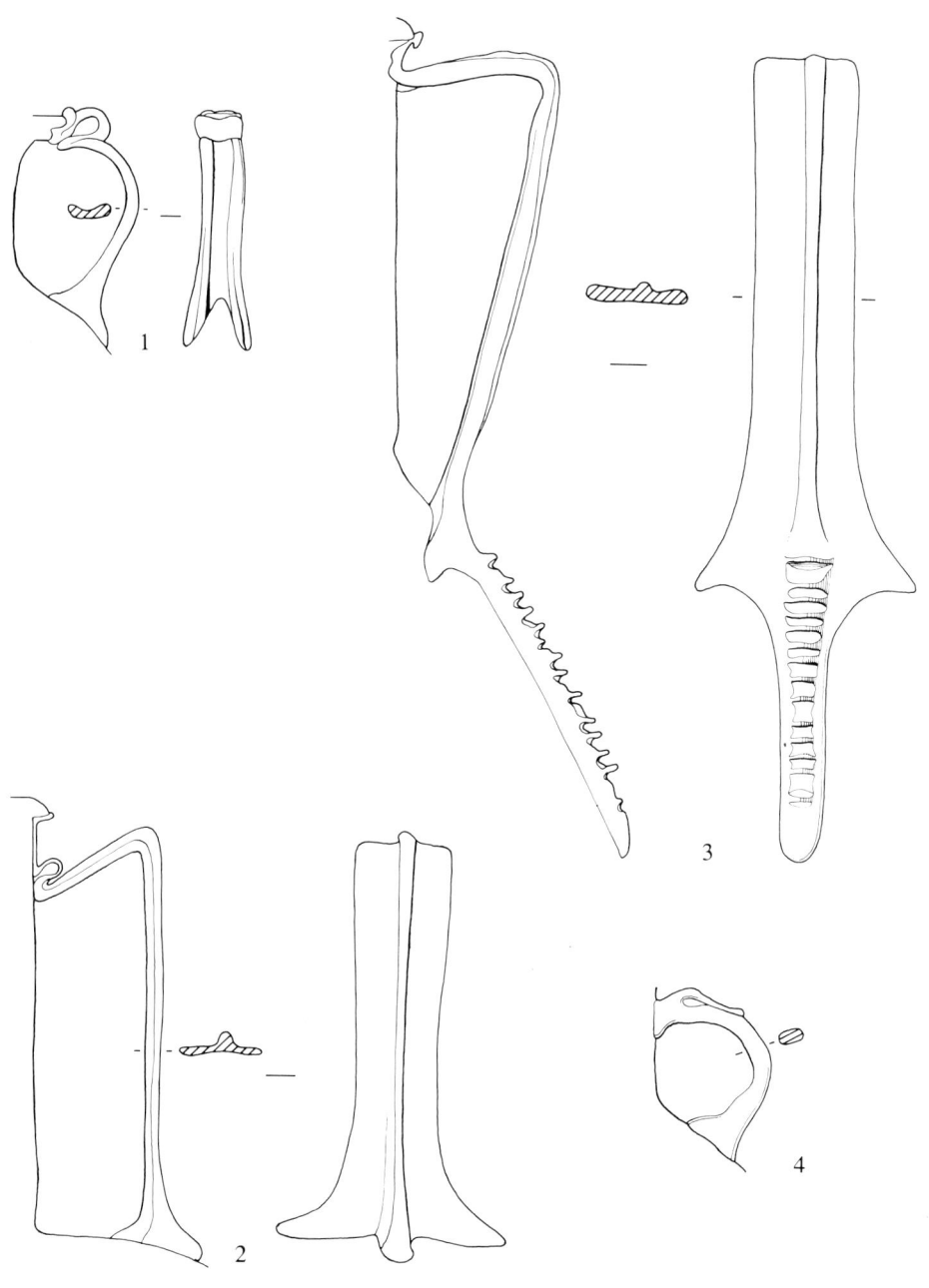

Fig 2.1–4   Scale 1:2

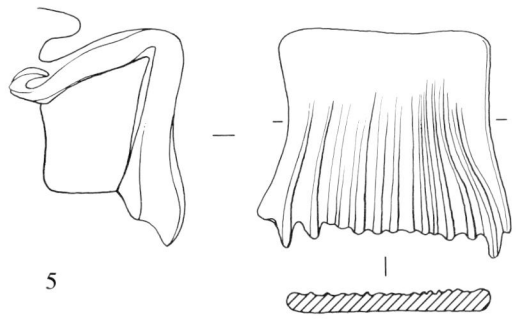

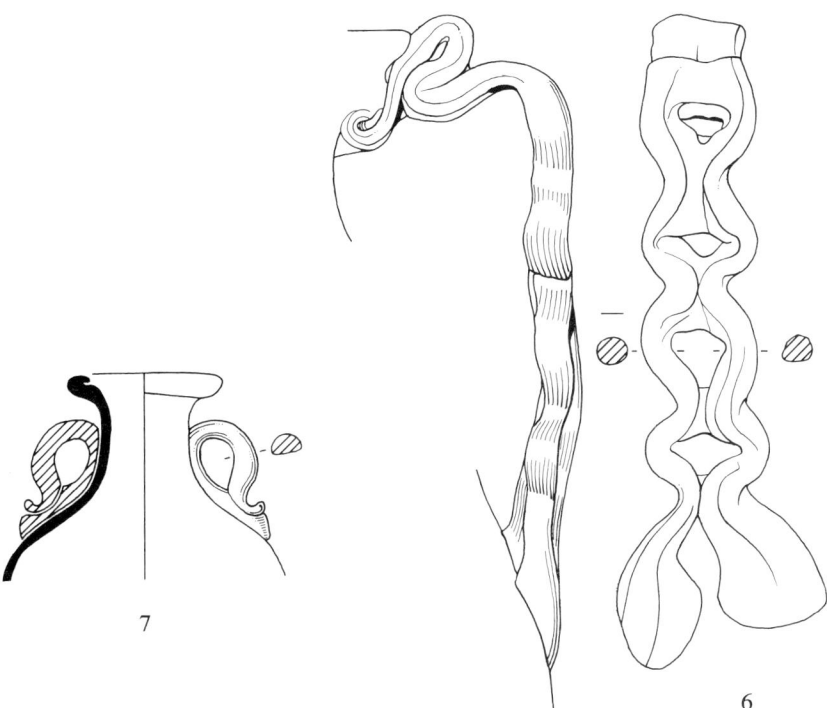

5

7

6

Fig 2.5–7   Scale 1:2

the Roman period, and are a characteristic feature of some 4th century forms of bowls, beakers, flasks and jugs (for example Figures 39, 55, 72).

A wide variety of applied bases are found on vessels of all periods in Roman Britain. An applied base may be recognised by the absence of a tubular hollow in the base ring,

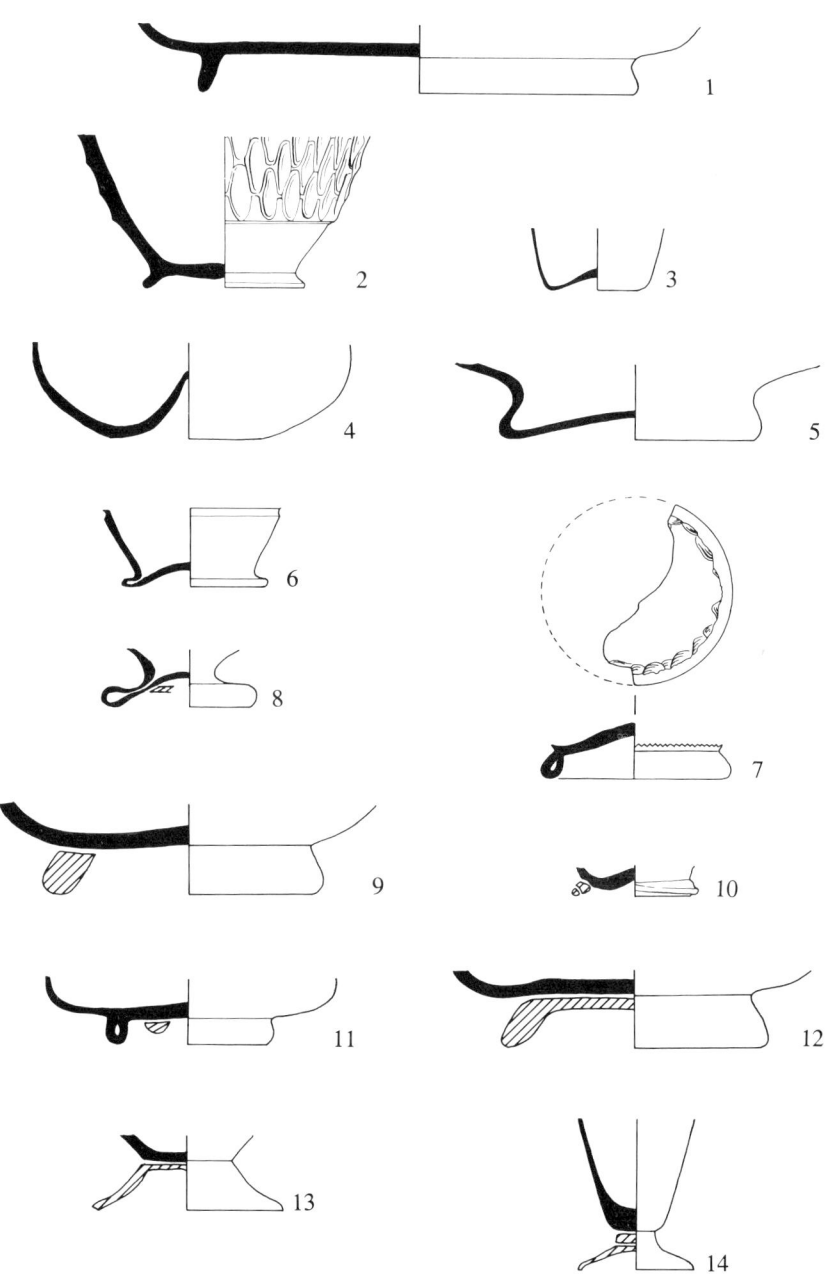

Fig 3.1–14   Scale 1:2

or by the indication of a join between the base ring and the main part of the vessel in section, or sometimes by a slightly raised ridge on the inside surface of the base of the vessel, corresponding to the position of the base ring on the outside surface.

On some vessels, a narrow ring of hot glass was applied to a flattened or slightly concave base (Figure 3.9). These 'true' base rings are a characteristic feature of tubular-rimmed bowls of the 1st–2nd centuries (see Figures 24–5). Base rings created by applying one or more circular or spiral trails of glass to the underside of the base (Figure 3.10) are found on some vessels in the 2nd–4th centuries (for example, Figures 38b, 56). In addition, a small circular trail applied as a second base ring within a tubular base ring (Figure 3.11) is almost always found on the colourless cylindrical cups which were very common in the late 2nd–3rd century (Figure 37). The inner trailed base ring usually has a pontil scar, and presumably served to thicken the base at the point of contact with the pontil iron.

Pad bases, where a disc of glass was applied to the underside of the base and the edges were manipulated to form a base ring, are not always easy to recognise, but they tend to be of much greater thickness within the base ring than outside it, and to have thick rounded edges (Figure 3.12).

A separately blown foot formed from a second bubble being applied to the base of the vessel, is found on a range of cups and bowls of the 1st–2nd centuries (Figure 3.13). The superfluous glass was then cracked-off, and the edge of the foot was ground smooth. These bases are also much thicker within the base ring than outside it, but are distinguishable from pad bases because the edges are cracked-off and ground (for example, Figures 32 a-b, 33). Sometimes a solid stem was applied to the bottom of the body, and a foot with a cracked-off and ground or fire-rounded edge was attached to the stem (Figure 3.14). Stems and feet are not very common in Britain, but they occur on some 1st century cups and on some late 2nd–3rd century beakers and flasks (for example, Figures 19b, 40).

Decoration

Decoration of a glass vessel takes place either during the forming process when the glass is hot, or when it has been annealed and is completely cold. Many glass vessels, particularly tablewares, have some form of decoration, and a single piece often has both hot and cold decoration. Common types of decoration found on Romano-British glass vessels are summarised below.

Decoration formed when the vessel was hot

Cased glass
In the early–mid 1st century, cased blown vessels were formed from two or more layers of glass in contrasting opaque and translucent colours. Some cased vessels, such as hemispherical cups with linear wheel-cut and abraded decoration (Figure 21), have the translucent colour outside (usually dark blue, dark green or yellow/brown) and a layer of opaque white inside, while cased vessels decorated with cameo-cutting always have an outside layer of opaque glass, which is usually white. Fragments of 1st century cased vessels have seldom been noted in Britain, though a few pieces are known on Claudian-Neronian sites. Cased blown vessels were also produced in the 4th century, but these are extremely rare in Britain. They were formed from two layers of contrasting translucent or transparent colours, the inner layer often being colourless or greenish colourless, and were decorated with facet-, relief-, or cameo-cutting.

Blobs, chips and trails (Figure 4 and Plate 2.4–5)
Applied blobs and lumps are found on several blown vessel forms of the second and third quarters of the 1st century, but they become rare after the early Flavian period. The ground colour is usually dark, often dark blue or yellow/brown, although blue/green and colourless examples are also known. The applied decoration is generally a contrasting opaque colour.

To produce marvered blobbed decoration, a partially inflated gather was rolled over chips of glass scattered on the marver block. These adhered to the surface and as this was reheated and blown into shape, the chips expanded to form extended blobs, which were marvered flush with the outside surface (Plate 2.4). Unmarvered blobbed decoration is also found on some 1st century vessels (Figure 4.1). This takes several forms, from tiny chips of glass in one or more contrasting colours which were partially embedded into the surface of the vessel to large lumps which stand proud of the surface of the vessel (Figure 19a).

Blobs in one or more contrasting translucent colours, such as turquoise, dark blue, purple, green and yellow/brown, were sometimes applied as decoration to 4th century cups and beakers. These stand slightly proud of the surface of the vessel (Figure 4.2). They were arranged as large round or oval blobs in a single row around the vessel, and as smaller blobs arranged in triangles or lozenges.

Applied blobs of the same colour as the vessel are less common, but both chips and lumps are sometimes found on 1st century drinking vessels, such as the colourless indented beaker from Wroxeter (see Figure 28b) and cups with stems and handles.

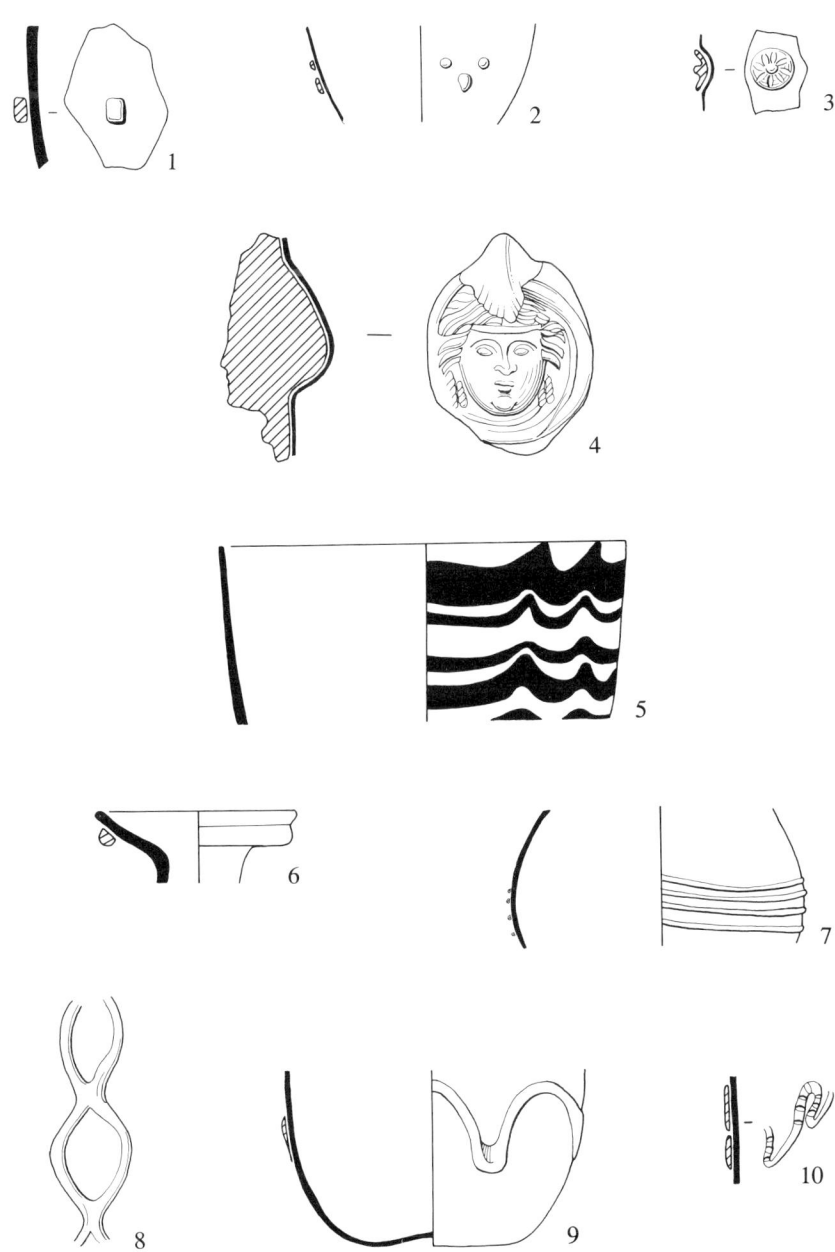

Fig 4.1–10   Scale 1:2

They also occur on a few 4th century vessels, and were sometimes impressed with a rosette or other design (Figure 4.3).

More elaborate blobs were produced by impressing a stamp decorated with a mask onto an applied disc of glass (see Cool and Price 1995, 118–120 for discussion). They are found on 1st century discoid, globular and conical jugs, usually at the base of the handle. Some masks have been interpreted as representations of Bacchus or Silenus (Figure 4.4), and many different designs are known. The mask often survives without the remainder of the vessel, and in these cases the broken edges of the body and handle have generally been carefully grozed.

Horizontal or spiral trails are known on some 1st century bowls and cups and also occur on a range of mid 2nd–4th century vessels. Trails were applied whilst the vessel was hot, and were either marvered flush with the surface (for example, Figures 4.5, 18), or left standing proud. Single horizontal trails occur on cylindrical cups, bowls, jugs and other forms in the 2nd–4th centuries (for example, Figures 4.6, 38 a-b, 40, 71a, 72, 84, 93). Bath flasks, beakers and jugs were sometimes decorated with a spiral trail running from neck to base (for example, Figures 4.7, 39). Spiral trails were also placed around the neck of jugs and flasks, and trails on the body were sometimes pinched together at intervals, producing a loose lattice of 'spectacle' trails (for example, Figure 4.8). Various types of spiral, looped and zig-zag trails occur on 4th century cups, beakers and jugs (for example, Figures 4.9, 48a).

An elaborate form of trailed decoration, consisting of irregular serpentiform trails scored diagonally, is found on a range of late 2nd and 3rd century vessels. This kind of trailing is usually called 'snake-thread' decoration. The trails were either self-coloured or opaque blue, yellow or white, and they occur on colourless, or more rarely blue/green or strongly coloured vessels (see Figure 4.10 and Plate 2.5). Fragments of snake-thread glass have been found on numerous settlement sites in Britain, but no intact vessels from burials have yet been found. This is remarkable, given the numbers found in burials elsewhere in the north-western provinces, particularly in the vicinity of Köln (Fremersdorf 1959, passim). Vessels with snake-thread decoration were probably made in the lower Rhineland area.

Tooling, folds and indents (Figure 5)

These types of decoration were not added or formed in a mould, but were created from the surface of the hot glass. Tooled points were formed when the vessel wall was pinched out to form lugs (see Figure 5.1) and single small projections (see Figure 5.2 and Plate 4.4). Tooled points featured strongly on a range of 3rd century colourless cups and bowls, as well as on flasks, beakers and other forms. They were often used in combination with other forms of decoration such as ribs, indents and horizontal abrasion (for example, Figure 45a). Very occasionally, the base edge of a vessel was manipulated into a ring of pulled-out points.

Vertical and diagonal tooled ribs occur principally on 1st–3rd century bowls, jugs and jars, and on 3rd century cups. The wall of the vessel was manipulated to raise ribs which range from shallow to quite prominent (for example, Figures 5.3, 25b, 58, 67, 71a, Front Cover). A few 1st–early 2nd century conical and convex jugs have ribs which are both vertical and diagonal (see Figure 66a Plate 2.1). These 'arrested' ribs are vertical on the lower neck, become diagonal on the upper body, and then change abruptly through pressure applied to the surface of the body by a tool (probably wooden) to become vertical again on the middle and lower body. On some 3rd century cups, the sides of the ribs have been gripped by a crimped tool (probably metal).

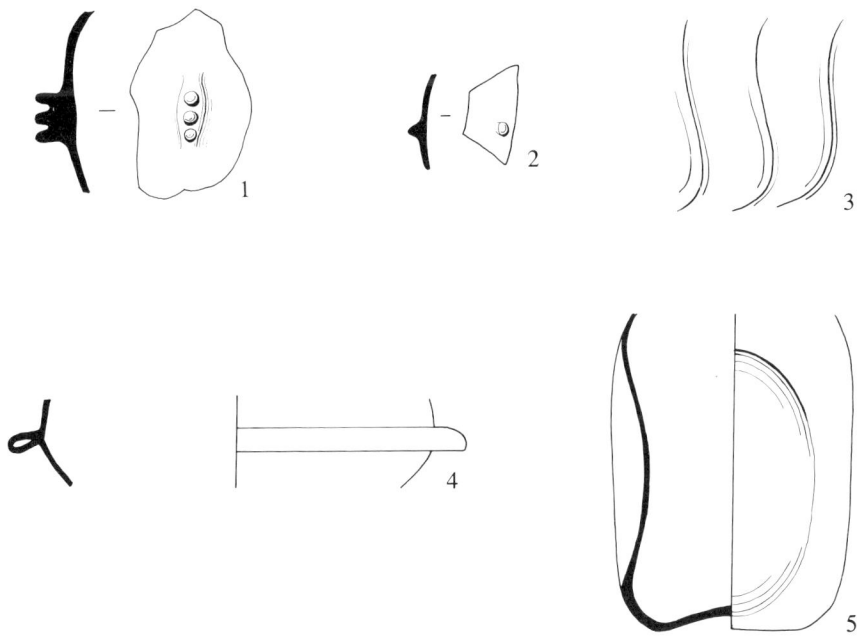

Fig 5.1–5 Scale 1:2

Horizontal folds form part of the vessel wall and are produced by applying pressure around the body to produce a projecting tubular flange (Figure 5.4). In some instances, the flange is then bent down to meet the body of the vessel and becomes a double, figure-of-eight fold. Fragments with folds below the rim or on the body are not uncommon in Britain in the 1st–3rd centuries, but only rarely is any further part of the vessel preserved. A blue/green convex bowl from Silchester has a projecting horizontal fold in the body (see Figure 43), and part of a small yellow/brown convex jug found in a context dated AD 50–70 at Richborough has a figure-of-eight fold in the upper body (Bushe-Fox 1932, 85 no 60 pl 15).

Oval indents are produced by applying pressure at various points on the body of the vessel, either with the edge or point of a tool or by blowing the gather inside a ring of vertical rods (Figure 5.5 Plate 3.5). Indents are found throughout the Roman period, on cups, bowls, flasks and unguent bottles (for example, Figures 28–9, 33, 53, 62a–b, 80). Some vessels have three or four deep indents, while others have numerous deep or shallow indents.

Decoration formed when the vessel was cold

Enamelled decoration
Powdered glass mixed with a binding agent was painted onto a vessel after it had been annealed and was cold, and the vessel was then re-heated to fuse the enamel to the

surface. This was never a common form of decoration in the Roman world, and comparatively few enamelled vessels have been recorded in Britain. In the mid 1st century, blue/green and coloured hemispherical cups (Figure 21) were occasionally decorated with vine leaves and other motifs. Fragments are known at Camulodunum (Harden 1947, 297 no 33 pl 87), and from Southwark and Mancetter.

Enamelled decoration is also found on colourless tablewares. In the later 1st century, a small number of conical beakers (Figure 26) had enamelled decoration rather than facet-cutting, and in the later 2nd–3rd century, some cylindrical cups (Figure 37) were painted with scenes of animal hunts, gladiatorial contests, fishes and other motifs (Plate 2.6). The cylindrical cups are concentrated in the north-western provinces and beyond the frontier in Denmark and Germany. Fragments have been found at several sites in Britain, mostly from the northern frontier region.

Cutting and abrasion (Figure 6)
All forms of wheel-cutting took place after the vessel had been annealed and was cold, using a rotating stone wheel, or small metal wheels and other engraving tools, or a flint or stone point. The majority of the vessels with cut and abraded decoration were colourless, though in the 1st century some were polychrome, brightly coloured or blue/green, and in the 4th century many were pale greenish or yellow/green.

Horizontal linear wheel-cutting and abrasion (Plate 4.2–3 and 5)
Horizontal linear cutting and abrasion (Figure 6.1), using a rotating stone or metal wheel is a simple form of wheel-cutting in common use on Roman glass vessels in Britain from the 1st to the late 4th century. Lightly abraded bands and deeper wheel-cut lines are found on early–mid 1st century cased and other polychrome, strongly coloured and blue/green cups and beakers (for example, Figures 21–3), and occasionally on blue/green and pale yellow/green cylindrical bottles (Figure 88c).

Colourless cups, bowls, flasks and bottles with single and closely grouped cut and abraded lines were produced at various times from the end of the 1st century to the 4th century (for example, Figures 32–5, 36b–c, 45a, 46, 49, 78, 82–4, 92–4 and Plate 4.3). Linear-cutting and abrasion were also used in combination with facet-cutting and other elaborate forms of cutting, particularly on beakers (for example, Figure 31) and on hemispherical bowls (for example, Figures 36a, 47b).

In the 4th century, horizontal bands of light abrasion were used on a wide range of pale greenish and yellow/green vessels, particularly bowls, cups and beakers (for example, Figures 48a–b, 50a, 52–3). At this period, the abrasion is often so slight that it is scarcely detectable.

Facet-cutting
Deep wheel-cutting, in the form of circular or oval facets which removed a substantial amount of glass from the surface (Figure 6.2), is found in Britain on some cast vessels produced in the late 1st-early 2nd century, and on blown vessels from the later 1st–4th century. Cast bowls and plates were sometimes decorated with circular or oval facets on the underside of the rim or base, as at Richborough (Yadin 1963, fig 40a) and Fishbourne (Price and Cottam 1996a, fig 6.27 no 30), or on all exterior surfaces, as on the bowl with wide rim and carved horizontal handles from Wroxeter (Charlesworth 1975a).

Blown vessels with facet-cut decoration are encountered more frequently. Facet-cut conical beakers (Figure 26a–b Plate 4.2) are among the earliest blown vessels produced in high quality colourless glass. They appeared in the late Neronian period, and

Fig 6.1–10   Scale 1:2

continued in use into the early 2nd century. The facets were usually arranged in rows to form interlocking diamond or hexagon shapes (Figure 6.2), although other designs, such as jigsaw facets, are known. Facet-cut decoration also occurs in combination with linear cutting (see previous section). In the 2nd and early 3rd century, hemispherical bowls were decorated with horizontal wheel-cut lines and circular, oval or narrow 'rice grain' facets (Figures 6.3–4, 36a). A wider range of facet-cut designs occurred in the 3rd century, when the basic facet shapes were joined by bar-shaped motifs, lozenges, circles with central bosses, 'ears of wheat', festoons and other features (Figures 6.5–6, 47a–b and Plate 4.5). Use of the same motifs continued in the 4th century, although they were often less deeply cut than on earlier vessels. With very few exceptions, the facet-cut vessels found in Britain were colourless or greenish colourless glass, apart from a rim fragment from a 4th century cased bowl in greenish colourless and purple which was found at Greyhound Yard, Dorchester, Dorset (Cool & Price 1993, 154 no 22).

Relief-cutting

The exterior surfaces of both cast and blown vessels were sometimes subjected to heavy cutting and grinding to leave decoration standing in high relief (Figure 6.7). Cast cups and bowls with relief-cutting are not very common, but they range widely in date. For example, a handled cup (scyphus) with gadroons in relief was found at Fishbourne in a Claudian-early Flavian context (Harden and Price 1971, 334 no 29, fig 138), while a generally similar cup from Exeter with the greek letter pi in relief was probably produced in the 4th century (Charlesworth 1979, 222 no 1, fig 70).

Relief-cut decoration occurs rather more frequently on blown tablewares, though it was never very common. Horizontal cordons occur on a range of cups and bowls, and are characteristically found below the rim, and on the upper and lower body (often flanking the zone of facet-cutting), on later 1st century–early 2nd century conical beakers (Figure 26a and d). Some of these conical beakers have more complex relief-cut motifs such as rosettes, shells and ovals (Figures 6.7, 26c), and fragments with under-cut and pierced motifs in very high relief (diatreta) have very occasionally been noted, at Blake Street, York (Cool 1995a, 1568 no 5923, figs 737–8), Guildhall Yard, London (information from John Shepherd) and Lincoln.

Cage-cups (diatreta) also occur in 4th century contexts, but fragments of these have seldom been noted in Britain. Small pieces are known from Silchester (Boon 1974, 233), Canterbury (Charlesworth & Price 1987, 222 no 13 fig 88) and Great Staughton villa, Huntingdonshire (Charlesworth 1994, 101 no 28 fig 8).

Cameo-cutting

This technique involved cutting away the outside layer or layers of a cased bichrome or polychrome vessel to create designs and figured scenes in relief, and gem-cutting tools were probably used. Comparatively few Roman cameo-cut vessels have survived, and only one fragment has been noted in Britain. This is an opaque white and dark blue convex body fragment with a cameo-cut vine leaf and other motifs pattern from Southwark, London (Lightfoot 1988, 374–8 no 83 fig 167).

Figured-cutting

Various combinations of wheel-cutting and abrasion were employed to create figured scenes on tablewares (Figure 6.8–10). In Britain, virtually all instances of figured-cut decoration are found on 4th century cups, bowls and beakers (Price 1995c). Fragments are known on urban and rural sites throughout Britain, but no examples have come from burials. This contrasts with finds from elsewhere in the north-western provinces, particularly in the Rhineland, where well preserved figure-cut vessels have been found in numerous burials. Late Roman figured-cut vessels were generally made in good quality, more or less colourless glass, rather than the bubbly and speckly glass used for ordinary late Roman tablewares. Several distinct styles and techniques of cutting have been recognised:

a) massed shallow wheel-cuts to create figures and features and short narrower wheel-cuts for details such as the hair and eyes (Figure 6.8). The scenes depicted include biblical episodes from the Old and New Testaments, dancing figures, and human busts or figures within circular frames. Examples from Britain include two hemispherical bowls with biblical scenes from Lullingstone villa, Kent (Figure 49; Cool and Price 1987, 113–7, 129–30 nos 338–9 fig 54), and a conical beaker with four figures from Frocester Court villa, Gloucestershire (Price 1979, 41 no 4 fig 16).

b) a combination of buffed areas and sharp wheel-cut lines was used on bowls and beakers with a range of scenes including pagan cults, the circus and hunting. This style is characterised by the use of short wheel-cuts to produce lozenge-shaped eyes on the figures (Figure 6.9). The most complete example in Britain is a hemispherical bowl with dancing figures from Colliton Park, Dorchester, Dorset (Harden 1969, 65 fig 8).

c) free-hand incisions, consisting of short and long lines perhaps produced with a flint burin, were used to create biblical, pagan or hunting scenes on shallow convex bowls and a few convex cups. The figures and features in the scenes are often outlined by single lines with short lines aligned diagonally against one edge (Figure 6.10). A motto in retrograde is often inscribed around the upper body of the bowl below the rim, indicating that the scene was arranged to be viewed from above. The most complete example known in Britain is a bowl showing a hare hunt (Figure 51a) from Wint Hill, Banwell, Somerset (Harden 1960a).

37

Glossary of Terms

These terms have been listed together to give the reader easy access to them. They are also explained individually elsewhere in the handbook.

Annealing: process of putting the finished vessels in a heated chamber or pit and then reducing the temperature gradually to ensure uniform cooling of the surfaces. This reduced the internal stresses in the vessels and made them less likely to crack or break.

Blowing (free-blowing): hot glass was gathered on the end of a blowing iron and inflated by blowing air into it through the blowing iron. At the same time, the vessel was shaping by marvering and by manipulation with metal and wooden tools.

Blowing iron: long narrow iron tube with expanded terminal, used to collect a gather of hot glass and then to inflate it.

Cage-cup or diatretum: a thick-walled vessel which was deeply undercut on the outside surface to form openwork patterns which were attached to the body by narrow bridges. The patterns included inscriptions, friezes of circular rings (cage-cups) or friezes with figured scenes or vegetal motifs.

Cased vessels: vessels formed from two or more layers of glass in contrasting colours.

Cast, Casting: a general term used to describe the methods of manufacture of non-blown vessels (see also sagging).

Constriction: horizontal concavity in the wall of a vessel, for instance, below the rim, at the base of the neck or in the lower body above the base, made by pressure from wooden or metal tools; see also tooling marks.

Crucible: an open ceramic container holding melted glass in the furnace.

Cullet: Broken fragments of vessel glass, collected for re-melting.

Egg and dart cutting: cutting sometimes found on the overhanging rim edge of cast colourless bowls (cf Figure 13b). The surface was ground away to produce narrow ribs with pointed terminals alternating with broad ovals.

Founding: melting the raw materials and heating them to a high temperature before working the glass.

Fritting: preliminary heating of the raw materials to fuse them partially and burn off impurities. Frit was the material produced by this process.

Gather: quantity of hot glass (sometimes called a gob or paraison) wound onto the expanded terminal of the blowing iron.

Grozing : process of chipping or snapping off pieces of glass from the uneven broken edges of a vessel or fragment to reshape it for secondary use.

Ingredients: three principal constituents, sand, soda and lime, occurring in virtually all Roman glass.

Jigsaw facet-cutting: an asymmetrical form of facet-cutting, produced by removing some of the junctions between oval or circular facets arranged in quincunx.

Kick: a high point at the centre of a concave base, produced by a pointed metal tool

Marvering: process by which a gather of hot glass was rolled on a flat stone or metal surface (the marver, or marver block) to shape the vessel, or to collect blobs and chips of glass onto the surface, or to smooth blobbed and trailed decoration into the surface.

Moile: the surplus part of the blown gather, which was either left on the blowing iron when the vessel was cut away for the rim to be finished, or was removed from the blowing iron with the unfinished vessel and then discarded after annealing when the rim of the vessel was cracked-off.

Mould-blowing: inflating a gather of glass in a multi-piece or single-piece mould to produce a fixed shape for the vessel and the decoration.

Optic-blowing: a gather was partly inflated in a mould or through a ring to transfer a pattern to the body of a vessel. The gather was then blown freehand and manipulated to achieve the final shape and decoration.

Pointillé: a cutting technique on some 4th century vessels which used massed small wheel-cut spots to produce dulled or textured areas.

Pontil, pontil iron: solid iron rod used to hold the base of a partially finished blown vessel while the body and rim were shaped, or handles and decoration applied.

Pontil mark: a small, often circular, scar in the centre of the base of a vessel, made by the pontil iron.

Post, post scar: large discontinuous circular scar left on the bottom edge of wide base rings, made by a pontil iron with a wide extension attached to the end.

Prismatic: a term used to describe square, rectangular, hexagonal and other bottles with angular-sectioned bodies.

Quincunx: facets arranged so that the first and third facets in rows one and three surround the second facet in row two.

Reeding: narrow, closely set vertical ridges on bottle handles.

Retrograde: arranged back to front. Retrograde inscriptions on some 4th century shallow convex bowls were intended to be read from inside the vessel.

Sagging: process of producing a vessel by placing a disc of glass over a former and heating it until it slumped to take the shape of the former (see also casting).

Tooling marks: short horizontal marks in the outside surface of a vessel, especially at the base of the neck, left from the use of wooden or metal tools to shape the vessel.

Wear, patterns of wear: dull or scratched patches resulting from use.

Weathering: cloudiness, or flaking black or iridescent deposits on the surfaces of vessels and fragments, caused by the glass reacting to moisture in the burial environment.

PART 2: GUIDE TO THE VESSEL FORMS

Introduction

The vessels have been grouped into five sections; *Cups and Bowls*; *Jars*; *Jugs*; *Flasks, Unguent Bottles and Bath-flasks*; *Bottles*. Within each group, the vessels are ordered according to shape and approximate date of use, and the largest group, *Cups and Bowls*, also has three subdivisions corresponding to the method of manufacture.

These groups have been devised for convenience. They are not fixed and they do not necessarily imply established or exclusive functions for each vessel form. Vessels in different groups sometimes share many of the same features.

The handbook is designed to provide a selection of the more common forms from Roman Britain. The references which accompany each form are a guide to further reading. They are not intended to be comprehensive, and other examples of most forms can be found both in published reports and in museum collections.

The dates given for each form are general, and are intended to apply only to finds from Britain. Vessels without an accompanying reference are unpublished.

The heights and rim diameters of the vessels are given in millimetres.

Key to colours

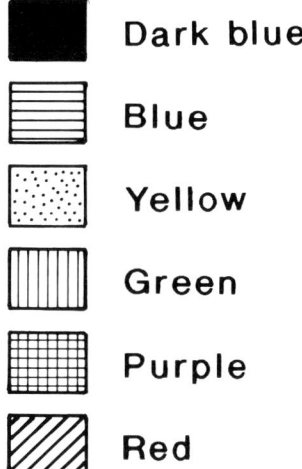

Dark blue

Blue

Yellow

Green

Purple

Red

Cups and bowls: cast

Ribbed bowl (pillar-moulded bowl)

Characteristics

Form

Vertical or sloping rim, edge rounded, deep, hemispherical or shallow convex body with vertical ribs, flat or slightly concave base.

Colours

Polychrome mosaic. Common combinations are translucent dark blue, purple or yellow/brown with opaque white or yellow rods or spirals; translucent dark green with opaque yellow and red rods or spirals.

Monochrome. Translucent dark blue and yellow/brown; purple is rare and dark green is unknown. Opaque colours are very rare. Blue/green is the most common colour.

Decoration

Most bowls have prominent vertical ribs, sometimes with a slightly diagonal slant, which extend to the base; some shallow examples have short, closely set ribs on the body only. The inside surface has horizontal grinding marks and is often decorated with wheel-cut lines on the lower body above the base and occasionally in the centre of the base or below the rim.

Other features

The inside surface, rim and area above the ribs outside are dull with grinding marks, the remainder of the outside surface (the ribs and base) is shiny. Small fragments are easily recognisable from the combination of ground and shiny surfaces. Tooling marks often occur at the tops of the ribs. The bowls occur in a wide range of sizes. Some large, thick-walled and carelessly finished bowls were produced in the second half of the 1st century. Shallow bowls are comparatively rare in Britain.

Range of measurements

Rim diameter c 100–220+mm. Height c 50–85mm.

Distribution

Very common. Found on most military and civil settlement sites with 1st century occupation. Complete bowls are sometimes found in burials. Fragments also occur at native sites.

Date range

AD 43–end of 1st century. A few blue/green bowls continued in use in the early 2nd century.

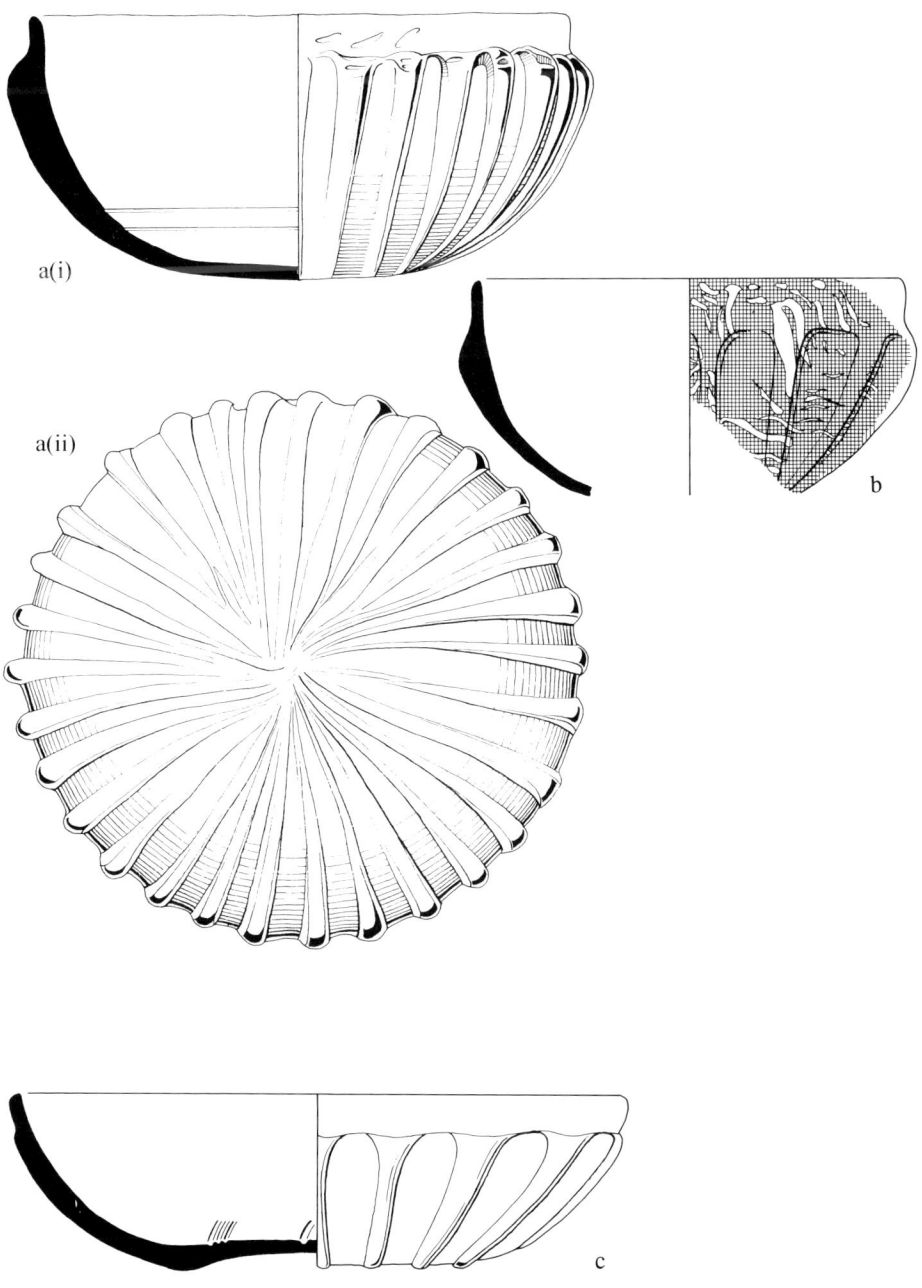

a(i)

a(ii)

b

c

Fig 7 Scale 1:2

Illustrated examples (Figure 7 and Plate 3.1)

a) *Stansted, Essex*: Blue/green, complete large hemispherical bowl, poorly finished, from cremation burial 247 at the Duckend Carpark site, dated to first quarter of 2nd century.

b) *Gloucester*: Polychrome mosaic, purple with opaque white rods, small hemispherical bowl, from the Neronian military site at Kingsholm (Price and Cool 1985, 45 no 1 fig 17).

c) *Colchester, Sheepen, Essex*: Blue/green, shallow bowl, from context dated to AD 49–61 (Harden 1947, 302 no 62 pl 88).

Other finds

Castleford, West Yorkshire: Fragments, one dark blue and at least 12 blue/green bowls, from Flavian military and later occupation (Cool and Price 1998, 152 nos 1–18 figs 50–51).

Colchester, Essex: Fragments, many polychrome and monochrome bowls, from Claudian-Flavian and later contexts (Cool and Price 1995, 15–26 nos 1–184 figs 2.2–7).

Colchester, Sheepen, Essex: Polychrome mosaic, yellow/brown with opaque white spirals, complete shallow bowl, from cremation group 3, Neronian burial (Charlesworth 1985a, MF 1:A7 (h) pl 10). Fragments, polychrome and monochrome bowls, from Claudian-early Neronian contexts (Harden 1947, 294, 302 nos 8, 10–14, 16–18, 61, 63–7 pls 87–8; Charlesworth 1985a, MF 3:F2,7,9 nos 11–15, 44–6, 65–81 figs 80–1).

Inchtuthil, Tayside: Blue/green, body and base, from legionary fortress occupied *c*.AD 83–86/7 (Price 1985a, 308 no 1, fig 93).

London: Fragments, polychrome and monochrome bowls; from Neronian-early Flavian and later contexts in Southwark St and Leadenhall Court (Shepherd 1995b, 121, 123–4 nos 6, 23–47 fig 38; Shepherd 1996, 104 nos 5–64 fig 62).

Murston, Kent: Blue/green, complete hemispherical bowl, from inhumation burial (Payne 1893, 40 pl 4 no 2).

Newstead, Borders: Fragments, polychrome and monochrome bowls, from fort with Flavian and Antonine occupation (Curle 1911, 272).

Radnage, Buckinghamshire: Polychrome mosaic, dark blue with opaque white spirals, complete shallow bowl (Front cover), from Flavian cremation burial (Skilbeck 1923, 334 pl 35 fig 1; Harden *et al* 1987, 51 no 27).

Richborough, Kent: Fragments, polychrome and monochrome bowls, from pre-Flavian-early 2nd century contexts (Bushe-Fox 1932, 84–5 nos 58–9 pl 15; Bushe-Fox 1949, 159).

Thornborough, Buckinghamshire: Blue/green, complete hemispherical bowl, from Neronian-early Flavian cremation burial (Price 1975, 18 no 1 fig 10)

Usk, Gwent: Fragments, polychrome (Plate 1.5) and many monochrome bowls, from Neronian-early Flavian contexts in legionary fortress (Price 1995a, 140–9 nos 1–2, 6–21 figs 42–3).

Wroxeter, Shropshire: Fragments, polychrome and monochrome bowls, from Neronian-Flavian military occupation.

York: Fragments, blue/green bowls, from Flavian and later contexts at Blake Street and the Minster site in the legionary fortress (Cool 1995a, 1650–1 nos 5845–5890 fig 734; Price 1995b, 353 nos 1–6 fig 141).

Further reading

Isings 1957, Form 3. For discussion in connection with finds from Colchester and Usk, see Cool and Price 1995, 14–26, and Price 1995a, 140–9.

Convex bowl

Characteristics

Form
Vertical or sloping rim, edge rounded, hemispherical or shallow convex body, slightly concave or flat base.

Colours
Polychrome mosaic. Opaque monochrome, including orange and pale blue. Translucent dark green and dark blue. Occasionally blue/green.

Decoration
Horizontal wheel-cut lines on inside and/or outside surfaces. Cordons in relief on body and/or base.

Other features
The inside and outside surfaces are dull and smooth, grinding and wheel-polishing marks are often visible. Some shallow blue/green bowls have the same combination of ground and shiny surfaces as pillar moulded bowls (see Figure 7).

Range of measurements
Rim diameters *c* 120–200mm.

Distribution
Not common; found on early Roman sites in southern Britain.

Date range
Second and third quarters of 1st century AD.

Illustrated examples (Figure 8)
a) *Colchester, Sheepen, Essex*: Polychrome mosaic, green ground, opaque yellow spirals with opaque red centres, fragmentary shallow bowl, from Claudian-Neronian context (Charlesworth 1985a, MF3:F2 no 1 fig 80).
b) *Colchester, Sheepen, Essex*: Dark green, complete hemispherical bowl, from cremation group 3, Neronian burial (Charlesworth 1985a, MF1:A6 (g) fig 15 no 6).

Other finds
Colchester, Essex: Fragments, polychrome mosaic and opaque monochrome, shallow and hemispherical bowls, from Claudian-early Neronian and later contexts (Cool and Price 1995, 27–30 nos 189–91 fig 2.9; Harden 1958a, 157 nos 3–4 fig 79).
Colchester, Sheepen, Essex: Fragments, dark green shallow bowls, from Claudian-Neronian occupation (Harden 1947 301 no 56 pl 88; Charlesworth 1985a MF3:F6 no 35 fig 80).
Fishbourne Palace, West Sussex: Fragments, dark green bowls, from Neronian-early Flavian and unstratified contexts (Harden and Price 1971, 328 no 12 fig 137 pl 25; Price and Cottam 1996a, 172 no 24 fig 6.27).
Verulamium, Hertfordshire: Rim and body, dark green shallow bowl, from 2nd century context (Charlesworth 1972, 196 no 1 fig 74).

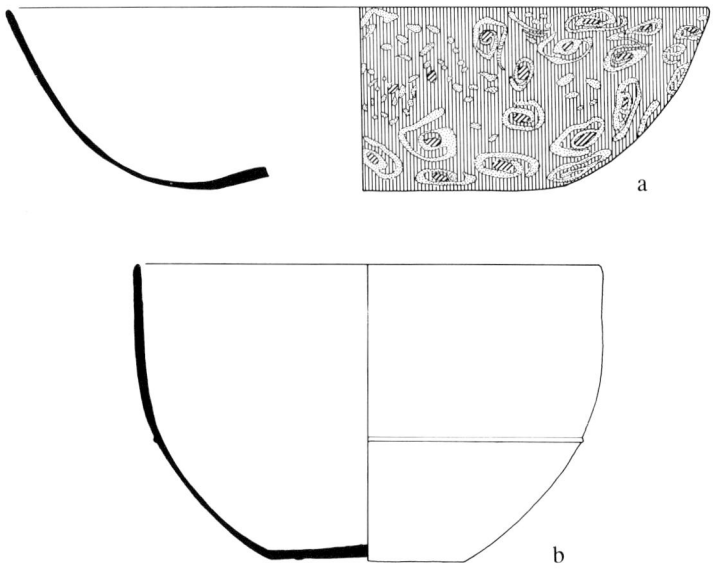

Fig 8 Scale 1:2

Winchester, Hampshire: Fragments, dark green and dark blue bowls, from Wolvesey Palace.
Bowls with shiny outside surfaces and ground inside surfaces.
Colchester, Essex: Rim and body, blue/green shallow bowl, from unstratified context (Cool and Price 1995, 26 no 184 fig.2.7).
Fishbourne Palace, West Sussex: Fragments, blue/green shallow and hemispherical bowls, from Claudian-early Flavian and unstratified contexts (Harden and Price 1971, 329 no 16 fig 137 pl 25; Price and Cottam 1996a, 171 no 17 fig 6.26).
Wimborne, Lake Farm, Dorset: Rim and body, blue/green shallow bowl, from Claudian-Neronian military occupation.

Further reading
Isings 1957, Form 1. For discussion in connection with finds from Colchester, see Cool and Price 1995, 27–31.

Constricted convex cup

Characteristics
Form
Everted rim, edge rounded, convex body with strong constriction, horizontal base, low diagonal base ring.

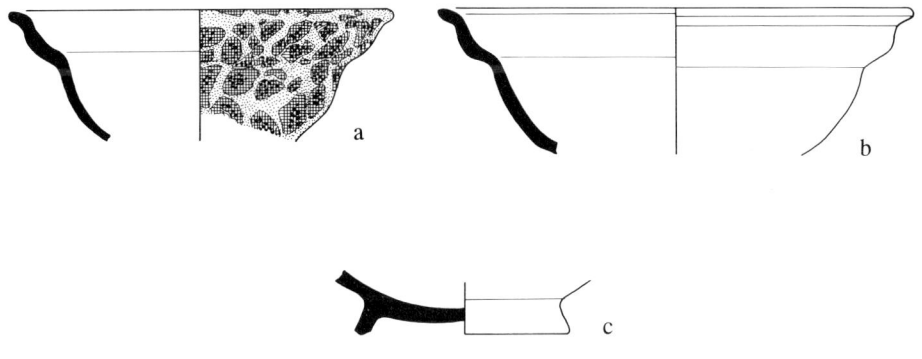

Fig 9 Scale 1:2

Colours
Polychrome mosaic. Opaque monochrome, particularly orange, light blue, white and red. Translucent monochrome, particularly dark blue and dark green.

Other features
The inside and outside surfaces are dull and smooth, grinding and polishing marks are often visible. These cups, shallow cylindrical bowls (see Figure 10) and some other forms are often called ceramic-form vessels. They are similar in appearance to contemporary metal and pottery vessels. This cup is closely comparable with the samian form Dragendorff 27.

Range of measurements
Rim diameters *c* 100–140mm. A wider and proportionately shallower version with a rim diameter of up to 230mm is occasionally found.

Distribution
Not common. Found on early Roman sites in southern Britain.

Date range
AD 43–65. Sometimes found in Flavian contexts.

Illustrated examples (Figure 9)
a) *Colchester, Sheepen, Essex*: Polychrome mosaic, opaque yellow ground, translucent purple patches with opaque white and green flecks, rim and body fragment, from Claudian-Neronian context, occupation to *c* AD 65 (Charlesworth 1985a, MF 3:F2 no 10 fig 80).
b) *Colchester, Sheepen, Essex*: , Dark green, rim and body fragment, from unstratified context, occupation to c. AD 65 (Harden 1947, 301 no 57 pl 88).
c) *Colchester, Essex*: Dark green, body and base fragment, from residual context (Cool and Price 1995, 35 no 203 fig 2.10).

Other finds
Bagendon, Gloucestershire: Dark blue, two fragments, from Claudian-Neronian occupation (Harden 1961, 200 no 11.1).
Caerleon, Gwent: Polychrome mosaic, green ground, opaque red and yellow flowers, rim and body, from Flavian-Trajanic context in barrack 12, Prysg Field (Price 1995d, 87 no 1 fig 9).
Canterbury, Kent: Opaque red, body, in residual Roman context, Marlowe Car Park (Shepherd 1995, 1228 no 24, fig 544).
Chichester, West Sussex: Opaque orange with red streaks, rim and body, from the Cattlemarket site (Price and Cool 1989a, 132 CM1 fig 19.1.1).
Llandovery, Powis: Polychrome mosaic, opaque red ground, translucent green and opaque yellow flowers, body and base (Plate 1.2).
Verulamium, Hertfordshire: Dark green, rim and body, from redeposited Antonine fire-debris in insula 27, house 2 (Charlesworth 1984, 147 no 8, fig 61.4). Polychrome mosaic, translucent purple and peacock blue ground, opaque white, red and yellow flowers and spirals, rim and body, from King Harry Lane site (Price 1989a, 42 no 268 fig 26).
Waddon Hill, Dorset: Opaque light blue, body, from Claudian military occupation (Harden 1960b, 95 no 4; 1979b, 87–8 no 24).

Further reading
Isings 1957, Form 2. For general accounts of early Roman ceramic-form glass vessels, see Price 1987b, 67–71, Grose 1991, 2–11. For discussion of these vessels in connection with finds at Colchester, see Cool and Price 1995, 30–5.

Cylindrical bowl

Characteristics
Form
Small horizontal rim, edge rounded, wide, low cylindrical body, flat base with projecting edge. A smaller and proportionately taller version is also known.

Colours
Sometimes in opaque monochrome. Translucent monochrome, particularly dark green, more common. Not recorded in polychrome mosaic.

Decoration
Cut grooves on rim edge, raised disc sometimes at the centre of the base on the inside surface, raised rings near the base edge on the outside surface.

Other features
The inside and outside surfaces are dull and smooth, grinding and polishing marks are often visible. These bowls, constricted convex cups (see Figure 9) and some other forms are often called ceramic-form vessels. They are similar in appearance to contemporary metal and pottery vessels. This bowl is closely comparable with the samian forms Dragendorff 22–23.

Fig 10 Scale 1:2

Range of measurements
Rim diameter *c* 80–180mm. Height *c* 25mm.

Distribution
Not common. Occasionally found on early Roman sites in southern Britain.

Date range
AD 43–AD 60/65.

Illustrated example (Figure 10)
Colchester, Sheepen, Essex: Dark green bowl, from cremation group 3, Neronian burial (Charlesworth 1985a, MF1:A6 (f) fig 15 no 5).

Other finds
Colchester, Essex: Dark blue, rim and body of unusual form, from unstratified context at Culver Street (Cool and Price 1995, 35 no 197 fig 2.10). Dark green bowl (Joslin Collection, Colchester Museum).
Gloucester: Dark green, complete profile, from Kingsholm (information from Hilary Cool).
London: Dark green, body and base, from Southwark St (Shepherd 1995b, 123 no 12 fig 38).
Verulamium, Hertfordshire: Dark green, complete profile, from occupation on floor of Neronian building in insula 17. Dark green base fragment, from mid 2nd century deposit in insula 22 (Charlesworth 1984a, 147 nos 7 and 11 fig 61 nos 3 and 7).

Further reading
Isings 1957, forms 22–23. For general accounts of early Roman ceramic-form glass vessels, see Price 1987b, 67–71, Grose 1991, 2–11. For discussion of these vessels in connection with finds at Colchester, see Cool and Price 1995, 30–5.

Two-handled cup (Scyphus)

Characteristics
Form
Vertical rim, edge rounded, convex or straight side, flat base, vertical base ring. Carved horizontal mouldings at rim edge, flanking two vertical handles, often with upper and/or lower projections (winged handles). Triangular or lozenge-shaped carved mouldings at junction of handles and body.

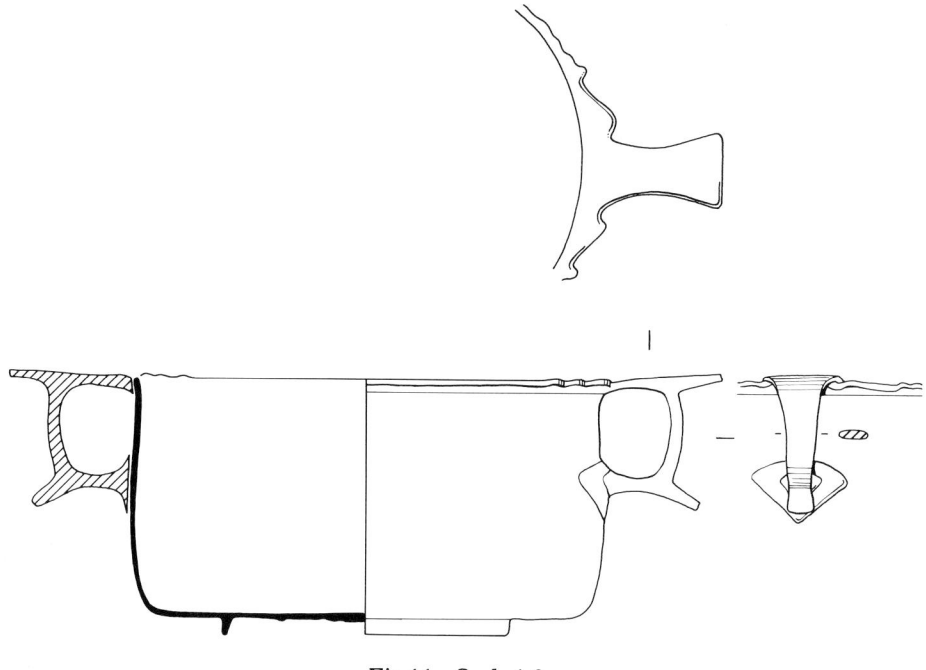

Fig 11   Scale 1:2

Colours
Occasionally in strong monochrome. Colourless and greenish colourless examples are more common.

Decoration
Some examples have horizontal raised cordons and wheel-cut lines below rim, and/or raised circles and central disc on underside of base.

Other features
All projecting elements, such as the handles, handle supports and base ring, were cut from the cast blank. The inside and outside surfaces are dull and smooth, grinding and polishing marks are often visible.

Range of measurements
Rim diameter *c* 100–130mm. Height 65–70mm.

Distribution
Not common.

Date range
AD 43–late 1st century. Examples in 3rd–4th century contexts (as at Exeter, noted below) represent a later phase of production. These sometimes have relief-cut decoration on the body.

Illustrated example (Figure 11)

London: Greenish colourless, cylindrical cup, from pit containing mid Flavian pottery at St Swithins House, Middle Walbrook Valley (Price 1991a, 159 no 610 fig 113).

Other finds

Colchester, Essex: Dark green, rim, edge of carved handle support, convex body, from Claudian/early Neronian contexts at Lion Walk (Cool and Price 1995, 34 no 193 fig 2.10).

Exeter, Devon: Colourless, rim, carved handle support, convex body with relief-cut decoration, from 4th century pit (Charlesworth 1979a, 222 no 1 fig 70).

Fishbourne Palace, West Sussex: Colourless, rim, handle and conical body with relief-cut godroons, from Claudian-early Flavian context. Colourless, handle and convex body with wheel-cut decoration, from context dated AD 100–270 (Harden and Price 1971, 334 and 336 nos 29 and 32 fig 138 pl 26).

London: Colourless, rim, carved handle support and convex body with triangular handle moulding, from context dated to AD 75–95 at Leadenhall Court (Shepherd 1996, 104 no 66 figs 61 and 63).

Segontium (Caernarvon), Gwynedd: Colourless, cylindrical body, handle with lozenge shaped moulding (Boon 1974b, 29–30 + fig).

York: Colourless, straight body and handle, and another handle (Harden 1962, 136 H G 222–3 fig 88).

Further reading

For discussion of these cups in connection with finds from Fishbourne and St Swithins House, London, see Harden and Price 1971, 332–6 and Price 1991a, 159–62.

Bowl with base ring

Characteristics

Form

Vertical or sloping rim, edge rounded, straight or convex body tapering in to horizontal base, vertical or diagonal base ring.

Colours

Some in polychrome mosaic and strongly coloured translucent monochrome. Colourless and greenish colourless examples are more common.

Decoration

Some examples have a horizontal wheel-cut line on the inside or outside of the rim, and/or raised horizontal cordons on the upper body and raised rings on the underside of the base. Facet- and relief-cutting are rare.

Other features

Deep and shallow conical and convex bowls have been included in this group. All projecting elements such as base rings and raised decoration were cut from the cast blank. The inside and outside surfaces are dull and smooth, grinding and polishing marks are often visible.

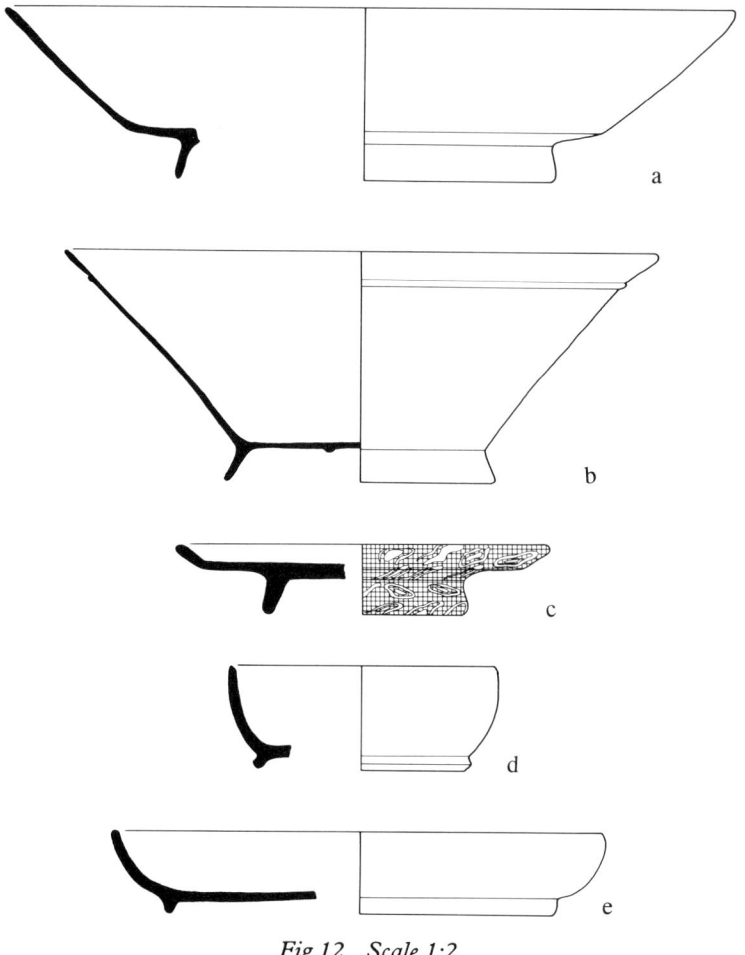

Fig 12   Scale 1:2

Range of measurements
Rim diameter *c* 70–240mm. Height *c* 40–120mm.

Distribution
Quite common.

Date range
Last quarter of 1st century-third quarter of 2nd century.

Illustrated examples (Figure 12)
a) *Watercrook, Cumbria*: Colourless, conical bowl, high base ring within wide base, from fort probably occupied from the last decade of the 1st century onwards (Charlesworth 1979b, 232 no 165 fig 93).

b) *Segontium, Gwynedd*: Colourless, conical bowl, raised ridges on body and underside of base, high base ring at junction of body and base, from Antonine drain deposit (Allen 1993, 220 no 10 fig 13.1).

c) *Piercebridge, Co. Durham*: Polychrome mosaic, translucent purple ground with opaque white roundels, shallow conical bowl, high base ring within wide base (Plate 1.4).

d) *London*: Greenish colourless, shallow convex bowl, low base ring at junction of body and base, from Cannon Street (Harden 1979c, 22 no 58 fig 12).

e) *London*: Greenish colourless, shallow convex bowl, low base ring at junction of body and wide base, from pit containing mid Flavian pottery at St Swithins House, Middle Walbrook Valley (Price 1991a, 159 no 611 fig 113).

Other finds
Chichester, West Sussex: Pale green shallow conical bowl (Down and Rule 1971, 47 fig 3.16).

Dorchester, Dorset: Colourless rim and body, conical bowl, from Greyhound Yard (Cool and Price 1993, 158 no 5 fig 84).

Fishbourne Palace, West Sussex: Colourless conical bowl with jigsaw and circular facets on the body and base (Price and Cottam 1996a, 172 nos 30–1 fig 6.27).

Park Street villa, St Albans, Hertfordshire: Colourless, rim and body, conical bowl with relief-cut papyrus leaves, from pit closed *c* AD 150 (Harden 1945, 70 no 2 fig 11).

Further reading
For discussion of these types of bowls in connection with the finds from St Swithins House, London and Segontium, see Price 1991a and Allen 1993. For more general discussion of cast colourless bowls in Britain, see Cool and Price 1995, 35–39.

Wide rimmed bowl/plate with base ring

Characteristics
Form
Wide horizontal rim, often with overhanging edge, straight or slightly convex body tapering in to horizontal base, diagonal or vertical base ring. There are two principal forms, a deep bowl and a shallow plate. The body of the plate is often only a shallow step joining the rim to the base.

Colours
Polychrome mosaic. Translucent monochrome, usually dark green or peacock blue. Opaque colours and blue/green examples are rare. Colourless/greenish colourless examples are most common.

Decoration
Low raised cordons are often found on the upper side of the rim at the angle with the overhanging edge and at the junction of rim and body. Wheel-cut lines are sometimes found on the upper side of the rim, and raised concentric circles at the centre of the base. A few bowls have egg-and-dart or notched cutting on the rim overhang, facet-cutting on the underside of the rim, on the body or on the underside of base. More complex decoration is very rare.

Other features
All the projecting elements, such as base rings, handles and raised decoration, were cut from the cast blank. The inside and outside surfaces are dull and smooth, grinding and polishing marks are often visible. These vessels are most frequently recognised by their distinctive rims. The overhanging edge is usually angular. Many variations of size, shape and production details occur. Bowls and plates with an overhanging rim edge tend to have high base rings sited within the area of the base, whereas examples without an overhang often have lower base rings close to the junction of body and base. A few examples have carved horizontal handles projecting from the rim.

Range of measurements
Rim diameter *c* 65–340mm. Height of plates *c* 20mm, height of bowls *c* 35–50+mm.

Distribution
Common.

Date range
Last quarter of 1st century–third quarter of 2nd century. Late dated examples include two bowls from Antonine contexts at Cramond, Central (Maxwell 1974, 198 nos 6–7 fig 16).

Illustrated examples (Figure 13 and Plate 4.1)
a) *London*: Dark yellow/brown, small plate, rim with overhanging edge, very shallow body, wide base, high diagonal base ring, from King William Street (Wheeler 1930, 122–3 no 4 fig 42).
b) *Colchester, Essex*: Colourless, bowl, rim with overhanging edge, convex body, high diagonal base ring, from Flavian–2nd century or later contexts (Cool and Price 1995, 39 no 212 fig 2.11).
c) *Gorhambury villa, St Albans, Hertfordshire*: Colourless, bowl, diagonal rim, conical body, low base ring, small central circle cut into upper surface of base (Neal et al. 1990, 201 no 4 fig 163).
d) *Walton-le-Dale, Lancashire*: Greenish colourless, small bowl, diagonal rim, convex body, low base ring, small central circle cut into lower surface of base (information from Christine Howard-Davis).

Other finds
Polychrome
Bakewell, Derbyshire: Translucent peacock blue ground with opaque yellow roundels, bowl with diagonal rim, from native settlement (Price 1985b).
Caersws, Powys: Translucent yellow/brown ground with yellow/brown and opaque yellow floral canes, bowl with diagonal rim, from early 2nd century context in vicus (Cool and Price 1989, 36 no 7 fig 20).
Carlisle, Cumbria: Translucent purple ground with green and opaque yellow floral canes, lower body and base, from Blackfriars Street, (Price 1990a, 165–6 MF 2/64 no 1 fig 159. Translucent purple ground with opaque yellow spirals, lower body and base, from Annetwell Street. Translucent dark green ground with opaque yellow roundels, shallow bowl with diagonal rim, from contexts containing Antonine and later material at The Lanes.

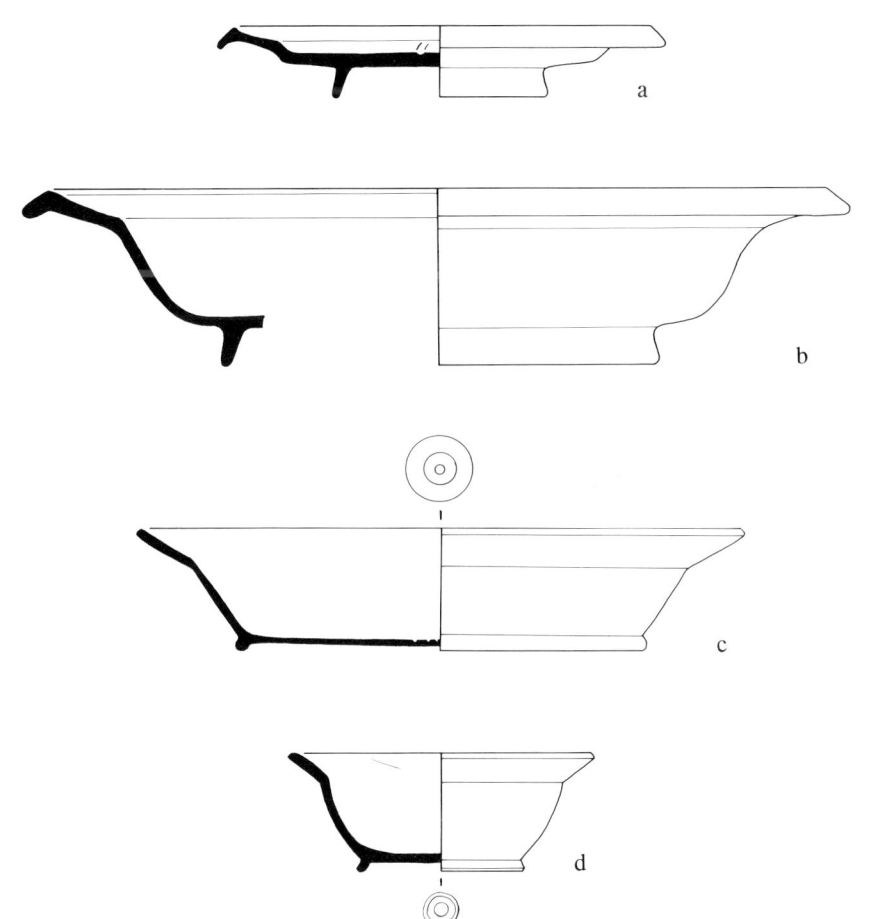

Fig 13   Scale 1:2

Catterick, North Yorkshire: Translucent purple ground with green and opaque yellow floral canes, rim with overhanging edge.

Fishbourne Palace, West Sussex: Two bowls with diagonal rims; translucent dark green ground with purple, opaque yellow, white and red canes; translucent dark yellow/brown ground with opaque yellow streaks, from residual/unstratified contexts (Harden and Price 1971, 324 and 326 nos 2 and 4 fig 137 pl 25).

Northchurch villa, Hertfordshire: Translucent purple ground, with green, opaque yellow and opaque blue floral canes and opaque white flecks, bowl, rim with overhanging edge, convex body. (Charlesworth 1974–76, 31 no 1 fig 19).

Strongly coloured opaque and translucent.

Birrens, Dumfries and Galloway: Translucent peacock blue, bowl, diagonal rim (Robertson 1975, 137 no 40 fig 48.3).

Castleford, West Yorkshire: Translucent peacock blue, bowl, diagonal rim, convex body, from mid 2nd century context in vicus. (Cool and Price 1998, 154 no 27 fig 51)

Ditchley villa, Oxfordshire: Opaque red, bowl, rim with overhanging edge (Harden 1936, 63–4 no 3 fig 12).

Kirkby Thore, Cumbria: Translucent dark green, small plate, horizontal rim (Charlesworth 1959a, 38–40 fig 3 no 3).

Colourless, Decorated

Cambridge: Convex bowl, horizontal rim, facet-cutting on underside of rim, facet-cut scene of a bird and plants enclosed in wheel-cut circle on underside of base, from Girton College cemetery, Roman cremation burial 2, dated to second or third quarter of 2nd century (Toynbee 1962, 185 no 140 pl 160; Fitzwilliam 1978, 46 no 86 fig).

Castleford, West Yorkshire: Small convex bowl, rim with overhanging edge, cutting on overhang and underside of rim, from mid 2nd century context in vicus. (Cool and Price 1998, 154 no 28 fig 51).

Fishbourne Palace, West Sussex: Convex bowl, rim with overhanging edge, cutting on overhang, small central circle on underside of base, from 2nd–3rd century context (Harden and Price 1971, 336 no 33, fig 138 pl 26). Base with cutting on underside (Price and Cottam 1996a, 172 no 32 fig 6.27).

London: Convex bowl, rim with overhanging edge, cutting on overhang, underside of rim, body and underside of base, from Hibernia Wharf, Southwark (information from John Shepherd).

Rim with overhanging edge, cutting on overhang and underside of rim, from Southwark Street (Shepherd 1995b, 125 no 60 fig 38).

Richborough, Kent: Rim with overhanging edge, cutting on overhang and underside of rim (Yadin 1963, 107–9 fig 40a).

Wroxeter, Shropshire: Convex bowl, rim with overhanging edge and carved horizontal handle, cutting on rim overhang, underside of rim, body and underside of base, from deposit dated before *c* AD 125 (Charlesworth 1975a).

York, Minster: Two convex bowls, one with cutting on rim overhang and underside of rim, one with horizontal rim and carved handle (Price 1995b, 355 nos 8–9 fig 142)

Colourless, Undecorated.

Ditchley villa, Oxfordshire: Wide convex bowl, rim with overhanging edge, complete profile (Harden 1936, 63–4 no 1 fig 12).

Gloucester: Rim with overhanging edge, from Flavian context in Westgate Street (Price 1980b, 111 no 1 fig 17).

Fishbourne Palace, West Sussex: Three bowls, one with diagonal rim, two with overhanging edges, from contexts dated *c* AD 75–100, and later (Harden and Price 1971, 332 and 336 nos 25–6 and 34 fig 138, pl 26).

London: Small bowl, rim with overhanging edge, from an early 2nd century pit, St Thomas Street, Southwark: (Townend and Hinton 1978, 389 no 101 fig 176). Rims, two bowls with overhanging edges, from Southwark Street (Shepherd 1995b, 125 nos 61–2 fig 38). Rim, bowl with diagonal rim, from context dated *c* AD 95–100, Leadenhall Court (Shepherd 1996, 104 no 65 fig 63).

Verulamium, Hertfordshire: Small plate with overhanging rim edge, from context dated AD 150–180, insula 28 (Charlesworth 1984a, 149 no 14 fig 61 no 8).

Wroxeter, Shropshire: Small bowl with diagonal rim, from deposit probably dated to mid 2nd century or earlier (Bushe-Fox 1914, 20 fig 12).

Further reading
For general accounts of cast colourless bowls and plates, see Price 1987b, 72–80, Grose 1991, 12–18. For discussion of these and other cast colourless bowls and plates in connection with finds from Colchester, see Cool and Price 1995, 35–39.

Cups and bowls: mould-blown

Mould-blown hemispherical ribbed bowl

Characteristics

Form
Straight or slightly curved rim, edge cracked-off and ground smooth, short straight or slightly concave shoulder, change of angle to convex body, tapering in to concave base.

Colours
Some dark blue and yellow/brown examples; blue/green, pale green and pale yellow/green more common.

Decoration
Close-set vertical ribs on body. One or two horizontal cordons are usual above the base edge. A frieze of bosses, arcading or leaf motifs very occasionally occurs on the lower body. Raised concentric circles, sometimes with central pellet, on base.

Other features
Several variations of these bowls have been noted. Some have a very pronounced change of angle on the upper body and there are differences in wall thickness, the angle of the rim, and the length, width and arrangement of the ribs. The bowls were produced in three-piece moulds; two vertical seams are visible on the body.

Range of measurements
Rim diameter *c* 90–110mm; height *c* 50–60mm.

Distribution
Fairly common on Claudian-early Flavian sites in southern Britain, occasionally found in northern England. Rare in burials.

Date range
c A 43–*c* AD 75/80.

Illustrated example (Figure 14 and Plate 2.2)
Usk, Gwent: Pale green, almost complete bowl, from late Neronian pit in legionary fortress (Price 1995a, 153 no 25 fig 43 pl 12).

Other finds
Brandon Camp, Herefordshire: Blue/green fragment, from military site occupied from *c* AD 55–60 (Price 1987c, 74 no 3).
Caersws, Powys: Yellow/brown, dark blue fragments, two or three bowls, from late 1st century contexts in vicus (Cool and Price 1989, 36–8 nos 12–4 fig 20).

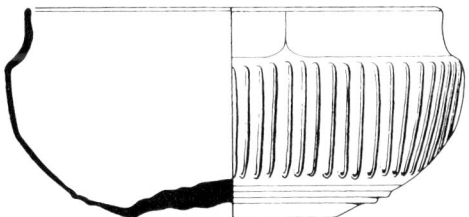

Fig 14   Scale 1:2

Carlisle, Cumbria: Dark blue, blue/green fragments, two cups, from Blackfriars Street (Price 1990a, 166 MF2/65 nos 6–7 fig 159).

Castleford, West Yorkshire: Blue/green fragments, two or three cups, one with a leaf frieze on the lower body, from Flavian contexts in fort (Cool and Price 1998, 154 nos 38–40 fig 52)

Colchester, Essex: Dark blue, pale green fragments, three cups, from residual contexts at Balkerne Lane, Culver Street and Gilberd School (Cool and Price 1995, 52–3 nos 243–5 fig 3.3).

Colchester, Sheepen, Essex: Pale yellow/brown fragment, from occupation to *c* AD 65 (Harden 1947, 300 no 48 pls 86–7).

Dorchester, Dorset: Blue/green fragment, from Greyhound Yard (Cool and Price 1993, 150, 158 no 10 fig 84).

Hallaton, Leicestershire: Green, complete bowl, from cremation burial (Page and Keate 1907, 212).

London: Pale blue/green, fragments, two cups; one with frieze of bosses and lattice on the lower body from Nicholas Lane (Wheeler 1930, 122 nos 5–6 fig 42).

Verulamium, Hertfordshire: Dark blue, yellow/green, blue/green, fragments, at least three cups, two from Neronian-early/mid Flavian contexts (Charlesworth 1972, 196 no 1 fig 74 no 2; Charlesworth 1984a, 150–1 nos 32–4 fig 61 nos 18–20).

Further reading
For general discussion of this and other 1st century mould-blown forms, see Price 1991b. For discussion in connection with finds from Colchester and Usk, see Cool and Price 1995, 51–3, and Price 1995a, 152–5.

Mould-blown ovoid cup

Characteristics
Form
Curved rim, edge cracked-off and ground smooth, convex body tapering to flat or slightly concave base.

Colours
Some strongly coloured examples; blue/green, pale yellow/green and greenish colourless are more common; cased examples are very rare.

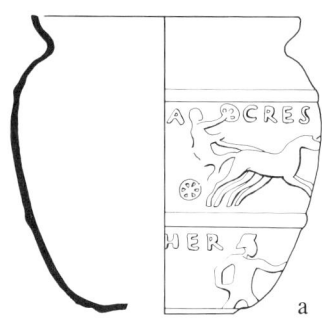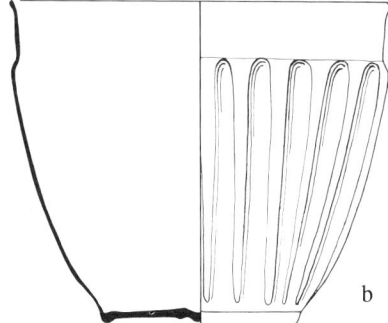

Fig 15   Scale 1:2

Decoration
Various schemes of decoration in relief on body, including vertical ribs, triangular bosses, scenes of chariot racing and gladiatorial combat in two friezes with named competitors, and other designs. Examples with Greek lettering are rare. Raised concentric circles on base.

Other features
Blown into a two- or three-piece mould; two vertical seams visible on body.

Range of measurements
Rim diameter *c* 70mm, height *c* 80mm.

Distribution
Not common. Mostly known in southern Britain, rare in northern England.

Date range
Few found in dated contexts. Probably third quarter of 1st century AD.

Illustrated examples (Figure 15)
a) *Hartlip villa, Kent*: Blue/green, fragmentary cup, two friezes showing chariot racing and gladiatorial combat (Harden 1982, 32 figs 3–4; RIB II,2 91 no 2419.18).
b) *Caerleon, Gwent*: Blue/green, fragmentary cup, vertical ribs, from late 1st–early 2nd century context in civilian settlement, (information from the late George Boon).

Other finds
Binchester, Co Durham: Pale blue/green, rim and upper body, horizontal zone containing Greek lettering (RIB II,2 96 no 2419.38).
Fishbourne Palace, West Sussex: Blue/green, rim and body, triangular bosses, from context dated AD 55–75 (Harden and Price 1971, 339 no 37 fig 138 pl 28).
London: Blue/green, fragmentary cup, chariot-racing and gladiators, worn mould, from Southwark (Harden 1982, 33, 35–6 no 2 fig 5; RIB II,2 92 no 2419.19).
Sea Mills, near Bristol, Avon: Blue/green body, triangular bosses and other motifs (Cool and Price 1987a, 95 no 7 fig 44).

Topsham, Devon: Blue/green, rim and upper body, two examples, chariot racing (Harden 1982, 36–7 nos 3–4 fig 6; RIB II,2 91 no 2419.16–17).
Usk, Gwent: Yellow/brown and opaque white cased body, triangular bosses, from residual context in legionary fortress (Price 1995a, 153 no 22 fig 43).

Further reading
See Harden 1982 for discussion of examples with chariot-racing and gladiators; see Price 1991 for discussion of this and other 1st-century mould-blown forms.

Mould-blown cylindrical cup (sports cup)

Characteristics
Form
Vertical or small curved rim, edge cracked-off and ground, cylindrical body, rounded base edge, flat or slightly concave base.

Colours
Some strong colours, especially dark blue, dark green and yellow/brown; blue/green, pale yellow/green and greenish colourless are more common. Cased examples are very rare.

Decoration
Horizontal cordons divide body into two or three zones of decoration, showing scenes from the circus or arena, usually chariot races or gladiators fighting, occasionally boxers or wrestlers. All versions have a narrow zone below the rim containing the names of the competitors. The main zone has either four charioteers with architectural features from the circus or four pairs of gladiators or four or more pairs of boxers. The lower body on some chariot-race and boxer cups has a narrow zone containing running animals, lattice or other motifs. Therefore concentric circles and a central pellet or hollow on the base. A few mould-blown cylindrical cups were decorated with quite different designs.

Other features
Usually produced in three-piece moulds; two vertical seams visible on body.

Range of measurements
Rim diameter *c* 75–80mm, height *c* 60–80mm.

Distribution
Fairly common on early sites in southern Britain, occasionally also in northern England. Rare in burials.

Date range
Approximately third quarter of 1st century AD (*c* AD 50/55–75/80).

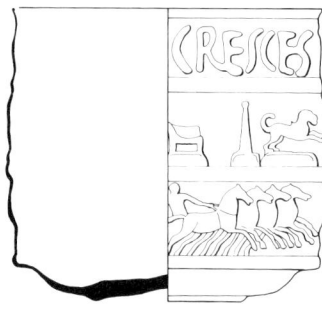

Fig 16   Scale 1:2

Illustrated example (Figure 16)

Colchester, Essex: Pale yellow/green, intact cup, chariot racing scenes in two zones, from cremation burial in West Cemetery (Harden *et al* 1987, 168 no 89).

Other finds

Canterbury, Kent: Dark blue, yellow/green,blue/green, fragments, six cups with chariot racing (Price 1995e; RIB II,2 88–9 no 2419.7–8, 10–11; and information from Pam Garrard).

Carlisle, Cumbria: Dark blue, fragments, cup with chariot racing, from context dated *c*.AD85–?105 at Annetwell Street (RIB II,2 88 no 2419.6). Blue/green, small fragments, cup with chariot racing, from The Lanes.

Colchester, Essex: Yellow/green, blue/green, fragments, at least nine cups with chariot racing and gladiators, from Neronian-early Flavian and later contexts at Balkerne Lane, Culver Street, Gilberd School and the General Post Office site (Cool and Price 1995, 43–50 nos 232–8 fig.3.1).

Colchester, Sheepen, Essex: Blue/green, fragments, three cups with gladiators, from contexts dated *c*.A D 49–61, and *c*A D 61–65 (Harden 1947 300 no 50–2 pl 86).

Gloucester: Pale yellow/green, blue/green, fragments, four cups with chariot racing and gladiators, from Neronian military site at Kingsholm (Price and Cool 1985, 45–6 nos 10–15 fig 17; RIB II,2 87, 93–4 no 2419.3, 25, 30).

Lincoln: Blue/green, fragments, two cups with chariot racing.

London: Dark green, dark blue, light blue, yellow/green, blue/green, fragments, at least 20 cups with chariot racing, gladiators and boxers, from Neronian-early Flavian and later contexts at various sites (Harden 1978; Shepherd 1996, 107 nos 92–8, fig 64; RIB II,2 90, 92–5 no 2419.12, 14–15, 21, 26, 28, 34; and information from Christine Jones and John Shepherd).

Richborough, Kent: Dark blue fragment, cup with chariot racing (Bushe-Fox 1932, no 64 pl 17).

York: Blue/green fragment, cup with chariot racing (Harden 1962, 136 fig 88 a).

Further reading

For general discussion of these and other 1st century mould-blown forms, see Price 1991b. For discussion in connection with finds from Canterbury and Colchester, see Price 1995e and Cool and Price 1995, 43–50.

Mould-blown conical beaker

Characteristics

Form
Straight or curved rim, edge cracked-off and ground smooth, tall, straight body tapering in to flat or slightly concave base, occasionally with tubular base ring.

Colours
Some strong colours, especially dark blue and yellow/brown; more commonly blue/green, pale yellow/green, and pale green; sometimes greenish colourless or colourless.

Decoration
Wide range of designs in relief on body, including oval bosses (often called almond-shaped knobs or lotus buds, and sometimes combined with lattice or pellets), and circular bosses, shells, rosettes, spirals and foliage. Base often has raised concentric circles.

Other features
Usually blown into two- or three-piece moulds, more rarely into four- and five-piece moulds; at least two vertical mould seams are visible on the body.

Range of measurements
Rim diameter *c* 65–75mm, height *c*120–150+mm.

Distribution

Not very common. Found on settlements in many parts of Britain, including lowland Scotland. Very rare in burials.

Date range

c A D 65/70-*c* AD 75/80.

Illustrated examples (Figure 17)

a) *Verulamium, Hertfordshire*: Colourless, fragment with shells and undulating line, from residual context (Charlesworth 1984a, 150 no 29 fig 61 no 15).
b) *Castleford, West Yorkshire*: Pale green, lower body and base edge with oval bosses, from late 1st century context in fort (Cool and Price 1998, 154 no 37 fig 52).

Other finds

Binchester, Co.Durham: Colourless with spirals, from late 1st century context in fort.
Caersws, Powys: Yellow/brown, dark blue, at least two beakers with oval bosses and lattice, from later 1st century contexts (Cool and Price 1989, 38 nos 15–7 fig 20).
Chester: Fragments with oval bosses and lattice, from Goss Street and Abbey Green.
London: Yellow/green fragment with oval bosses and cordon above base, from late 1st century context at Leadenhall Court (Shepherd 1995b, 107 no 88 fig 63).
Stoke Bruerne (probably), Northamptonshire: Greenish, complete beaker with circular bosses and lattice. Curved rim and tubular pushed-in base ring; three mould-seams on body (Brown 1968).
Verulamium, Hertfordshire: Yellowish, at least two beakers with oval bosses and lattice,

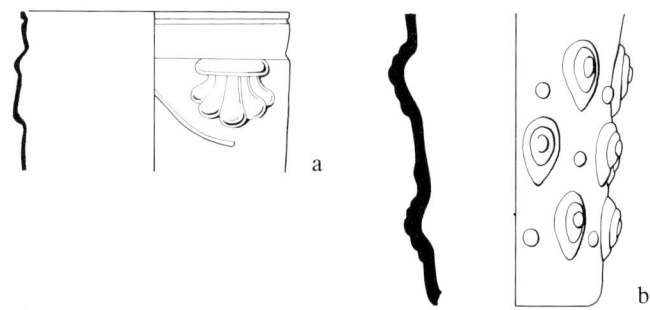

Fig 17   Scale 1:2

one with curved rim from pit dated AD 60–75, the other from early 2nd century, residual and unstratified deposits in insula 14 (Charlesworth 1972, 196–8 nos 2, 4–6 fig 74 no 3).

Usk, Gwent: Pale green with oval bosses and pellets, colourless with foliage, fragments of two beakers, from unstratified context and late Neronian-early Flavian deposit in legionary fortress (Price 195a, 153 and 155 nos 23 and 27 fig 43).

Winchester, Hampshire: Colourless fragment with horizontal foliage motifs, from late 1st century context at Brook Street.

Wroxeter, Shropshire: Colourless fragments, at least two beakers with oval bosses and lattice, and with foliage motifs.

York: Light green fragment with oval bosses and circular pellets (Harden 1962, 136 H.G.273 fig 88). Colourless fragment with square meander from the Minster site (Price 1995b, 355 no 13 fig 142).

Further reading
Isings 1957, Form 31. For general discussion of this and other 1st century mould-blown forms, see Price 1991b. For discussion of this form in connection with finds at Caersws and Usk, see Cool and Price 1989, 32–3, and Price 1995a, 150–1.

Cups and bowls: blown

Trailed ribbed cup (zarte Rippenschale)

Characteristics
Form
Strongly curved rim, edge cracked-off and ground smooth, convex body, small flat base, thickening towards centre.

Colours
Strongly coloured translucent, blue/green or greenish colourless ground with opaque white trails.

Decoration
Opaque white spiral trail wound from the centre of the base and round the body to the area below the rim. Narrow vertical pinched ribs on the body.

Other features
The trail was applied before the vessel was blown to full size and before the ribs were formed. It is thicker on the base than on the body and is distorted by the ribs.

Range of measurements
Rim diameters *c* 60mm–*c* 100mm.

Distribution
Not common. Found in small numbers on early sites in southern England and the Midlands.

Date range
AD 43–AD 60/65.

Illustrated example (Figure 18)
Colchester, Sheepen, Essex: Blue/green, opaque white trails, from a Claudian-early Neronian pit (Harden 1947, 295 no 20 pl 88).

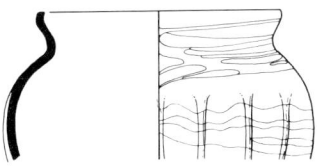

Fig 18   Scale 1:2

Other finds
With opaque white trails
Colchester, Essex: Three, blue/green and yellow green, from insecurely dated or residual contexts (Cool and Price 1995, 60 nos 254–56).
Colchester, Sheepen, Essex: At least six yellow/brown, blue/green and greenish colourless, from Claudian-early Neronian and residual contexts (Harden 1947, 295 nos 20a–21c pls 87–8; Charlesworth 1985a, MF 3:F3 nos 20–2 fig 80).
Chichester, West Sussex: Two, yellow/brown and greenish colourless (Charlesworth 1978a, 267 no 13 fig 10.22; Charlesworth 1981b, 293 no 8 fig 15.1).
Dorchester, Dorset: Yellow/brown, from Greyhound Yard (Cool and Price 1993, 158 no 13 fig 84).
Ham Hill, Somerset: Yellow/brown.
Longthorpe, Cambridgeshire: Light green (Charlesworth 1974a, 89–90 fig 48 no 6).
Mancetter, Warwickshire: Three, pale green, blue/green and yellow/brown, from Claudian-Neronian military occupation.
Waddon Hill, Dorset: Two, purple and blue/green, from Claudian military occupation (Harden 1979b, 87 nos 2 and 9).
Wimborne, Lake Farm, Dorset: Two, pale green and pale yellow/brown, from Claudian-Neronian military site.

Further reading
Isings 1957, form 17, Haevernick 1981, xi–xxviii, 171–9. For discussion of these and other polychrome blown vessels in connection with finds from Colchester, see Cool and Price 1995, 56–61.

Cup with stepped rim and stemmed base (cantharus)

Characteristics
Form
Slightly out-splayed stepped rim, edge fire-rounded, deep convex body tapering in, applied solid stem and blown base. Few handles survive on pieces from Britain, but examples from elsewhere in the western provinces have two curved handles attached to the rim edge and the body, or no handles.

Colours
Polychrome, strong coloured monochrome and blue/green.

Decoration
Trails and blobs in contrasting colours at rim or on body; sometimes cased.

Other features
Small fragments are not very diagnostic; they may come from various cup forms.

Range of measurements
Rim diameters *c* 90–140mm.

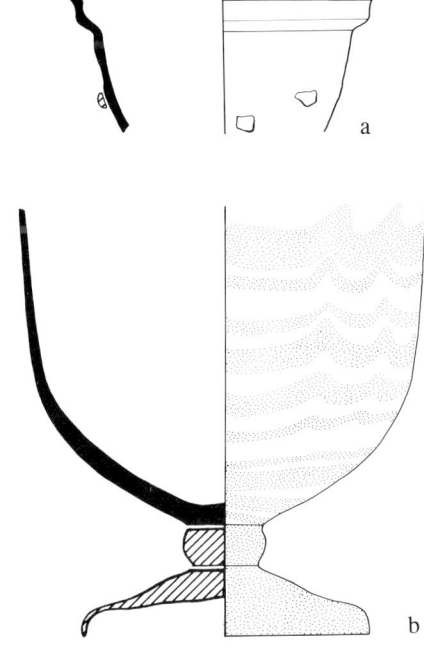

Fig 19   Scale 1:2

Distribution
Not common. Noted on some early sites in southern Britain.

Date range
AD 43–*c* AD 65.

Illustrated examples (Figure 19)
a) *London*: Pale green with unmarvered opaque white blob, from late 1st century context at Toppings and Sun Wharves (Schwab 1974, 103 no 4 fig 50).

b) *Colchester, Sheepen, Essex*: Yellow/brown with marvered opaque white trails, from Claudian-early Neronian context (Charlesworth 1985a, MF 3:F2–3 no 16 fig 80).

Other finds
Abergavenny, Gwent: Dark blue body with marvered opaque white trail, from pre-Flavian context at the Orchard site (Price 1993a, 216 no 3 illustration 16).

Colchester, Essex: Blue/green rim and upper body with unmarvered opaque blue blobs, from context dated *c* AD 49/55–60/1 at Balkerne Lane. Blue/green rim fragments from contexts dated AD 49–60/1 and *c* AD 49/55–60/1 at Culver Street and Lion Walk (Cool and Price 1995, 60 no 253 fig 4.1, 100 nos 699–700 fig 6.5).

Colchester, Sheepen, Essex: Yellow/brown and opaque white cased body fragment with handle attachment; pale green rim and upper body with unmarvered opaque blue blob, from Claudian-Neronian context (Harden 1947, 297 no 35 pl 87, Charlesworth 1985a, MF 3:F3 no 27 fig 80).

Exeter, Devon: Dark green stepped rim, from residual context (Charlesworth 1979a, 223 no 4 fig 70); blue/green rim and handle, from Neronian-early Flavian occupation (Allen 1991, 222 no 14 fig 93).

Lincoln: Blue/green body, stem and foot, from Neronian-early Flavian military phase at North Row (Harden 1949, 77 no 6 pl 10). Yellow/green rim fragment from Cottesford Place.

London: Blue/green stepped rim, from mid to late 1st century context at Leadenhall Court (Shepherd 1996, 109 nos 138–140).

Wroxeter, Shropshire: Dark blue stepped rim with marvered opaque white trails. Yellow/green stepped rim, from Neronian-early Flavian military occupation.

Further reading

Isings 1957, forms 36, 38; van Lith 1991. For discussion of the polychrome and monochrome examples in connection with finds from Colchester, see Cool and Price 1995, 56–60, 100–101.

Deep cup with stepped rim and one handle (modiolus)

Characteristics

Form

Several types of rim are found. Some examples have a stepped rim with fire-rounded edge, similar to the cantharus (see Figure 19). Others, such as the illustrated example, have a stepped rim with a tubular edge bent up, out and down, a deep cylindrical body tapering in to a pushed-in base ring and concave base. A vertical curved ribbon handle is applied to the body and attached to the underside of the rim.

Colours

Strongly coloured or blue/green.

Decoration

A figure-of-eight fold forming a horizontal band is sometimes present below the rim. The body is often undecorated, although ribs and horizontal wheel-cut lines sometimes occur.

Other features

Similar cups are also known in metal and pottery. Rim and body fragments can often be mistaken for other forms of cups.

Range of measurements

Wide range of heights, rim diameters *c* 120–140mm.

Distribution

Rare; occasionally found at early sites in southern Britain.

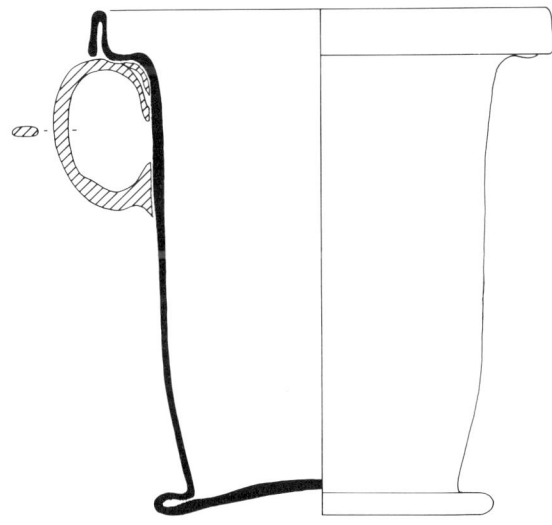

Fig 20   Scale 1:2

Date range
Uncertain. Examples from dated contexts suggest *c* AD 43–AD 65/70.

Illustrated example (Figure 20)
Stevenage, Boxfield Farm, Hertfordshire: Dark yellow/brown, from Neronian-early Flavian cremation burial.

Other finds
Ashdon, Bartlow Hills, Essex: A yellowish vessel with blue handle described as nearly complete, found in burial with coin of Hadrian (Gage 1834, 7 pl 3 fig 8).
Exeter, Devon: Nearly complete, blue/green, narrow vertical ribs, handle missing, in Neronian-early Flavian pit (Journal of Roman Studies 43, 1953, 124 pl 23).
Gloucester: Blue/green stepped rim with tubular edge, from Neronian military assemblage at Kingsholm (Price and Cool 1985, 50 no 48 fig 19 – illustrated upside down).

Further reading
Isings 1957, form 37. Kern 1963. Haevernick 1981, 367–74).

Convex cup with wheel-cutting and abrasion (Hofheim cup)

Characteristics
Form
Vertical or slightly inturned rim, edge cracked-off and ground smooth, slightly convex or straight upper body, convex lower body tapering in to flat or concave base, sometimes with a high central kick.

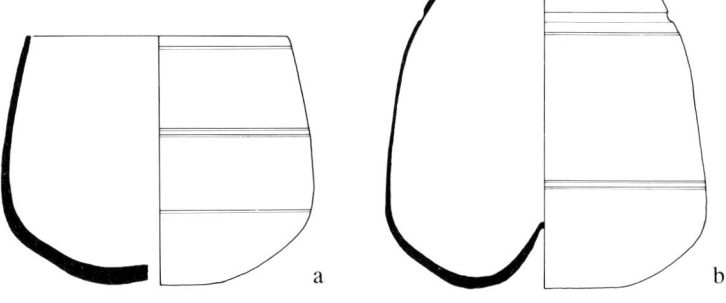

Fig 21   Scale 1:2

Colours
Polychrome exmples are rare, strongly coloured monochrome, pale green and greenish colourless are quite frequent, blue/green is most common.

Decoration
Polychrome cups were made in cased glass, or with marvered splashes and trails (see Figure 4.5), or enamelled decoration. Monochrome cups are by far the most common, and are always decorated with horizontal wheel-cut or abraded lines. There is often a broad wheel-cut line on the upper body. Vertical ribs are rare.

Other features
Often called 'Hofheim cups', after the Rhineland military site where over thirty examples were found (Ritterling 1912/13, 365–6 forms 1–2, Abb 93). The rim edge, although carefully finished, is sometimes uneven. High kicked bases occur in the second half of the 1st century.

Range of measurements
Rim diameters *c* 60–80mm, heights *c* 65–80mm.

Distribution
Very common on sites in southern Britain . Also found at a few Flavian sites in northern Britain.

Date range
AD 43-*c* AD 75.

Illustrated examples (Figure 21)
a) *Exeter, Devon*: Blue/green, from unstratified context (Allen 1991, 222 no 9 fig 93).
b) *Wroxeter, Shropshire*: Blue/green, from drain deposit in the Forum containing early Flavian samian.

Other finds
Caerleon, Gwent: Blue/green, from Flavian-Trajanic context in barrack 12, Prysg Field (Price 1995d, 83, 87 no 3 fig 9). At least two, blue/green, from 2nd century contexts at Roman Gates (Allen 1992, 179 nos 4–5, figs).

Colchester, Essex: At least 35 polychrome, strongly coloured, pale green, greenish colourless and blue/green, from Claudian, Neronian-early Flavian and later contexts (Cool and Price 1995, 66–8 nos 279–331 fig 5.2).

Colchester, Sheepen, Essex: Polychrome, strongly coloured, greenish colourless and blue/green, from Claudian-early Neronian deposits (Harden 1947, 303 nos 68–76 pl 88; Charlesworth 1985a, MF 3: F7 nos 48–52 fig 81 & F9 nos 82–4 fig 82).

Exeter, Devon: Blue/green with ribs (Journal of Roman Studies 43, 1953, 124 pl 33). Strongly coloured, greenish and blue/green, from Claudian-early Flavian and later contexts (Harden 1952, 93 nos 3–4; Charlesworth 1979a, 223 nos 5–6 fig 70; Allen 1991, 222 nos 10–13, fig 93).

Fishbourne Palace, West Sussex: Strongly coloured, pale green and blue/green; several from contexts dated AD 43–75 (Harden and Price 1971, 345–6, nos 46–8, 50–1, fig 139, Price and Cottam 1996a, 176, 178 nos 54–5, 61, 73 fig 6.28).

Gloucester: At least seven strongly coloured, greenish colourless and blue/green, in Neronian military assemblage at Kingsholm (Price and Cool 1985, 46, 48 nos 21–23c, 41–45b, figs 18–9).

Inchtuthil, Tayside: Yellow/green, from fortress occupied *c* AD 83–86/7 (Price 1985a, 308–10 no 2 fig 93).

London: Blue/green cups, from late 1st century and later contexts at Southwark Street and Leadenhall Court (Shepherd 1995b, 129 nos 124–30 fig 39, Shepherd 1996, 107 nos 102–10 fig 64).

Mancetter, Warwickshire: Fragments, polychrome, strongly coloured and blue/green, from Claudian-Neronian military occupation.

Ribchester, Lancashire: Three, greenish colourless and blue/green.

Usk, Gwent: cased, strongly coloured, greenish colourless and blue/green, in Neronian-early Flavian contexts in legionary fortress (Price 1995a, 159–162 nos 32, 37–45, fig 43).

Wimborne, Lake Farm, Dorset: At least four, blue-green, from Claudian-early Neronian military site.

Wroxeter, Shropshire: At least eleven strongly coloured and blue/green, from Neronian-early Flavian military occupation.

York: Fragments, at least five strongly coloured, light green and blue/green, in Flavian and later contexts at Blake Street in the legionary fortress (Cool 1995a, 1651–2, 1656 nos 5895, 5898, 5914–6, 6030–9 fig 735).

Further reading
Isings 1957, form 12. For discussion in connection with finds from Colchester and Usk, see Cool and Price 1995, 64–8, and Price 1995a, 159–62.

Beaker on solid base

Characteristics
Form
Curved rim, edge cracked-off and ground, cylindrical, thick-walled upper body, slightly convex lower body tapering in, out-splayed base edge, thick flat base, often with internal dome.

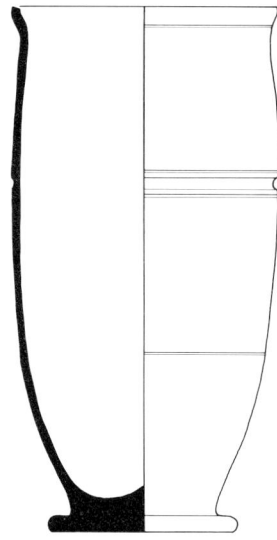

Fig 22   Scale 1:2

Colours
Yellow/green, pale green, most commonly blue/green.

Decoration
Horizontal wheel-cut and abraded lines

Other features
Rim and upper body often quite thick-walled, but small body fragments are difficult to distinguish from Hofheim cups and other beakers

Range of measurements
Rim diameters *c* 70mm, heights *c* 140mm.

Distribution
Not common. Found on some sites in southern England and the Midlands.

Date range
AD 43–*c* AD 65/70.

Illustrated example (Figure 22)
Colchester, Sheepen, Essex: Blue/green, from Claudian-early Neronian context (Harden 1947, 303 no 77 pl 88).

Other finds
Colchester, Essex: Blue/green rim, body, base fragments, at least five beakers, from Claudian-Neronian and later contexts (Cool and Price 1995, 69 nos 336, 343, 348–51 fig 5.3).
Colchester, Sheepen, Essex: Blue/green fragments, two beakers, from Claudian-early

Neronian contexts (Harden 1947, 303 no 78 pl 88, Charlesworth 1985a, MF3:F9 no 87 fig 83).

Dorchester, Dorset: Blue/green, rim, body, base fragments, at least one beaker, from Greyhound Yard (Cool and Price 1993, 162 nos 93–4 fig 86).

Gloucester: Yellow/green body fragment, from Neronian military assemblage at Kingsholm (Price and Cool 1985, 48 no 32 fig 18).

Lincoln: Blue/green rim and body fragment, from late Neronian-early Flavian legionary levels at North Row (Harden 1949, 77 no 5 pl 10).

London: Blue/green, fragments of two beakers, from pre-Flavian and late 1st century contexts at Borough High Street, Southwark, and Leadenhall Court (Townend and Hinton 1978b, 151 no 1 fig 60; Shepherd 1996, 108 no 112 fig 64).

Mancetter, Warwickshire: Blue/green, fragments of two beakers, from Claudian-Neronian military occupation.

Milton Keynes, Bancroft villa, Buckinghamshire: Blue/green base fragment (Allen 1994, 358 no 370 fig 182).

Richborough, Kent: Blue/green rim and body, from pit dated AD 75–100 (Bushe-Fox 1949, 159 no 378 pl 59).

Usk, Gwent: Blue/green base fragment, from late Neronian-early Flavian pit in legionary fortress (Price 1995a, 164, 167 no 52 fig 44).

Wilcote, Oxfordshire: Blue/green rim and body fragment, from Claudian ditch (Cool 1993, 160, no 10 fig 82).

Wimborne, Lake Farm, Dorset: Blue/green rim and body fragments, from Claudian-early Neronian military site.

Wroxeter, Shropshire: Pale green and blue/green fragments, from Neronian-early Flavian military site.

Further reading
Isings 1957, form 34; for discussion in connection with finds of these and similar beakers from Colchester, see Cool and Price 1995, 68–9.

Conical or ovoid beaker with pushed-in base

Characteristics
Form
Vertical rim, edge cracked-off and ground smooth, tall, straight or slightly convex side tapering in to small out-splayed, pushed-in base ring and domed base.

Colours
Pale yellow/brown, pale green, greenish colourless.

Decoration
Horizontal wheel-cut lines, some quite broad, and horizontal abrasion.

Other features
The quality of the glass, ie the lack of specks and bubbles, helps to distinguish body fragments from similar 4th century beakers. Rim and upper body fragments are often similar to those of Hofheim cups.

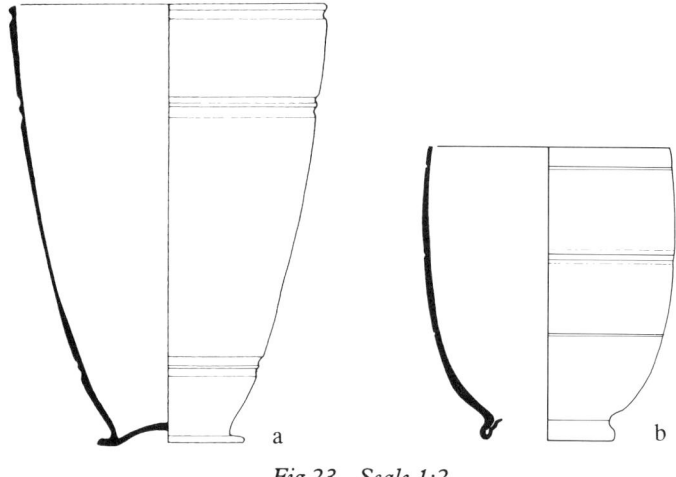

Fig 23   Scale 1:2

Range of measurements
Rim diameters *c* 60–85mm, heights *c* 80–120mm.

Distribution
Not common. Noted in southern England and the Midlands.

Date range
Last third of the 1st century AD.

Illustrated examples (Figure 23)
a) *Usk, Gwent*: Greenish colourless, conical, from late Neronian-early Flavian pit in legionary fortress (Price 1995a, 162 no 46 fig 43).
b) *Dorchester, Dorset*: Pale green, ovoid, from Greyhound Yard (Cool and Price 1993, 160 no 27 fig 85).

Other finds
Carlisle, Cumbria: Pale green, conical, rim fragment, from context dated *c* AD 72–86 in Flavian fort at Annetwell Street.
Leicester: Pale yellow/brown, ovoid, complete profile.
Wroxeter, Shropshire: Greenish colourless, ovoid, from late Neronian or early Flavian military occupation.
York: Greenish colourless, ovoid, from early Flavian and later contexts at Blake Street (Cool 1995a, 1653–4 no 5952 fig 736). Pale green, conical, rim fragment, from Coppergate.

Further reading
For discussion in connection with finds from Usk and York, see Price 1995a, 160, and Cool 1995a, 1565.

Shallow tubular rimmed bowl

Characteristics

Form
Narrow vertical tubular rim, edge bent out and down, short cylindrical upper body, rounded change of angle, horizontal or gently tapering lower body, horizontal base with applied diagonal base ring.

Colours
Strongly coloured monochrome, particularly dark blue and green. Blue/green.

Other features
Shallow bowls often have quite narrow tubular rims, but they are not easy to recognise from small fragments, as the rims and bases are very similar to those on other bowl and cup forms (for example, Figures 25, 55–6). A large pontil or post mark is found on the bottom edge of the base ring.

Range of measurements
Rim diameters *c* 130–180mm.

Distribution
Not common. Found on some sites in southern Britain.

Date range
AD 43-AD 60/65. Shallow tubular-rimmed bowls are not as long lived as the deeper versions.

Illustrated example (Figure 24)
Colchester, Sheepen, Essex: Dark green, from unstratified context on site occupied in Claudian-Neronian period (Charlesworth 1985a, MF 3:F6 no 37 fig 80).

Other finds
Colchester, Essex: Dark green and three blue/green, from Claudian-early Neronian and later 1st century contexts (Cool and Price 1995, 94, 97 nos 635, 679–81 fig 6.3).
Colchester, Sheepen, Essex: Dark green, from Claudian-Neronian context (Harden 1947, 304 no 80 pl 88).
Fishbourne Palace, West Sussex: Two, blue/green, from Claudian-early Flavian and late 1st century contexts (Harden and Price 1971 352 nos 66–66a fig140). One dark blue, two dark green (Price and Cottam 1996a, 174–5 nos 40, 48–9 fig 6.27).
Gloucester: Dark blue, from Neronian military occupation at Kingsholm (Price and Cool 1985, 46 no 24 fig 24).

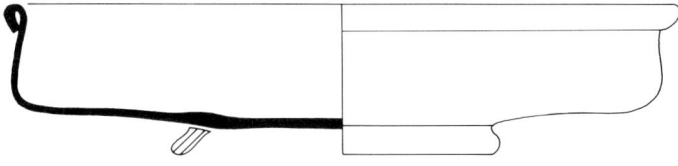

Fig 24   Scale 1:2

Mancetter, Warwickshire: Two, dark blue and blue/green, from Claudian-Neronian military occupation.

Usk, Gwent: Blue/green, in mid-2nd century pit (Price 1995a, 169 no 66, fig 44).

Further reading
Isings 1957, form 45. Tubular rimmed bowls are discussed in connection with finds from Colchester and Usk, see Cool and Price 1995, 94–96, and Price 1995a, 166.

Deep tubular rimmed bowl

Characteristics
Form
Vertical tubular rim bent out and down (occasionally also rolled-in, forming a double fold), cylindrical or slightly concave upper body, strong rounded change of angle, wide slightly convex lower body, horizontal base with applied vertical or diagonal base ring.

Colours
Polychrome examples are rare. Quite often found in strong monochrome colours, including dark blue, yellow/brown, yellow/green, purple, but not in dark green. Blue/green most common.

Decoration
Vertical or diagonal ribbing on body of some bowls from the end of the 1st century onwards. Opaque white marvered blobs on polychrome examples.

Other features
Deep bowls often have quite broad tubular rims. The form is generally identified by the rim, although small fragments may be indistinguishable from other bowl and cup forms with tubular rims (for example, Figures 24, 55–6). The outside surface of the base ring sometimes has diagonal tooling marks. A large pontil or post mark is usual on the bottom edge of the base ring.

Range of measurements
Rim diameters *c* 100–250mm.

Distribution
Very common on settlements in Britain; occasionally found in burials.

Date range
c AD60/65–third quarter of 2nd century.

Illustrated examples (Figure 25)
a) *Stansted, Essex*: Yellow/green, fragmentary bowl, from cremation burial 249 at the Duckend Carpark site, dated to second quarter of 2nd century.
b) *Chichester, West Sussex*: Blue/green, with ribs (Charlesworth 1978a, 267 no 14 fig 10.22).

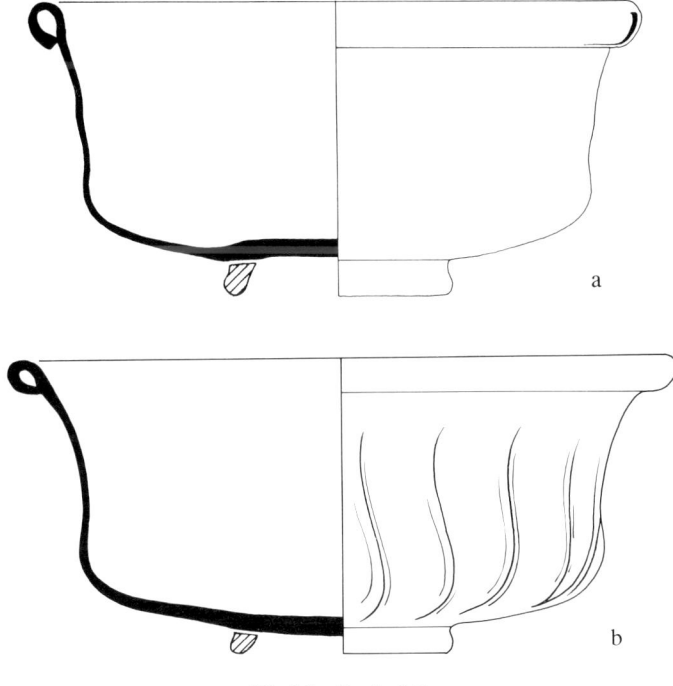

Fig 25   Scale 1:2

Other finds

Carlisle, Cumbria: Blue/green, complete profile, in Flavian-Trajanic context at Blackfriars Street (Price 1990a, 172–4 no 39 fig 162). Yellow/brown, complete profile, from The Lanes.

Colchester, Essex: Fragments, dark blue, yellow/brown, yellow/green, pale green and blue/green, in Flavian and later contexts (Cool and Price 1995, 94–8 nos 630, 636, 646–9, 651–4, 656 fig 6.2–3).

Faversham, Kent: Blue/green, with ribs, complete, from burial (Harden *et al* 1968, 84 no 110).

Gloucester: Fragments, polychrome (Plate 2.4), yellow/green, blue/green, in Neronian military assemblage at Kingsholm (Price and Cool 1985, 46, 48, 50 nos 17, 37, 47 figs 17–19).

Harlow, Felmongers, Essex: Fragments, yellow/brown and blue/green, in pit dated by samian to *c* AD 160–70 (Price 1987a, 188, 202 nos 4–5 fig 1).

Hemel Hempstead, Hertfordshire: Yellow/brown, with ribs, complete, in pit with Trajanic samian (Charlesworth 1974–76b, 117 fig 64a pl 41).

Long Melford, Suffolk: Dark blue, complete, in ditch with Neronian samian (Avent and Howlett 1980, 246, fig 41).

Newstead, Borders: Yellow/brown, purple and blue/green fragments, in Flavian and later fort (Curle 1911, 272).

Plymouth, Cornwall: Yellow/brown with ribs, complete, from Mount Batten (the Stamford Hill cemetery). The bowl was destroyed in the 2nd World War, but the description and illustration identify it as a deep tubular rimmed bowl with ribs (Cunliffe 1988, 95 fig 53).

Richborough, Kent: Rim and body, blue/green, from pit dated to AD 70–100 (Bushe-Fox 1932, 85 no 63, pl 15).

Stonea, Cambridgeshire: Rim and body, yellow/brown with ribs, from mid–late 2nd or 3rd century context (Price 1996b, 398 no 4 fig 124).

Verulamium, Hertfordshire: Fragments, strongly coloured and blue/green bowls, from later 1st-mid 2nd century and later contexts (Charlesworth 1972, 199 nos 1–18, fig 74 nos 6–11; 1984, 151–3 nos.53–70, fig 62 nos 21–29).

Further reading
Isings 1957, form 44. For discussion of tubular-rimmed bowls in connection with finds from Colchester and Usk, see Cool and Price 1995, 94–6, and Price 1995a, 166.

Conical beaker with ground exterior surfaces and facet-cut/relief decoration

Characteristics
Form
Formed from a thick blown blank from which the details of the rim, body and base were ground. Vertical rim, edge cracked-off and ground smooth, straight side tapering in to diagonal foot, small flat base. Outside surface cut away, leaving areas in relief.

Colours
Colourless

Decoration
Wheel-cut and ground decoration. Horizontal cordons occur at the rim and often on the upper and lower body, and a small raised disc is occasionally found at the centre of the underside of the base.

Most examples have a single decorative zone (sometimes in relief) of horizontal rows of circular or oval facets closely set in quincunx to form diamonds or hexagons. Other arrangements of facets are also known. The decorative area is sometimes divided into two zones, or some of the facet edges are ground away to create an irregular pattern of jigsaw-facets.

A small group of beakers has individual motifs in relief, such as shells, ovals and rosettes, and a very few have motifs such as leaves, stems and buds which are deeply undercut, sometimes producing openwork patterns (cage cups or diatreta).

A few have no decoration between cordons on the upper and lower body.

Other features
Tall and narrow, and short and wide versions were produced. Fragments have a distinctive combination of surfaces, glossy on the inside, ground and polished on the outside. Vessels are often thick-walled, especially near the base. They sometimes deteriorate badly in the ground, fracturing into tiny fragments.

Range of measurements
Rim diameters *c* 80–110mm, heights 70–180mm.

Distribution
Facet-cut beakers are common on settlements throughout Britain, but have rarely been recorded in burials. The other varieties are rare.

Date range
c AD 65–first or second quarter of 2nd century.

Illustrated examples (Figure 26)
Facet-cut
a) *Castleford, Yorkshire*: Short and wide, with large circular facets arranged to form diamonds, from context dated AD 140–180 in vicus (Cool and Price 1998, 162 no 133 fig 55).
b) *London*: Tall, with two zones of oval facets, in pit apparently sealed by Hadrianic fire-debris at St Swithins House, Middle Walbrook Valley (Price 1991a, 165–7 no 618 fig 166).
Relief-cut
c) *London*: Conical beaker with rosettes, ovals and tear shaped motifs in relief, from Old Jewry.
Cordons
d) *Rough Castle, Stirlingshire*: Short and wide, base missing, from Antonine Wall fort, occupied *c* AD 140–160 (Charlesworth 1978–80, 268–9 no 273 fig 12).

Other finds
Facet-cut
Abergavenny, Gwent: Fragment, tall beaker with diamond facets from the Orchard Site. (Price 1993a, 218 no 4 illustrn 16).
Barnwell, Cambridgeshire: Intact short and wide beaker with diamond facets (Plate 4.2), from burial (Harden *et al* 1987, 194 no 104).
Birdoswald, Cumbria: Almost complete profile, short and wide beaker with three rows of facets, from post-Roman context (Price and Cottam 1997a, 348 no 11 fig 248).
Castleford, West Yorkshire: Fragments, at least ten tall and short beakers with diamond facets, in late 1st and 2nd century contexts in the fort and vicus (Cool and Price 1998, nos 98, 105–6, 112–3, 116–7, 134–46, 161–2 figs 54–6).
Cardean, Tayside: Complete profile, tall and narrow beaker with diamond facets, from Flavian fort (Wilson 1969, 202 pl 14 no 1).
Chichester, West Sussex: Fragments, two beakers with diamond facets (Charlesworth 1974b, 134 nos 11–12 fig 8.13).
Exeter, Devon: Fragment with jigsaw facets, from context probably dated *c* AD 60–65 (Charlesworth 1979a, 224 no 12 fig 70).
Colchester, Essex: Fragments, at least five beakers with diamond and jigsaw facets, from late Neronian-Flavian and later contexts (Cool and Price 1995, 74–5 nos 395–402 fig 5.6).
Fishbourne Palace, West Sussex: Fragments, at least six beakers with diamond, hexagon and jigsaw facets, from Flavian and later contexts (Harden and Price 1971, 342–4 nos 41–44 fig 139; Price and Cottam 1996a, 176 nos 58–9 fig 6.28).
Flint, Pentre Farm, Clwyd: Fragment, short and wide beaker with three rows of large diamond facets (Price 1989b, 78, 81 no 5 fig 29).
London: Fragments, diamond facets and diagonal grooves, from Southwark Street

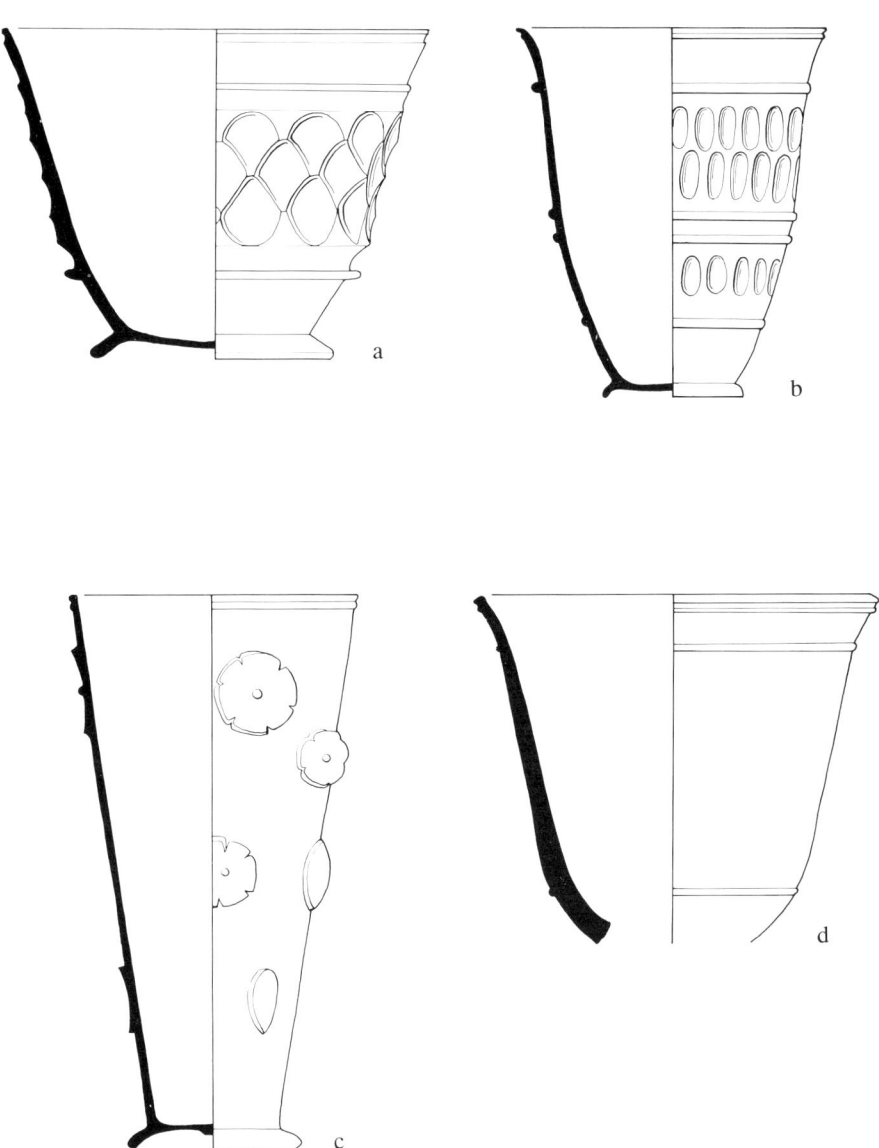

Fig 26   Scale 1:2

(Shepherd 1995b, 125–6 nos 71–5, 77 fig 38. Fragments, tall and narrow beakers with jigsaw facets, from late Neronian and later 1st century contexts at Leadenhall Court (Shepherd 1996, 104–5 nos 67–72 figs 61.63).

Strageath, Tayside: Fragments, tall and narrow with large oval facets, probably from the Flavian occupation of the fort (Price 1989c, 194, 197 no 2 fig 100).

York: Fragments, three beakers with diamond and jigsaw facets, in 2nd–3rd century contexts at Blake Street in the legionary fortress (Cool 1995a, 1569 nos 5928–30 fig 737)

Relief-cut and undercut.

Fishbourne Palace, West Sussex: Fragment with undercut ivy leaf, from context dated AD 75–100 (Harden and Price 1971, 336 no 30 fig 138 pl 26).

Gloucester: Fragment with ovals and shells in relief, from Berkeley Street.

London: fragment with undercut leaf, from Guildhall Yard (information from John Shepherd). Tall beaker with ovals, from a late 1st–early 2nd century rubbish pit in Ironmonger Lane (*Glass in London*, 1970, 8 no 18). Fragment with ovals and rosettes, from Leadenhall Street (Wheeler 1930, 122 no 7, fig 42). Fragment with shell, from Southwark Street (Shepherd 1995b, 125 no 59 fig 38).

Lincoln: Fragment with undercut vine leaf, from Flaxengate.

York: Fragments with ovals and undercut bud and stem, from 2nd century contexts at Blake Street in legionary fortress (Cool 1995a, 1652–3, nos 5923–7 fig 737).

Cordons.

York: Rim and body, from Antonine building at Blossom Street.

Further reading
For general discussion of facet-cut, relief-cut and relief- and undercut beakers, see Oliver 1984; von Saldern 1991; Koster and Whitehouse 1989. For discussion of the forms in connection with finds from Colchester, see Cool and Price 1995, 71–5.

Arcaded beaker

Characteristics

Form
Vertical rim, edge cracked-off and ground smooth, tall, straight upper body tapering in, convex lower body, small tubular pushed-in base ring, domed base.

Colours
Colourless, greenish colourless, pale green.

Decoration
One or more horizontal wheel-cut lines below rim. On body, vertical or diagonal trails usually joined at top and bottom to form long, round-ended loops (arcades).

Range of measurements
Rim diameters *c* 75–100mm, heights *c* 140mm+.

Distribution
Not common. Found at settlements in many parts of Britain

Date range
Last third of 1st century AD

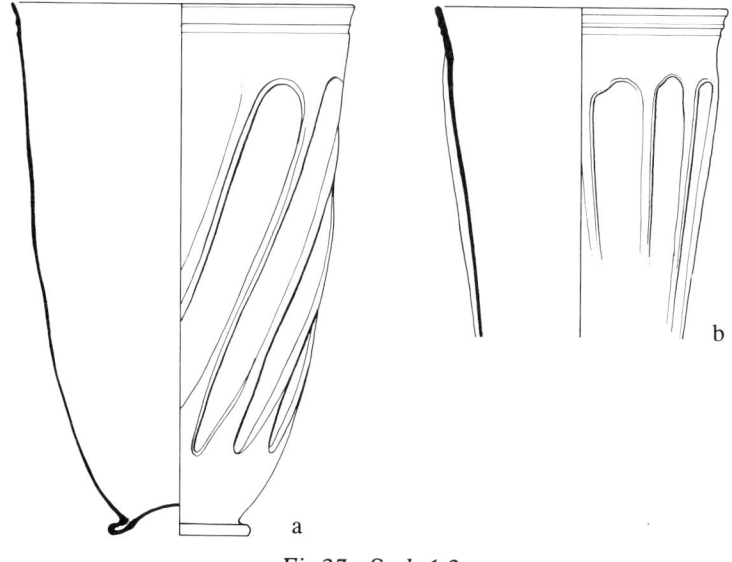

Fig 27   Scale 1:2

Illustrated examples (Figure 27)

a) *Wroxeter, Shropshire*: Complete profile, greenish/colourless, diagonal arcading, from drain deposit in forum containing early Flavian samian.

b) *Wroxeter, Shropshire*: Rim and body, greenish/colourless, vertical arcading, from same deposit.

Other finds

Colchester, Essex: Fragment, pale green, in context dated *c* AD 49/55-*c* AD 75 (Cool and Price 1995, 71 no 394 fig 5.5).

Caerleon, Gwent: Fragment, colourless, from Flavian-Trajanic context in legionary fortress (Nash-Williams 1929, 257 no 4 fig18).

Corbridge, Northumberland: Fragment, colourless, from Flavian pit at Red House (Charlesworth 1979c, 58 no 2 fig 20).

Elginhaugh, Lothian: Fragment, colourless, from mid-Flavian fort.

Gloucester: Fragment, colourless, from Berkeley Street.

Gorhambury villa, Hertfordshire: Fragment, colourless (Neal *et al* 1990, 203 no 33 fig 163).

Leckie Broch, Central: Fragment, colourless (information from Dominic Ingemark).

Segontium, Gwynedd: Fragment, colourless (Allen 1993, 222 no 25 fig 13.2).

Wroxeter, Shropshire: Fragment, colourless.

Usk, Gwent: Fragment, colourless, from late Neronian-early Flavian pit in legionary fortress (Price 1995a, 163 no 48 fig 44).

Further reading

Isings 1957, form 33. For discussion of the form in connection with finds from Colchester and Usk, see Cool and Price 1995, 71 and Price 1995a, 163.

Indented beaker with concave base

Characteristics
Form
Vertical, or slightly out-turned rim, edge cracked-off and ground smooth, tall straight indented body, small concave base.

Colours
Colourless, pale yellow/green, blue/green.

Decoration
One or more horizontal wheel-cut or abraded lines often found below the rim. The body usually has four long vertical oval indents, though more sometimes occur. Unmarvered chips are very unusual.

Other features
Often found in very small pieces. The most diagnostic part is the lower body and base; body fragments may come from other indented forms. Early indented beakers may be confused with similar late Roman indented conical beakers, although the quality and colour of the glass helps to distinguish the types.

Range of measurements
Rim diameters *c* 65–90mm, heights *c* 130–160mm.

Distribution
Fairly common. Found at settlements in many parts of Britain. Not known in burials.

Date range
AD 65/70–early 2nd century.

Illustrated examples (Figure 28)
a) *York, Blake Street*: Blue/green, from early 2nd century context in legionary fortress (Cool 1995a, 1656 no 6040 fig 740).
b) *Wroxeter, Shropshire*: Colourless with self-coloured unmarvered chips, from drain deposit in forum containing early Flavian samian.

Other finds
Colchester, Essex: Colourless and blue/green, fragments of two examples, from later 1st–early 2nd century contexts (Cool and Price 1995, 71 nos 390, 393 fig 5.4).
Corbridge, Northumberland: Blue/green, two beakers, from Flavian military occupation at Red House (Charlesworth 1959b, 164–6 fig 22 nos 1–2).
Doncaster, South Yorkshire: Fragments, three beakers, from a late 1st century ditch (Buckland 1986, 17 fig 11).
Dorchester, Dorset: Greenish colourless fragments, from Greyhound Yard (Cool and Price 1993, 160 nos 30–31 fig 85).
London: Blue/green fragments, from contexts dated to last quarter of 1st century AD at Leadenhall Court (Shepherd 1996, 108 129–31 fig 65).

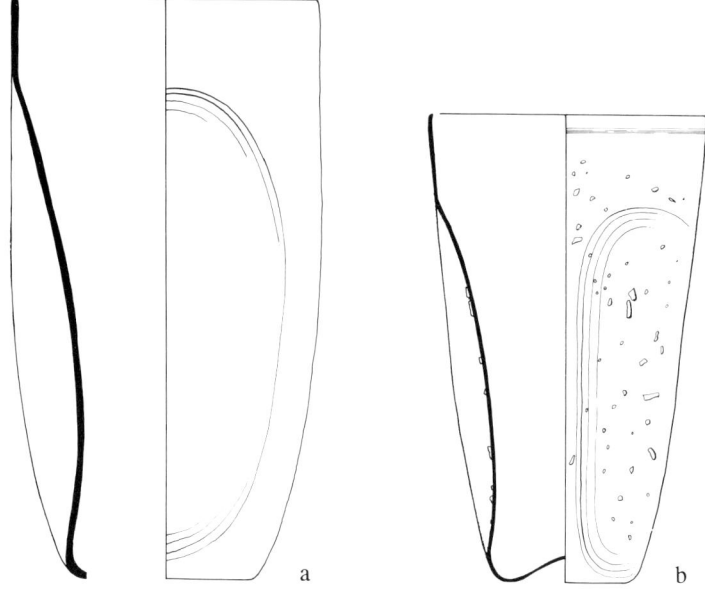

Fig 28   Scale 1:2

Usk, Gwent: Small fragments, pale yellowish green, blue/green and greenish colourless, from Neronian-early Flavian contexts in legionary fortress (Price 1995a, 163–4 no 49, 49a-b fig 44).
Wroxeter, Shropshire: Fragment, light green.

Further reading
Isings 1957, form 32. For discussion of these and other indented forms in connection with finds from Colchester and Usk, see Cool and Price 1995, 69–71, and Price 1995a, 163–4.

Indented cup

Characteristics
Form
Vertical rim, edge cracked-off and ground smooth, convex thin-walled indented body, lower body tapering in, small tubular pushed-in base ring and domed base. Also known with concave base.

Colours
Colourless, greenish colourless, pale green, pale yellow/green.

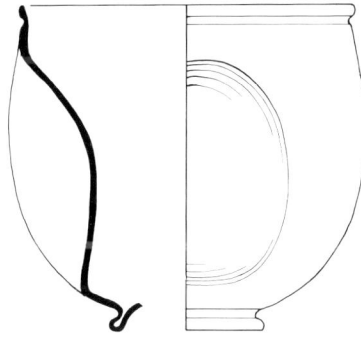

Fig 29   Scale 1:2

Decoration
Horizontal wheel-cut or abraded line often found below the rim. Four wide oval indents on the body.

Other features
These cups are shorter and have wider convex bodies than the indented beakers (see Figure 28).

Range of measurements
Rim diameters *c* 80–90mm, heights *c* 80–100mm.

Distribution
Quite common at settlements in many parts of Britain. Very rare in burials.

Date range
c AD 65–early 2nd century. The cup from Richborough is notably earlier than other dated examples.

Illustrated example (Figure 29)
Colchester, Essex: Colourless, from context dated *c* AD 60/75–100/150 (Cool and Price 1995, 71 no 388 fig 5.4).

Other finds
Caerleon, Gwent: Fragment, colourless, from later 2nd century context at Roman Gates (Allen 1992, 183 no 27 fig). Fragment, greenish colourless, in context dated *c* AD 74/5–90 at Legionary Museum site (Zienkiewicz 1992, 5 no 8 fig 1).
Colchester, Essex: At least three more cups, light green and colourless, from late 1st–early 2nd century contexts (Cool and Price 1995, 70–1 nos 387, 389 & 392 fig 5.4).
Corbridge, Northumberland: Fragment, colourless (Allen 1988, 293 no 41 fig 132).
Dorchester, Dorset: Fragment, light green, from Greyhound Yard (Cool and Price 1993, 160 no 29 fig 85).
Exeter, Devon: Fragment, colourless (Allen 1991, 228 no 61 fig 96).
Fishbourne Palace, West Sussex: Fragments, colourless (Price and Cottam 1996a, 166, 176 nos 66–7 fig 6.28).

Manchester: Fragment, colourless (Price 1974, 131 no 85 fig 48).

Richborough, Kent: Colourless, from mid 1st century well (Bushe-Fox 1926, 49 no 8 pl 19).

Segontium, Gwynedd: Fragment, colourless, in residual context (Allen 1993, 222 no 24 fig 13.2).

Strageath, Tayside: Fragment, colourless, in Antonine occupation (Price 1989c, 195, 198 no 7 fig 100).

York: Fragments, colourless, from early-mid 2nd century context at Blake Street (Cool 1995a, 1571 and 1653 no 5949).

Further reading
For discussion of these and other indented drinking vessel forms in connection with finds at Colchester and Usk, see Cool and Price 1995, 69–71, and Price 1995a, 163–4.

Thin-walled wheel-cut cup with domed base

Characteristics
Form
Slightly out-turned rim, edge cracked-off and ground, straight upper body, curved change of angle, lower body tapering in, small pushed-in base ring and domed base.

Colours
Colourless, sometimes with greenish tinge.

Decoration
Horizontal wheel-cut lines, often below the rim and above the change of angle.

Other features
Fragments can be distinguished from other varieties of colourless wheel-cut cup because of the thin walls, especially in the upper body, and the pushed-in base ring and domed base.

Range of measurements
Rim diameters *c* 80–100mm, heights *c* 70–100mm.

Distribution
Common finds on settlements; rare in burials.

Date range
Late 1st–early to mid 2nd century. A late dated example came from a pit in Park Street, Towcester containing samian dated to AD 155–65 (Price 1980a, 64 no 4 fig 14).

Illustrated examples (Figure 30 and Plate 4.3)
a) *Stansted, Essex:* Almost complete cup, from cremation burial 247 at the Duckend Carpark site, dated to first quarter of 2nd century.
b) *Gorhambury villa, Hertfordshire:* Almost complete cup (Neal *et al* 1990, 203 no 34 fig 163).

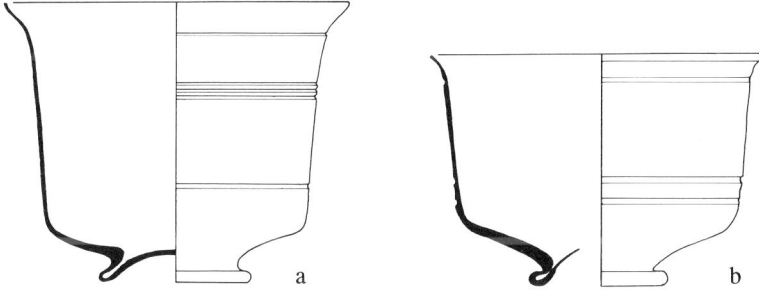

Fig 30   Scale 1:2

Other finds
Ashley, Northamptonshire: Fragments, from early 2nd century context (Taylor and Dix 1985, 94 fig 6).
Caerwent, Gwent: Fragment, strong change of angle (Boon 1972/3, 121 no 31d fig 4).
Caersws, Powys: Fragments, at least two cups, from several late 1st–early 2nd century contexts in vicus (Cool and Price 1989, 39–40 nos 39–41 fig 20).
Castleford, West Yorkshire: Fragments, several cups, one from a late 1st century context in fort, most from mid 2nd century contexts in vicus (Cool and Price 1998, 161–4 nos 99–100, 118–9, 123–4, 160–72 figs 55–6).
Colchester, Essex: Fragments, several cups, in Flavian and 2nd century contexts (Cool and Price 1995, 81–2 nos 434–5, 442, 445–6, fig 5.10).
Fishbourne Palace, West Sussex: Fragment, in 2nd–later 3rd century context (Harden and Price 1971, 347 no 56A fig 140).
Shakenoak, Oxfordshire: Fragments, two examples, from 2nd–early 3rd century deposit in Building A (Harden 1968a, 76 no 6 fig 26 no 4).
Wroxeter, Shropshire: Almost complete, from late 1st–early 2nd century pit (Bushe-Fox 1916, 34 no 1 pl 23 fig 1).
York: Body and base fragments, from Barrack 2, in last 1st–3rd century, and later contexts at the Minster site (Price 1995b, 358, 363 nos 30, 55 figs 143–4).

Further reading
For discussion of this and other wheel-cut drinking vessels, in connection with finds from Colchester, see Cool and Price 1995, 79–82.

Beaker with shallow facet-cutting

Characteristics
Form
Curved rim, edge cracked-off and ground smooth, tall slightly convex body, tapering in, small base with separately blown foot with out-splayed, cracked-off and ground edge.

Colours
Colourless, sometimes with greenish tinge.

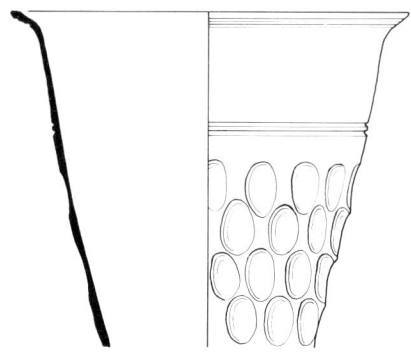

Fig 31   Scale 1:2

Decoration
One or two horizontal wheel-cut lines below rim. Three to five rows of widely spaced shallow oval facets in quincunx on body. One or more horizontal wheel-cut lines on lower body.

Other features
The exterior surface of these beakers is not ground, and so only the facets have wheel-polishing marks, in contrast to the conical beakers with deep facet-cutting and relief-cutting (see Figure 26).

Range of measurements
Rim diameters c 75–100mm, heights c 80–130mm+.

Distribution
Fairly common, but less frequently noted than beakers with deep facet cutting.

Date range
Late 1st century–early/mid 2nd century.

Illustrated example (Figure 31)
Verulamium, Hertfordshire: Rim and body, from Antonine fire debris, dated AD 150–155/60 (Charlesworth 1972, 206–8 no 1 fig 77 no 42). The base illustrated in the publication does not join the rim and body, and has been omitted.

Other finds
Birrens, Dumfries and Galloway: Body fragment, five rows of facets (Robertson 1975, 135 no 33 fig 47 no 4).
Castleford, West Yorkshire: Body fragments, 2 beakers, in mid-2nd century and later contexts in the vicus (Cool and Price 1998, 162–4 nos 147–8 fig 56).
Chichester, West Sussex: Rim and body fragment (Charlesworth 1981b, 293 no 12 fig 15.1).
Corbridge, Northumberland: Rim and body fragment (Charlesworth 1959c, 42 fig 3 no 7).

Dorchester, Dorset: Rim and body fragment, from Greyhound Yard (Cool and Price 1993, 160 no 52 fig 85).

Verulamium, Hertfordshire: Rim and body of second beaker, found with Antonine fire debris, dated AD 150–155/60 (Charlesworth 1972, 206–8 no 2 fig 77 no 41).

York: Body fragments, two beakers, in 2nd–3rd century and later contexts at the Minster site (Price 1995b, 357 nos 22–3 fig 142).

Further reading

For discussion of this form in connection with the finds from Dorchester, see Cool and Price 1993, 152.

Biconical/cylindrical wheel-cut cup with separately blown foot

Characteristics

Form

Out-turned rim, edge cracked-off and ground smooth, straight upper body, either cylindrical or expanding out slightly, strong change of angle, straight or slightly convex lower body tapering in, base with separately blown foot with out-splayed, cracked-off and ground edge.

Colours

Colourless, greenish colourless.

Decoration

Single or close-set bands of horizontal wheel-cut lines, usually at rim, and on upper and lower body.

Other features

A wide range of body shapes is included in this group; on some, the proportions of the upper and lower part sare approximately equal while on others, the lower part is very short. These cups are generally much thicker-walled than the cups with base rings and domed bases (see Figure 30).

Range of measurements

Rim diameters *c* 60–10mm, heights *c* 50–120mm.

Distribution

Common on settlements in Britain; rare in burials.

Date range

2nd century AD, chiefly in the second and third quarters.

Illustrated examples (Figure 32)

a) *Harlow, Felmongers, Essex*: Complete profile, from pit containing samian dated to AD 160–70 (Price 1987a, 202 no 8 fig 2).

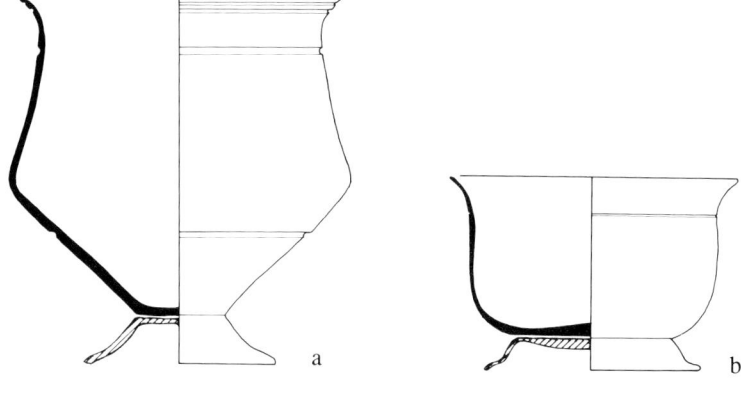

Fig 32   Scale 1:2

b) *London*: Complete profile, from pit dated to the last quarter of the 2nd century at St Thomas Street, Southwark (Townend and Hinton 1978a, 389 no 114 fig 176).

Other finds

Alcester, Warwickshire: Almost complete profile, found in pit with samian dated to *c* AD 150–160 (Price and Cottam 1994, 224 no 11 fig 104).

Cambridge: Complete, very long upper body; from Girton College cemetery, Roman cremation burial 2, dated to second or third quarter of 2nd century (Fitzwilliam 1978, 39 no 74 fig).

Castleford, West Yorkshire: Complete profile and fragments, several examples, in contexts dated to *c* AD 140–80 in vicus (Cool and Price 1998, 166 nos 176–82 fig 57).

Colchester, Essex: Almost complete profile and fragments, from mid 2nd century and later contexts (Cool and Price 1995, 80–82 nos 426–7, 431–3, 436, 439–41 fig 5.10)

Crundale, Kent: Complete profile (Charlesworth 1959c, 49 pl 2 no 2).

Ditchley villa, Oxfordshire: Rim and body, greenish colourless (Harden 1936, 64 G2 fig 12).

Hardnott, Cumbria: Complete profile, from the south angle tower (Charlesworth 1959a 37 fig 3).

Harlow, Felmongers, Essex: Almost complete profile and fragments, three cups, found in same pit as the example illustrated in Figure 32a, above (Price 1987a, 202–3, nos 8–11 fig 2).

Verulamium, Hertfordshire: Nearly complete profile and fragment, two cups, from contexts in insula 14 containing Antonine fire debris, dated AD 150–155/60 (Charlesworth 1972, 208 no 2 fig 77 no 43–4); fragments, at least three cups, from early–mid 2nd century and later contexts in insula 28 (Charlesworth 1984a, 155 nos 93–4, 96 fig 63 nos 45–6, 48).

Further reading

For discussion of this and other wheel-cut cup forms in connection with finds at Felmongers, Harlow and Colchester, see Price 1987a and Cool and Price 1995.

Indented beaker with curved rim

Characteristics

Form
Out-turned rim, edge cracked-off and ground smooth, tall, slightly convex indented body, tapering-in, small base, separately blown foot with out-splayed, cracked-off and ground edge, or tubular pushed-in base ring.

Colours
Colourless.

Decoration
Horizontal wheel-cut line and/or band of abrasion below rim. Four long oval indents on body.

Other features
Not easy to identify unless substantial parts survive; body fragments are often very similar to colourless indented beakers with concave bases (see Figure 28), and lower body fragments with pushed-in base rings and domed bases are often very similar to colourless indented cups (see Figure 29).

Range of measurements
Rim diameters of *c* 50–65mm, heights *c* 130–140mm.

Distribution
Not common.

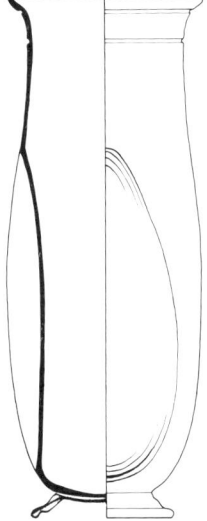

Fig 33   Scale 1:2

93

Date range

Uncertain. In use in mid-later 2nd century.

Illustrated example (Figure 33)

Harlow, Felmongers, Essex: Nearly complete, separately blown foot, from pit containing samian dated to AD 160–170 (Price 1987a, 203 no 15 fig 2).

Other finds

Birdoswald, Cumbria: Body fragments, part of two indents, from late 4th century context (Price and Cottam 1997a, 348 no 10).

Castleford, West Yorkshire: Almost complete profile; tubular base ring, from late 1st–mid 2nd century contexts in vicus. (Cool and Price 1998, 164–6 nos 173–5 figs 56–7)

Harlow, Felmongers, Essex: Rims and upper bodies, two examples, from the same pit as beaker in Figure 33 (Price 1987a, 204 nos 16–7 fig 2).

Verulamium, Hertfordshire: Rim and upper body fragment, in disturbed late 3rd–early 4th century context (Charlesworth 1984a, 156 no 104 fig 63 no 55).

Further reading

Isings 1957, Form 35. For discussion in connection with the finds at Felmongers, Harlow, see Price 1987a, 191–2.

Cylindrical wheel-cut cup with flat base

Characteristics

Form

Out-turned rim, edge cracked-off and ground, straight body, usually cylindrical, sometimes tapering in slightly, flat base, either thickening towards centre to produce an uneven, slightly convex surface with a small central concavity, or thin and flat/slightly concave.

Colours

Colourless.

Decoration

Horizontal wheel-cut lines, below rim and on body, wheel-cut circle on underside of thin flat/slightly concase bases.

Other features

Not easy to distinguish from other colourless wheel-cut cups or other vessels unless substantial parts survive. The thickened base is a diagnostic feature.

Range of measurements

Rim diameters *c* 70–80mm, heights *c* 50–65mm.

Distribution

Quite common; very occasionally present in burials.

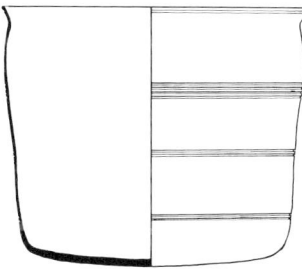

Fig 34   Scale 1:2

Date range
Uncertain; 2nd century, chiefly second and third quarters.

Illustrated examples (Figure 34)
Braughing, Skeleton Green, Hertfordshire: Complete, from cremation burial 33, dated to mid-late 2nd century (Charlesworth 1981a, 268–9 B 33d fig 105 no 3).

Other finds
Braughing, Skeleton Green, Hertfordshire: Fragmentary, apparently without wheel-cutting, from cremation burial 45, dated to mid–late 2nd century (Charlesworth 1981a, 271 B 45 fig 106 no 13).
Camelon, Lothian: Body and base fragment, from Antonine context.
Castlecary, Lothian: Complete profile, cup with wheel-cut circle on underside of base, from fort on Antonine Wall occupied *c* A.D.140–160 (Christison et al 1902/3, 337 fig 35; Charlesworth 1959c, 44 fig 7 no 6).
Castleford, West Yorkshire: Body and base fragments, several examples, mostly from mid-2nd century contexts in the vicus (Cool and Price 1998, 162, 166 nos 126–7, 186–90 figs 55, 57).
Fishbourne Palace, West Sussex: Lower body and base with wheel-cut circle, from 2nd–later 3rd century context (Harden and Price 1971, 349 no 59 fig 140).
Flint, Pentre Farm, Clwyd: Body and base fragment, in residual context (Price 1989b, 81 no 9 fig 29).
Heybridge, Essex: Almost complete cup, from 2nd century cremation burial.
Winchester, Hampshire: Two examples, one with almost complete profile apart from rim, from a 2nd-late 3rd century context.
York: Two examples, one very large, one with wheel-cut circle on underside of base, from 2nd century contexts at Blake Street (Cool 1995a, 1654 nos 5953–4 fig 740).

Further reading
For discussion of this and other forms of wheel-cut cups in connection with finds from Colchester and Blake Street, York, see Cool and Price 1995, 79–82 and Cool 1995a, 1572–3.

Convex wheel-cut cup

Characteristics

Form

Out-turned curved rim, edge cracked-off and ground smooth, sometimes with a constriction above the wide globular or ovoid body, concave base, or occasionally, separately blown foot with cracked-off and ground edge.

Colours

Colourless; rarely in other colours.

Decoration

Single or groups of several horizontal wheel-cut or abraded lines, on rim and body.

Other features

Some of these cups are thin-walled. The curved rim with constriction above the convex body is a diagnostic feature; otherwise, these cups are difficult to identify from small fragments.

Range of measurements

Rim diameters *c* 60–85mm, heights *c* 70–90mm.

Distribution

Quite common, occasionally found in burials.

Date range

Mainly mid/later 2nd century.

Illustrated example (Figure 35)

Braughing, Fordstreet, Hertfordshire: Globular cup, from cremation burial with samian dated to *c* AD 150–80 (Harden 1977, 102 no 23 fig 43 pl 9b).

Other finds

Castleford, West Yorkshire: Rims and bodies, at least two examples, in mid 2nd century and later contexts in the vicus (Cool and Price 1998, 164 nos 165–6 fig 56).

Colchester, Essex: Rims and bodies, two examples, in late 2nd–early 3rd century and later contexts (Cool and Price 1995, 80–1 nos 427 & 430 fig 5.10).

Fishbourne Palace, West Sussex: Rim and body, from 2nd–later 3rd century context (Harden and Price 1971, 347 no 56 fig 140).

Flint, Pentre Farm, Clwyd: Rim and body, in residual context (Price 1989b 81 no 8 fig 29).

Harlow, Felmongers, Essex: Rim and body, ovoid, from pit containing samian dated to *c* AD 160–170 (Price 1987a, 203 no 13 fig 2).

London: Complete profile, brown globular cup, from pit dated to last quarter of 2nd century at St Thomas Street, Southwark (Townend and Hinton 1978a, 389 no 115 fig 176).

Neath, Glamorgan: Rim and body, from late Trajanic or Hadrianic context (Charlesworth and Price 1992, 198 no 21 fig 6).

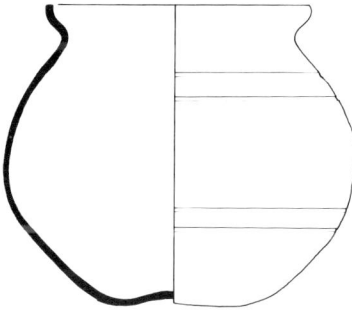

Fig 35   Scale 1:2

Prestatyn, Clwyd: Rim and body, contexts dated c AD 90–160 (Allen 1989, 118–9 no 12 fig 54).

Segontium, Gwynedd: Rim and body, in 2nd–3rd century context (Allen 1993, 220 no 16 fig 13.2).

Verulamium, Hertfordshire: Rim and body, from context dated AD170–180 in insula 21 (Charlesworth 1984a, 155 no 95 fig 63 no 47).

Winchester, Hampshire: Rims and bodies.

Further reading
For discussion of this and other forms of wheel-cut cups in connction with finds from Colchester, see Cool and Price 1995, 79–82.

Convex bowl with linear and facet-cutting

Characteristics
Form
Out-turned rim, edge cracked-off and ground smooth, convex body, flat or slightly concave base. Shallow and approximately hemispherical versions are known.

Colours
Colourless.

Decoration
Horizontal wheel-cut lines on rim and body. Sometimes also with oval facets, and occasionally with more complex facet-cutting.

Range of measurements
Hemispherical bowl; rim diameters *c* 110–120mm, heights *c* 50–60mm.
Shallow bowl; rim diameters *c* 150–200mm, heights *c* 35–45mm.

Distribution
Fairly common. Occasionally found in burials.

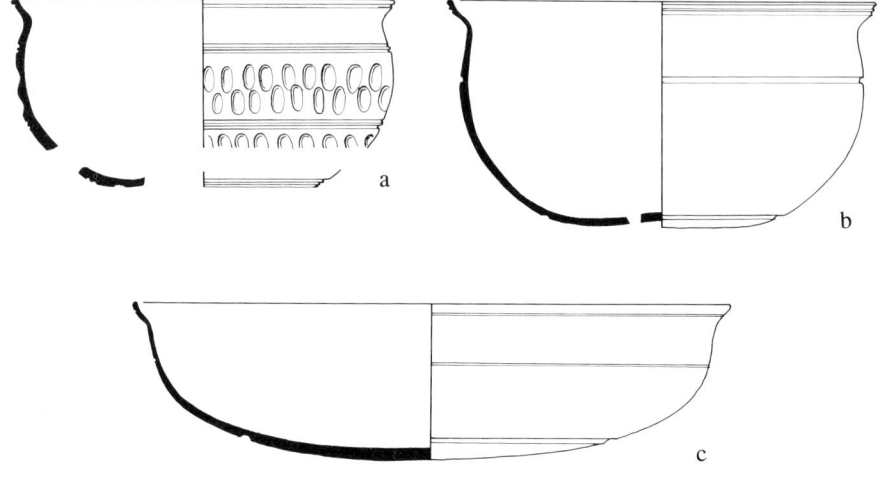

Fig 36   Scale 1:2

Date range
Uncertain. In use in mid/late 2nd century AD.

Illustrated examples (Figure 36)
a) & b) *Towcester, Northamptonshire*: Two approximately hemispherical bowls, from pit containing samian dated AD 55–165 in Park Street (Price 1980a, 63–4 nos 1–2 fig 14).
c) *Braughing, Skeleton Green, Hertfordshire*: Shallow bowl, from cremation burial 33, dated to mid-late 2nd century (Charlesworth 1981, 268 B 33a fig 105 2a).

Other finds
Birrens, Dumfries and Galloway: Rim and body, hemispherical bowl with at least four rows of interlocking facets, from mid/late 2nd century or later context (Birley 1937/8, 334 fig 35; Charlesworth 1959c, 41–2 fig 3 no 5; Robertson 1975, 135 no 33 fig 47 no 5).
Braughing, Skeleton Green, Hertfordshire: Fragments, two further shallow bowls with horizontal wheel-cut lines, from cremation burial 33 dated to mid-late 2nd century (Charlesworth 1981, 268 B 33b-c fig 105 2b).
Caister-on-Sea, Norfolk: Rim and convex body fragments with narrow vertical oval facets, circular facets and bands of horizontal wheel-cut lines (Price and Cool 1993, 141 nos 4–5, 7–8 fig 129).
Colchester, Essex: At least three hemispherical bowls with narrow vertical oval facets and horizontal wheel-cut lines (Cool and Price 1995, 78 nos 412–4 fig 5.8).
Corbridge, Northumberland: Fragments, shallow bowl with horizontal ground ridges separating bands of broad and narrow oval facets and oval and small circular facets with short wheel cuts (Allen 1988, 292 no 36 fig 132).
Milton Keynes, Holne Chase, Buckinghamshire: Body fragments, convex bowl with three rows of interlocking oval facets (Price 1987d, 149 no 215 fig 48).

Ospringe, Kent: Shallow bowl with wheel-cut lines and oval facets, in cremation burial 99 dated *c* A D 140–190 (Whiting *et al* 1931, 35 no 340 pl 32).

Verulamium, Hertfordshire: Rim and upper body, shallow bowl with horizontal wheel-cut lines, in context dated *c* AD 135–45/50; lower body, shallow bowl with horizontal wheel-cut lines and three bands of circular facets and geometric design elements, from context dated *c* AD 140–70 (Charlesworth 1972, 206, 210 no 16 fig 78 no 56; 1984a 156 no 106 fig 63 no 57).

Whitton, South Glamorgan: Body, convex bowl, horizontal bands of wheel-cut lines (Price 1981, 156 nos 17–18 fig 66).

York: Rim and body, deep bowl with horizontal wheel-cut lines, from late 2nd–3rd century context at Blake Street (Cool 1995a,1654 no 5955 fig 740).

Further reading
For discussion in connection with the finds from Towcester, Corbridge and Colchester see Price 1980a, 63–4, Allen 1988, 292, and Cool and Price 1995, 76–9.

Cylindrical cup with fire-rounded rim and double base ring

Characteristics
Form
Vertical or slightly in-turned rim, edge fire-rounded, straight, or occasionally very slightly convex side, strong change of angle, horizontal lower body, flat or slightly concave base with tubular base ring and small, thick trailed ring near centre of base.

Colours
Colourless, greenish colourless. Occasionally blue/green.

Decoration
Usually none. Very occasionally decorated with painted or incised scenes. Painted cups have a horizontal row of small dots below the rim and representations of animals, gladiators and other motifs on the body. Incised cups, often with letters, figures and fishes, are also known.

Other features
The outer base ring is occasionally a thick circular trail. A small blob of glass is sometimes found at the centre of the underside of the base. The inner trailed ring generally shows a pontil scar. Blue/green cups appear to have had single tubular base rings, as base fragments with an inner trailed ring are not known.

Range of measurements
Rim diameters range from *c* 70–140mm, though most are *c* 80–110mm, heights 60–100mm.

Distribution
Perhaps the commonest form of drinking vessel of any period in Roman Britain before

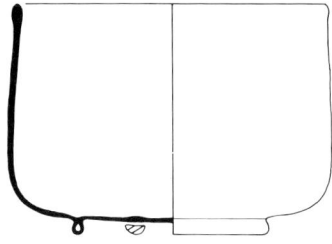

Fig 37   Scale 1:2

the 4th century. Occur in virtually all assemblages of the period, sometimes in very large numbers. A few are known from burials.

Date range
Third quarter of 2nd century–mid 3rd century.

Illustrated example (Figure 37)
Verulamium, Hertfordshire: from a late 2nd century well deposit (Wheeler and Wheeler 1936, 186 no 24 fig 29).

Other finds
Airlie, Angus: Complete cup, from burial in sandstone cist (Curle 1931–2, 291, 386–7 fig 3; Charlesworth 1959c, 44 pl 1 no 4).
Birdoswald, Cumbria: At least five cups, including painted fragments, from contexts dated *c* 220–70 and later (Price and Cottam 1997a, 348–9 nos 5, 17–20, 24 fig 248).
Brougham, Cumbria: Three cups from cremation burials, dated *c* AD 220/30–270/80 (Cool 1990, 170 fig 1 no 1).
Caerleon, Gwent: Fragments, more than 40 cups, from the fortress baths and elsewhere in the fortress and civil settlement, including fragments with painted and incised decoration, many from 2nd–3rd century contexts (Allen 1986, 111 nos 68–72, fig 43; Allen 1992, 184 nos 28–28a; Zienkiewicz 1992, 6–7 nos 18–9 fig 2; Price 1995d, 81–3, 87 no 2 fig 9).
Caerwent, Gwent: Fragments, about twelve cups (Boon 1972/3, 121 nos 40a–c fig 4).
Carlisle, Cumbria: At least 32 cups, including two blue/green, from late 2nd century and later contexts at Blackfriars Street (Price 1990a, 170–2, 174 nos 22–30, 41 fig161).
Chichester, West Sussex: Fragments, at least six cups, from 3rd century and later contexts (Charlesworth 1974b, 134 no 15 fig 8.13; Charlesworth 1978a, 269 nos 20–4 fig 10.22; Price and Cool 1989, 140 EP1 fig 19.4; Cool and Price 1993, 177 no CS2 fig 15.3).
Colchester, Essex: Fragments, at least 39 cups, including a piece from Middleborough in a mid–2nd century or earlier context (Cool and Price 1995, 82–85 nos 465, 476–535 fig 5.12).
Dorchester, Dorset: Fragments, at least five cups, from Greyhound Yard (Cool and Price 1993, 153, 162 nos 63–5 figs 85–6).
Harlow, Felmongers, Essex: Small rim fragment; in pit dated by samian to *c* AD 160–70. One of the earliest dated examples (Price 1987a, 204 no 19 fig 2).

London: At least five cups, including one blue/green, from Southwark Street (Shepherd 1995b, 126–8 nos 89–110 fig 39).

Piercebridge, Co Durham: At least sixty-one cups, including 5 blue/green.

Shakenoak villa, Oxfordshire: Several cups, in late 2nd-early 3rd century and later contexts (Harden 1968a, 78 no 19; 1971, 104 nos 117–121 fig 44 no 56; 1973, 100 no 188 fig 52; 1978b, 90 no 267, 92 nos 281–3).

Stonea, Cambridgeshire: Fragments, 16 cups, including 3 blue/green, in late 2nd–3rd century and later contexts (Price 1996b, 400–401 nos 16–23, 32–4 figs 127–9).

Verulamium, Hertfordshire: More than 50 examples, including incised fragments (Allen 1988, 293 no 44; Charlesworth 1984a, 155 nos 91–2 fig 63 nos 43–4, 156–8 nos 112–31 fig 64 nos 62–69, 158–9 nos 141–9 fig 65 nos 76–7).

Vindolanda, Northumberland: At least five cups, three colourless, one from context dated to c AD 235–250/60, and two blue/green, one from context dated c AD 235 (Price 1985c, 207 nos 8–11, 209 nos 24–5 fig 77).

Winterton villa, Lincolnshire: At least twelve cups (Charlesworth 1976a, 248 nos 15–20 figs 133–4, and unpublished).

York: Numerous cups (including painted and incised fragments) from sites in fortress and colonia (Harden 1962, 137 H.G.202.6 fig.88; Charlesworth 1976b, 17 nos 49–51 fig 13; Charlesworth 1978b, 55, 56–7 nos 169, 172, 279 fig 30; Cool 1995a, 1574–5, 1654, nos 5983–8, 5990–1 fig 742); Price 1995b, 363, nos 51–4 fig 144).

Further reading
Isings 1957, form 85. The form is discussed in detail in connection with finds from Brougham (Cool 1990) and Colchester (Cool and Price 1995, 82–5).

Cylindrical cup with fire-rounded rim and trailed decoration

Characteristics
Form
Slightly out-turned rim, edge fire-rounded, straight side, strong change of angle, horizontal lower body, flat or slightly concave base, with tubular pushed-in or applied base ring, sometimes rather narrow. Low trailed ring often found near centre of base.

Colours
Colourless, greenish colourless. Very rarely blue/green.

Decoration
Horizontal self coloured marvered trail on upper body and at change of angle and/or on lower body. Trails of contrasting colour are occasionally found below the rim, and these vessels may have further trailed decoration, such as 'snake thread' trails, on the main part of the body.

Other features
The inner trailed ring generally shows a pontil scar.

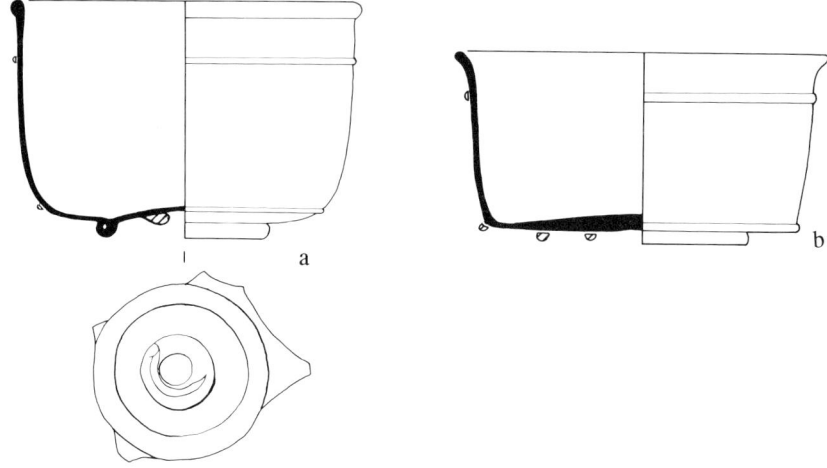

Fig 38   Scale 1:2

Range of measurements
Rim diameters *c* 70–140mm, heights *c* 60–100mm.

Distribution
Quite common. Occasionally found in burials.

Date range
Third quarter of 2nd century–mid 3rd century.

Illustrated examples (Figure 38)
a) *York*: Fragmentary cup, from late 2nd–late 3rd century and later contexts at Blake Street (Cool 1995a, 1575, 1654 no 5992 fig 742).
b) *Castleford, West Yorkshire*: Fragmentary cup from context dated *c* AD 140–80 in vicus (Cool and Price 1998, 166 no 195 fig 57).

Other finds
Baldock, Hertfordshire: Complete cup, from burial 104, dated to *c* AD 200 (Westell 1931, 274 no 4828 fig 6).
Carlisle, Cumbria: Rim and body fragment, blue/green with opaque white trail below rim, from Castle Street (Cool and Price 1991, 168, 171 no 641 fig 153).
Castleford, West Yorkshire: At least four further cups from mid-2nd century contexts in fort and vicus. (Cool and Price 1998, 161, 166–8 nos 96, 115, 196–8 figs 54, 58).
Chichester, West Sussex: Rim and body fragment (Charlesworth 1974b, 134 no.14, fig.8.13).
Colchester, Essex: Fragments, at least 7 cups, from mid 2nd–early 3rd century and later contexts (Cool & Price 1995, 82, 85 nos 466–75 fig 5.12).
Corbridge, Northumberland: Two examples (Allen 1988, 293 nos.42–42a fig.132).
Housesteads, Commandant's House, Northumberland; Three cups from a 2nd century drain deposit (Charlesworth 1971a, 34 figs.1–2, 3 (base only); Charlesworth 1975b, 24).

Segontium, Gwynedd: At least two cups from Hadrianic-Antonine contexts (Allen 1993, 220–2 nos.20 & 22 fig.13.2).

Shakenoak villa, Oxfordshire: At least one cup from a mid 3rd century or later context (Harden 1971, 102–4 nos 112–5 fig 44 no 55).

Stonea, Cambridgeshire: Fragments, at least three cups, in mid–late 2nd or later contexts (Price 1996b, 399–400 nos 13–5 fig 126.

Verulamium, Hertfordshire: At least nine cups, mostly from 3rd century and later contexts (Charlesworth 1972, 213 no 6 fig 79 no 69; 1984a, 158 nos 132–9 figs 64–5 nos.70–74).

Vindolanda, Northumberland: At least two cups, colourless and blue/green (Price 1985c, 207 no 6, 208–9 no 23 fig 77).

West Deeping, Rectory Farm, Lincolnshire: Rim and body, blue/green.

Further reading
Isings 1957, form 85. These cups are discussed in connection with finds from Colchester (Cool and Price 1995, 82–5).

Convex cup or beaker with trails

Characteristics
Form
Vertical or slightly out-turned rim, edge fire-rounded, convex body, tubular pushed-in base ring, concave base.

Colours
Blue/green, colourless.

Decoration
Self-coloured narrow unmarvered spiral trails on upper and lower body, sometimes with undecorated area around the middle of the body.

Other features
Pontil mark on the base. Small fragments are not very diagnostic, as many vessels have similar rims and bases and trailed decoration.

Range of measurements
Rim diameters *c* 50–80mm, heights *c* 120–150mm.

Distribution
Not common.

Date range
Not certain. In use in 2nd century AD.

Illustrated example (Figure 39)
Verulamium, Hertfordshire: Tall pale blue/green example from late 2nd century well deposit (Wheeler and Wheeler 1936, 186 no 27 fig 29 no 27).

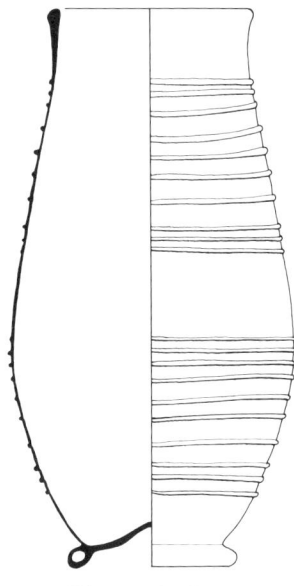

Fig 39   Scale 1:2

Other finds

Chichester, West Sussex: Rim and upper body, blue/green (Charlesworth 1974b, 134 no 18 fig 8.13).

Corbridge, Northumberland: Rim and upper body, blue/green (Allen 1988, 289 no 13 fig 131).

Cramond, Lothian: Rim and upper body, colourless (Maxwell 1974, 198 no 5 fig 16).

Neath, Glamorgan: Rim and upper body, blue/green, from abandonment phase of timber fort, mostly Flavian but some early 2nd century finds (Charlesworth and Price 1992, 196 no 13 fig 6).

Verulamium, Hertfordshire: Rim, upper body and base, blue/green, from King Harry Lane (Price 1989a, 42 no 278 fig 26).

Further reading

These vessels have not received much attention. See the brief note in connection with the find at King Harry Lane (Price 1989a, 48).

Cylindrical beaker with stem and foot

Characteristics

Form

Vertical or slightly out-turned rim, edge fire-rounded, tall, narrow, straight side, lower body tapering-in, solid globular stem and wide foot with fire-rounded edge.

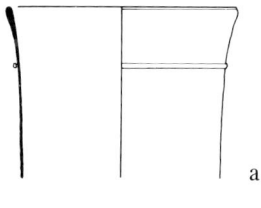

a

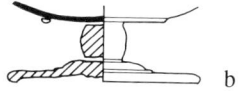

b

Fig 40   Scale 1:2

Colours
Colourless, blue/green.

Decoration
Trails, self-coloured or in contrasting colours, most frequently opaque white, yellow or blue. Horizontal trail sometimes present below the rim, on the lower body and on the base. Looped serpentine ('snake-thread') trails, scored across or impressed with criss-cross patterns on a few beakers. More elaborate decorative features, such as long vertical trails with impressed shell motifs, standing proud of the body and joined to it with pinched folds at intervals, have occasionally been recorded.

Other features
Similar stems and feet are also found on some flasks. There is a small pontil mark at the centre of the base.

Range of measurements
Rim diameters *c* 60–80mm, heights not known from fragments in Britain.

Distribution
Not very common.

Date range
Second half of the 2nd century–early 3rd century.

Illustrated examples (Figure 40)
a) *South Shields, Tyne and Wear:* Rim and body, colourless beaker with opaque blue and yellow trails.
b) *Lullingstone, Kent:* Body, stem and foot, colourless with self-coloured trail on lower body, from late Antonine context (Cool and Price 1987a, 131 nos 350–1 fig 54).

Other finds
Aldborough, Yorkshire: Lower body, stem and foot, blue/green with opaque white and blue snake-thread trails (Charlesworth 1959c, 54 pl 3 no 4).
Caerwent, Gwent: Lower body, stem and foot, colourless (Boon 1972/3, 116 no 17 fig 2).
Colchester, Essex: Two stems and feet, colourless, in early 3rd century and later contexts (Cool and Price 1995, 85–6 nos 541–2 fig 5.13).
Cirencester, Gloucestershire: Stem and foot, colourless with two opaque yellow trails, unstratified context in Parsonage Field (Charlesworth 1971b, 85 no 15 fig 11).
Silchester, Hampshire: Lower body, stem and part of foot, colourless with opaque white and yellow snake-thread trails (Thorpe 1935, 35 fig 2k).
Dorchester, Dorset: Body fragment, colourless with blue snake-thread trails, and two feet, colourless, one with self-coloured trail, from Greyhound Yard (Cool and Price 1993, 158 no 16 fig 84, 162 nos 66–7 fig 86).
London: Lower body, stem and foot, colourless, from Southwark Street (Shepherd 1995b, 125–6 no 76 fig 38).
Whitton, South Glamorgan: Body fragments, colourless with opaque white and blue snake-thread trails (Plate 2.5), from mid 3rd century context (Price 1981, 154–5 no 8 fig 66).
York: Lower body, stem and foot, colourless with vertical trail on lower body; in residual context at Fishergate (Hunter and Jackson 1993, 1336 no 4673 fig 647). Foot, colourless, from Church Street sewer deposit (Charlesworth 1976b, 17 no 52 fig 13). Stems and feet, at least two colourless vessels, from late 2nd–3rd century and later contexts at Blake Street (Cool 1995a, 1655 nos 5996–5999 fig 742). Lower body, colourless with self-coloured horizontal trail, from the Minster site (Price 1995b, 361 no 48 fig 144).

Further reading
Isings 1957, form 86. See discussion in connection with finds from Lullingstone (Cool and Price 1987, 112–3), Colchester (Cool and Price 1995, 85–6) and the Minster, York (Price 1995b, 350).

Bowl with out-turned fire-rounded rim

Characteristics
Form
Out-turned rim, edge fire-rounded, straight upper body, tapering in slightly, convex lower body, concave base with tubular pushed-in base ring or applied pad base ring.

Colours
Colourless, greenish colourless, blue/green. Very occasionally yellow/brown appearing black.

Decoration
A horizontal trail or ridge is sometimes found on the underside of the rim.

Other features
Pontil mark on base. Difficult to recognise from small fragments, as the rim, body and base are similar to other vessels.

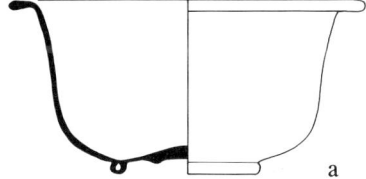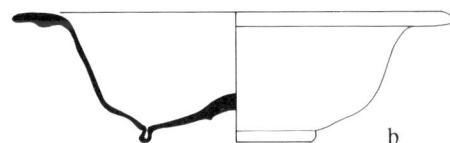

Fig 41   Scale 1:2

Range of measurements
Rim diameters *c* 90–300mm, heights *c* 30–45mm.

Distribution
Not very common.

Date range
Uncertain, probably in use in late 2nd–3rd centuries AD.

Illustrated examples (Figure 41 and Plate 3.6)
a) *Colchester, Essex*: Small blue/green bowl, from early 4th century burial, grave 100, in Butt Road cemetery; the bowl is probably earlier (Cool and Price 1995, 100 no 693 fig 6.4).
b) *Hauxton, Cambridgeshire*: Greenish colourless bowl with ridge on underside of rim, probably from cemetery in use in 2nd–3rd centuries (Harden 1958b, 12 no 3 fig 7 pl 3c).

Other finds
Birdoswald, Cumbria: Rim and body fragments, at least two colourless bowls with trails on underside of rim, from late 3rd–late 4th century contexts (Price and Cottam 1997a, 348 nos 6–9 fig 248).
Caerwent, Gwent: Fragmentary blue/green bowl with rim edge bent down (Boon 1972/3, 119 no 26 fig 3).
Castleford, West Yorkshire: Rim fragment with ridge, yellow/brown appearing black, from mid-2nd century context in vicus (Cool and Price 1998, 148, 157 no 62 fig 53).
Colchester, Essex: Four rim fragments with ridges, colourless and yellow/brown appearing black, from late 1st century, later 2nd–3rd century and late 3rd–4th century contexts (Cool and Price 1995, 100 nos 694–7 fig 6.4).
Fishbourne Palace, West Sussex: Two rim fragments, blue/green, from mid–late 3rd century and unstratified contexts (Harden and Price 1971, 353 nos 72–3 fig 141).
Hauxton, Cambridgeshire: Greenish colourless bowl with ridge on underside of rim, very similar to the example illustrated in Figure 41b, probably from cemetery in use in 2nd–3rd centuries (Harden 1958b, 12 no 4 fig 7 pl 3d).
Lincoln: Blue/green rim fragment, from late Roman and later deposit at Saltergate. Greenish colourless rim fragment with trail, redeposited in late 4th–early 5th century modifications to defences at the Park.
Shakenoak, Oxfordshire: Fragments, rim and body similar to the bowl in Figure 41a, green, from late 4th century context (Harden 1973, 102 no 202 fig 52).
Wallsend, Northumberland: Fragments, rim with applied trail and body, colourless. Very similar to Figure 41b (information from Denise Allen).

York: Blue/green bowl with applied pad base, rim and body similar to Figure 41a from late 2nd century levelling deposit at Tanner Row in the colonia.

Further reading
Isings 1957, form 42. For discussion in connection with finds from Colchester, see Cool and Price 1995, 99–100.

Small cylindrical bowl with high tubular base ring

Characteristics
Form
Slightly out-turned rim, edge fire-rounded, straight upper body, curved change of angle, horizontal lower body, slightly convex base with high tubular pushed-in base ring.

Colours
Colourless, blue/green.

Other features
Pontil mark on base. Difficult to recognise from small fragments, as the rim and body fragments are closely comparable with other bowls (for example, see Figure 41a). The high base ring is more diagnostic, though it also occurs on other vessels.

Range of measurements
Rim diameters *c* 90mm, heights *c* 60–70mm. Larger versions also known.

Distribution
Not very common.

Date range
Uncertain. In use in 3rd century.

Illustrated example (Figure 42)
Brougham, Cumbria: Blue/green bowl, from cremation burial dated *c* A D 250–270 (Cool 1990, 171 fig 2 no 7).

Other finds
Birdoswald, Cumbria: Colourless base, from late 4th century context (Price and Cottam 1997a, 348 no 21 fig 248).
Brading villa, Isle of Wight: Pale blue/green base (Tomalin 1987, 43 no B11+fig).
Caerleon, Gwent: Blue/green base, from Roman Gates site (Allen 1992, 182 no 18 fig).
Carrawburgh, Northumberland: Greenish colourless base from Coventina's Well (Allason-Jones and McKay 1985, 41 no 139+fig).
Castor, Normangate Field, Cambridgeshire: Colourless base.
Colchester, Essex: Blue/green base, from context dated *c* A D 250–300 (Cool & Price 1995, 171 no 1542 fig 10.2).
Lincoln: Blue/green base, from post-Roman context at Flaxengate.

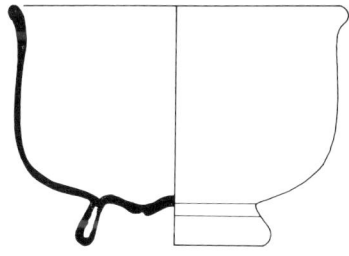

Fig 42   Scale 1:2

Further reading
Isings 1957, form 87. See discussion in connection with the find at Brougham (Cool 1990, 171–2).

Bowl with horizontal fold in body

Characteristics
Form
Vertical or slightly out-turned rim, edge fire-rounded, straight upper body, horizontal fold, convex lower body, concave base with tubular base ring.

Colours
Colourless, blue/green. Occasionally yellow/brown or yellow/green.

Other features
Pontil mark on base. Rim and base very similar to other small bowl forms (for example, see Figures 41–42). The single projecting fold in the body is the most diagnostic feature; double (figure-of-eight) folds occur in the bodies of other vessel forms.

Range of measurements
Rim diameters *c* 110mm, heights *c* 55mm.

Distribution
Body fragments quite common. Complete profiles rare.

Date range
Uncertain. Probably late 2nd–4th centuries AD.

Illustrated example (Figure 43)
Silchester, Hampshire: Complete blue/green bowl (Boon 1974a, 232, fig 36 no 7).

Other finds
Carlisle, Cumbria: Blue/green body with fold, large bowl, from Bowling Green site.
Chichester, West Sussex: Blue/green body with fold, from early–mid 4th century context at Chapel Street (Cool and Price 1993, 178 no CS12 fig 15.3).

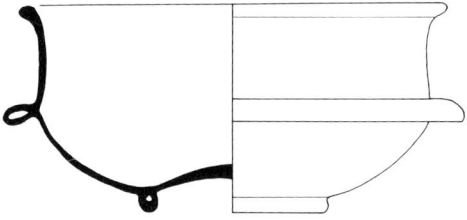

Fig 43   Scale 1:2

Colchester, Essex: Blue/green body with fold, post-Roman context (Cool and Price 1995, 103 no 706 fig 6.6).

Felixstowe, Suffolk: Yellow/green, complete bowl (British Museum, Department of Prehistoric and Romano-British Antiquities; 53.8–15.24).

Gorhambury, Hertfordshire: Blue/green, rim and body fragments (Neal *et al* 1990, 203 nos 51–4 fig 164).

Mucking, Essex: Blue/green body with fold.

Lincoln: Colourless body with fold, from the Park.

Piercebridge, Co. Durham: Blue/green, rim and body with fold.

Sandy, Bedfordshire: Colourless body with fold.

Usk, Gwent: Blue/green body with fold, context not closely dated (Price 1995a, 169 no.68 fig 44).

Further reading
See discussion in connection with the find from Colchester (Cool and Price 1995, 102–3).

Shallow bowl with out-splayed tubular rim

Characteristics
Form
Out-splayed rim, tubular edge bent out and down, shallow straight side tapering in, sharp change of angle, convex lower body, flat, convex or slightly concave base with tubular base ring.

Colours
Blue/green, greenish colourless.

Other features
Tubular rimmed bowls are common at several periods; see Figures 24–5 and 55 for 1st –2nd century and 4th century types. Similar folded rims may also come from blown window panes.

Range of measurements
Rim diameters 160–200+mm, heights *c* 40–50mm.

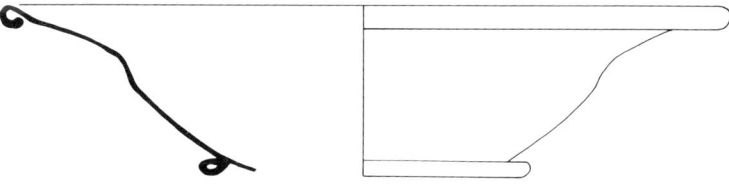

Fig 44   Scale 1:2

Distribution
Rim fragments are quite frequently found. Complete profiles are rare.

Date range
Not closely dated within 2nd–4th centuries AD.

Illustrated example (Figure 44)
Canterbury, Kent: Blue/green fragmentary bowl, from topsoil, south of St George's Street (Charlesworth and Price 1987, 223 no 16 fig 88).

Other finds
Caerwent, Gwent: Blue/green rim, perhaps from oval bowl (Boon 1972/3, 119 no 24 fig 3).
Chichester, West Sussex: Blue/green rim with mortar attached, perhaps from window pane (Charlesworth 1978a, 270–2 no 48 fig 10.23).
Colchester, Essex: Blue/green rims, three bowls, from mid 1st, 3rd–4th and unstratified contexts (Cool and Price 1995, 99 nos 683–5 fig 6.3).
Dorchester on Thames, Oxfordshire: Greenish/colourless rim, context dated AD 220–50 (Charlesworth 1984b, 153 no 9 fig 38).
Flint, Pentre Farm, Clwyd: Blue/green rim, from mid 3rd century or later context (Price 1989b, 82–4 no 28 fig 30).
Lincoln: Blue/green rims, at least three bowls, from Holmes Grain Warehouse and the Park.
London: Blue/green rim and body, from 1st-mid 2nd century context at Borough High Street , Southwark (Townend and Hinton 1978c, 462 no 150 fig 207).
Verulamium, Hertfordshire: Greenish rim, from context dated c AD 125–145 (Charlesworth 1984a, 167 no 257 fig 67 no 111).
Vindolanda, Northumberland: Blue/green rim and body from bowl or window pane, found with mid 3rd century material (Price 1985c, 210 no 29 fig 77).
Winchester, Hampshire: Rim and body, blue/green, from bowl or window pane, from context dated AD 150–70 at Wolvesey Palace.

Further reading
See discussion of these and other bowls with tubular rims in connection with finds from Colchester (Cool and Price 1995, 94–99).

Convex cup with out-turned fire-rounded rim

Characteristics

Form
Slightly out-turned rim, edge fire-rounded, convex body tapering in, slightly concave or thick flat base.

Colours
Colourless.

Decoration
Horizontal abraded lines, pinched or tooled decoration, indents. Narrow vertical ribs, lugs or small points are quite common. Ribs and points often are used together, sometimes also with indents.

Other features
Part of the rim surface is often lightly ground. Pontil mark on base. Small body fragments may come from other drinking vessels with tooled decoration, such as the beaker with applied foot from Verulamium (Wheeler and Wheeler 1936, 186 no 26 fig 29), or flasks.

Range of measurements
Rim diameters *c* 65–90mm, heights 65–80mm.

Distribution
Decorated body fragments quite common. Occasionally found in burials.

Date range
Uncertain. Possibly in use at end of 2nd century AD. More common in 3rd century.

Illustrated examples (Figure 45, Plate 4.4)
a) *Brougham, Cumbria*: Cup with horizontal abraded lines, tooled points and ribs, from cremation burial dated to *c* AD 220/30–270/80 (Cool 1990, 170 fig 1 no 2).
b) *Brougham, Cumbria*: Cup without decoration from similarly dated burial in the same cemetery (Cool 1990, 171 fig 1 no 6).

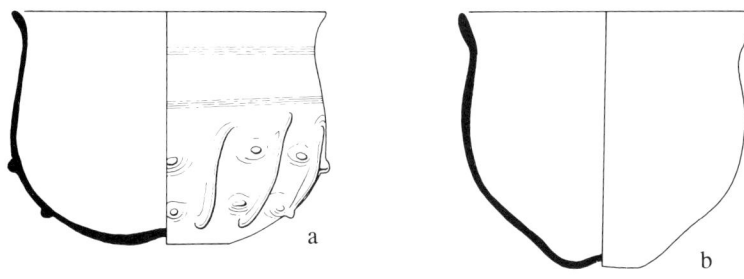

Fig 45   Scale 1:2

Other finds

Braintree, Essex: Body fragment with horizontal abraded lines and vertical ribs with tooled points, from context dated to *c* 330–70 (Rodwell 1976, 38 no 6 fig 19).

Brougham, Cumbria: Three cups with combinations of horizontal abraded bands, tooled points, vertical ribs, tooled lugs with points and oval indents, from cremation burials dated to *c* AD 220/30–270/80 in same cemetery as Figure 45a–b (Cool 1990, 170 fig 1 nos 3–5).

Chilgrove villa 2, near Chichester, Sussex: Body fragment with tooled lug and points, from 4th century context (Down 1979, 163 no 5 fig 56).

Colchester, Essex: Fragmentary cup without decoration, from Grave 693, dated AD 270–300/20, in the Butt Road cemetery; body fragments with combinations of wheel-cut lines, tooled points, ribs and lugs, from 2nd–3rd century and later contexts (Cool and Price 1995, 87 nos 543–550a, fig 5.14).

Collingham, Dalton Parlours villa, West Yorkshire: Rim and body fragment without decoration and body fragment with lugs and points, both unstratified (Price 1990b, 103 nos 8 & 12 fig 78).

Dorchester, Dorset: Rim, body and base fragments, at least two cups, from Greyhound Yard (Cool and Price 1993, 162 nos 68–71 fig 86).

East Grimstead villa, Wiltshire: Tall ovoid cup without decoration, from the main drain (Sumner 1924, 43, pl 8 no 3).

Fishbourne Beach, Isle of Wight: Body and base fragments, four rows of points in horizontal band.

Malton, North Yorkshire: Body fragments with a horizontal abraded band, points and lugs (Price and Cottam 1997b, 123 no 11 fig 46).

Papcastle, Cumbria: Rim and body fragment with horizontal abraded band (information from Chris Howard-Davis).

Sparsholt villa, Hampshire: Fragmentary cup with horizontal abraded bands, tooled ribs and points from a latrine pit, probably deposited before *c* AD 270–295 (information from Denise Allen).

Stonham Aspel, Suffolk: Fragmentary cup with two rows of points (Charlesworth 1967, 240–1, a, fig 38).

Verulamium, Hertfordshire: Rim and body without decoration, and base, from King Harry Lane (Price 1989a, 42, 44 nos 280 & 284 fig 26).

Vindolanda, Northumberland: Rim and body without decoration, unstratified, and five small body fragments with pinched points, from contexts dated to *c* AD 235–50/60 and *c* 250/60 (Price 1985c, 207–8 nos 7, 15 fig 77).

Wallsend, Northumberland: Fragmentary cup with points (information from Denise Allen).

York: Rim, body, base fragments, at least four cups, from late 2nd–3rd century and later contexts at Bishophill, Blake Street and the Minster site (Charlesworth 1978b, 57 no 177 fig 30; Cool 1995a, 1655 nos 6001, 6015–6 fig 742; Price 1995b, 363 no 60 fig 144).

Further reading

See discussion in connection with finds from Brougham and Colchester (Cool 1990, Cool and Price 1995, 86–7).

Cylindrical cup with vertical ground rim

Characteristics

Form
Vertical rim, edge cracked-off and ground flat, straight upper body, convex lower body, small, thick, flat or slightly concave base.

Colours
Colourless, greenish colourless.

Decoration
Horizontal abraded band on upper body. Other decoration, such as self-coloured trails, very rare.

Other features
Small pontil mark on base. This feature is very unusual on vessels with ground rims. The most diagnostic part of the vessel is the rim; body fragments are similar to cylindrical cups with fire-rounded rims (see Figure 37) and base fragments are similar to some other cups (for example, see Figure 45b).

Range of measurements
Rim diameters *c* 80mm, heights 60–80mm.

Distribution
Quite common.

Date range
Uncertain. Possibly in use at end of 2nd century AD. More common in 3rd century.

Illustrated example (Figure 46)
Brougham, Cumbria: Green-tinged colourless, from cremation burial dated to *c* AD 220/30–270/80 (Cool 1990, 172 fig 2 no 8).

Other finds
Alcester, Warwickshire: Rim, from late 4th century context (Price and Cottam 1994, 224 no 14 fig 104).
Caerleon, Gwent: Rim, from context dated *c* AD 200 at the Legionary Museum site (Zienkiewicz 1992, 7 no 22 fig 2).
Chesterton, Cambridgeshire: Rim and body with straight and meandering trails.
Colchester, Essex: Three rims, from contexts dated AD 225–275/325 and 4th century (Cool and Price 1995, 82 no 438 fig 5.10, and 92 nos 574–5, fig 5.16).
Malton, Yorkshire: Fragments, at least two cups (Price and Cottam 1997b, 122 nos 6–7 fig 46).
Maryport, Cumbria: Rim fragment (Price 1976b, 52 no 5 fig 9).
Rudston villa, Yorkshire: Rim fragment (Charlesworth 1980, 125 no 2 fig 84).
Winterton villa, Lincolnshire: Fragments, two cups, one from a context dated AD 180–220.
Witcombe villa, Gloucestershire: Rim and base fragments, two cups. (Price and Cottam 1998, 75, 78, 80 nos 12–13, 22 fig 22).

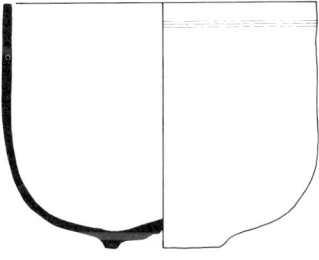

Fig 46   Scale 1:2

York: Rim and body, colourless, from 4th century context at the Minster site (Price 1995b, 358 fig 143). Complete profile, colourless, from late 2nd–3rd century context at Tanner Row.

Further reading
See discussions in connection with the finds from Brougham (Cool 1990) and the Minster, York (Price 1995b, 349).

Hemispherical/deep convex bowl with facet-cutting

Characteristics
Form
Slightly curved rim, edge cracked-off and ground smooth, convex body, small flat or slightly concave base. Cylindrical body with flat base found very occasionally.

Colours
Colourless, greenish/colourless.

Decoration
All-over or zoned decoration in various combinations and styles of facet-cutting, using circular, oval or 'rice-grain' facets, set in quincunx or in vertical lines. Some circular facets have central bosses. Many design elements occur, including lozenges formed from long oval facets infilled with cross-hatched diagonal lines, arcading formed from narrow vertical and diagonal lines enclosing long oval facets, 'ears of wheat' formed from vertical oval facets and diagonal 'rice grain' facets and I-motifs formed from two horizontal oval facets joined by a narrow vertical line.

Other features
The bowls are easily recognised from small decorated body fragments. The lower body and base of deep bowls are often thick-walled. There is some overlap in the chronology and design elements between these bowls and the convex facet-cut bowls (see Figure 36a).

Range of measurements
Rim diameters 80–120mm, heights 70–120mm.

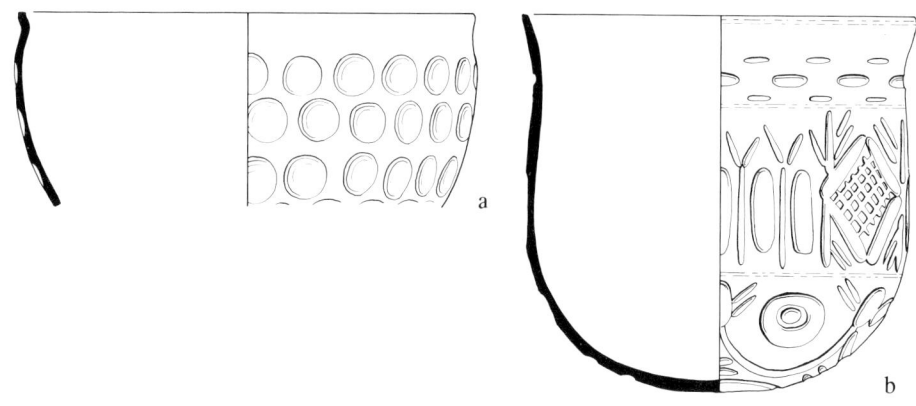

Fig 47   Scale 1:2

Distribution
Quite common.

Date range
Uncertain, because of lack of securely dated finds. Possibly present in late 2nd century AD, certainly in use during the 3rd and early 4th century.

Illustrated examples (Figure 47 and Plate 4.5)
a) *Colchester, Essex*: Rim and body, hemispherical bowl with all-over pattern of circular facets in quincunx, from unstratified context in insula 2 (Hull 1958, 79 fig 35 no 1).
b) *London*: Deep bowl with zones of horizontal oval facets, arcading and lozenges and 'ears of wheat' circular facets with central bosses and swags, separated by horizontal abraded bands, from King William Street (Wheeler 1930, 121–2 no 1, fig 42).

Other finds
Birdoswald, Cumbria: Body fragments, three convex bowls with circular and oval facets, wheel-cut circles and other motifs, in unstratified contexts (Price and Cottam 1997a, 348 nos 12–14 fig 248).
Caister-on-Sea, Norfolk: Rim and body, hemispherical bowl, with in-filled lozenges and oval facets, from 3rd-late 4th century and later contexts (Price and Cool 1993, 141 no 6 fig 129).
Canterbury, Kent: Body, circular and oval facets and short wheel-cuts, from context dated AD 290–320, at Rose Lane (Charlesworth and Price 1987, 222 no 12 fig 88). Rim and body fragments with circular and oval facets, and other motifs, from late 2nd-mid 4th century and residual contexts, at Marlowe Car Park (Shepherd 1995a, 1231 nos 50–56, 58–62 fig 544).
Catsgore, Somerset: Body with round facets and short cut lines, possibly arcading, from early/mid 3rd–early/mid 4th century context (Price 1984, 30 no 1 fig 14).
Colchester, Essex: Rim and body fragments, bowls with circular and oval facets and other motifs, from 2nd, 3rd, 4th century contexts (Cool and Price 1995, 78–9 nos 415–25 fig 5.8).
Great Bedwyn, Castle Copse, Wiltshire: Rim and body, hemispherica bowl, with in-filled lozenges and oval facets (Grose 997, 301–2 nos 438–9 fig 142).
London: Two further deep bowls, with oval and circular facets, some with central

116

bosses, and arcades, ears of wheat, herringbone and I-motifs, from King William Street (Wheeler 1930, 122 nos 2–3 fig 42).

Piercebridge, Co Durham: Body, circular facets with central bosses and I-motifs (Charlesworth 1959c, 44 fig 3 no 9).

Richborough, Kent: Rim and body with circular facets, triangles and other motifs (Bushe-Fox 1928, 52 no 75 pl 25).

Silchester, Hampshire: Rim and body, hemispherical bowl, with horizontal rice grain facets, in-filled lozenges and arcades (Boon 1974a, 232 fig 36 no 4).

Verulamium, Hertfordshire: At least seven deep bowls with horizontal and vertical oval facets, circular facets, some with central bosses, lozenges, arcading and other motifs, from building 5, insula 14, in a pit and cellar deposit dated *c* AD 280–315 (Charlesworth 1972, 206 (xiii) nos 8–13, 208–10 fig 78 nos 48–53). Body, five rows of circular facets in quincunx, from robber trench (Charlesworth 1984a, 154 no 84 fig 62 no 36)

Witcombe villa, Gloucestershire: Body fragments, at least two bowls with circular facets and I-motifs (Price and Cottam 1998, 76, 80 nos 26–29 fig 22).

York: Cylindrical bowl with Z-motifs, arcading and lozenges and horizontal oval facets separated by horizontal wheel-cut lines; and two convex body and base fragments with circular facets, triangles and I-motifs (Harden 1962, 137 HG 210, HG 162, HG 211 fig 88). Base fragments with circular and 'rice-grain' facets, from context dated *c* AD 160–280 at Blake Street (Cool 1995a, 1655 no 6013 fig 744). Body fragment with oval facets and other motifs, from late 4th century context at the Minster site (Price 1995b, 357 no 24 fig 142).

Further reading
See discussion in connecton with finds from Colchester (Cool and Price 1995, 76–9).

Convex cup with straight or curved rim

Characteristics
Form
Vertical or curved rim, edge cracked-off and usually left unworked, convex body, small slightly concave base.

Colours
Greenish colourless, pale green, pale yellow/green.

Decoration
Light horizontal bands of abrasion are almost always present. In addition, unmarvered looped self-coloured trails or coloured blobs or trails occur on some cups. Horizontal wheel-cut lines and mould-blown cups with arcading and honeycomb patterns are found occasionally.

Other features
The glass is generally thin and rather bubbly with small specks. The rim edges of some cups have been ground smooth. For thicker-walled convex bowls, see Figure 52.

Range of measurements
Rim diameters *c* 70–90mm, heights *c* 65–80mm.

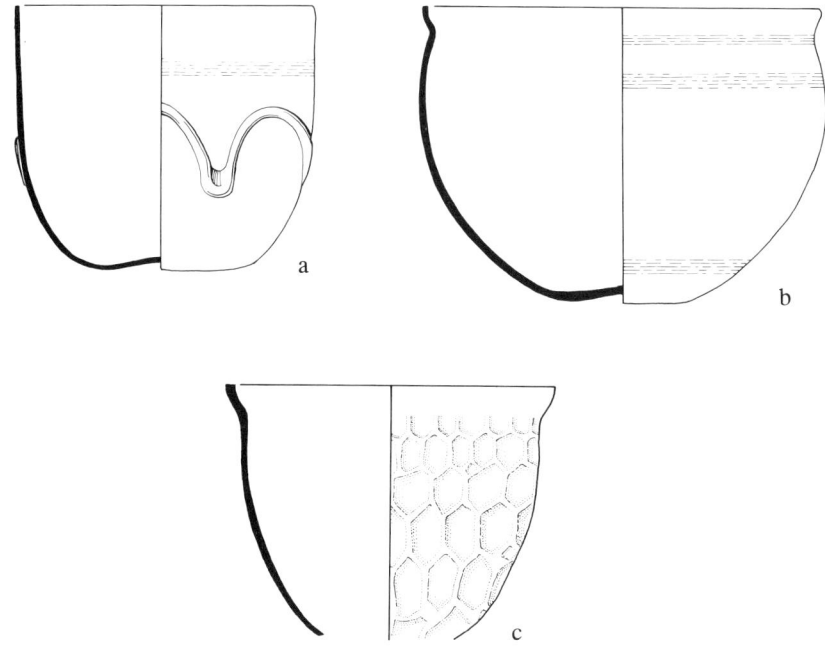

Fig 48   Scale 1:2

Distribution
Very common. Sometimes found in burials.

Date range
4th century AD. A few are known in the last years of the 3rd century. The mould-blown examples probably belong to the second half of the 4th century.

Illustrated examples (Figure 48 and Back cover)
a) *Colchester, Essex*: Almost complete greenish colourless cup with vertical rim, abraded band and festooned trail, from grave 180 dated *c* AD 360–80 at Butt Road cemetery (Cool and Price 1995, 90 no 553 fig 5.16).
b) *Towcester, Northamptonshire*: Fragments, rim, body and base, pale green cup with curved rim and horizontal abraded bands, from context dated *c* AD 330–70+ in Alchester Road suburb (Price and Cool 1983, 119 no 11a-b fig 46).
c) *Fishbourne Beach, Isle of Wight*: Rim and body, mould-blown pale greenish cup with curved rim and hexagonal honeycomb pattern (Price and Cottam 1995, 240 fig 21.4 no 1).

Other finds
Barnsley Park villa, Gloucestershire: Vertical and curved rim fragments with horizontal abraded bands, four greenish colourless and yellow/green cups; also body fragments with festooned trails, from later 4th–5th century contexts (Price 1982a, 175–7 nos 3, 11–12, 14–17 fig 59).
Caister-on-Sea, Norfolk: Rim, body and base fragments, at least fifteen greenish, colour-

less and yellow/green cups with abraded, trailed and blobbed decoration, showing several variations in profile (Price and Cool 1993, 144 149 nos 50–77, 99 figs 130–1).

Carlisle, Cumbria: Rim and body, yellow/green cup with curved rim and abraded decoration, from Blackfriars Street (Price 1990a, 179 fig 164 no 72).

Colchester, Essex: Rim, body and base fragments, at least nine greenish colourless and yellow/green cups with abraded and trailed decoration, from late 3rd–4th century and post-Roman contexts (Cool and Price 1995, 90 nos 554–60, 563–7 fig 5.16).

Dorchester, Dorset: At least three greenish and greenish colourless cups, with abraded decoration and trails, wheel-cut lines and no decoration, from Greyhound Yard (Cool and Price 1993, 162 no 72 fig 86, 164 nos 136–40 fig 87).

Portchester, Hampshire: Rim and body fragments, two yellow/green cups with abraded lines and blobs (Harden 1975, 371 no 10b-c fig 198).

Towcester, Northamptonshire: Fragments, at least seven pale greenish cups with vertical or curved rims and abraded and trailed decoration, from contexts dated *c* A D 330–70+ in the Alchester Road Suburb (Price and Cool 1983, 119–20 nos 12–25 fig 46).

Verulamium, Hertfordshire: Greenish thick-walled cup with curved rim and abraded bands, from house 5, insula 14, cellar deposit dated *c* AD 280–315; rim fragments, two colourless cups, from house 2 insula 27, context dated AD 375–8, and house 1 insula 28, unstratified (Charlesworth 1972, 210 no 4 fig 79 no 61; 1984a, 161 nos 152–3 fig 65 nos 78–9).

Winchester, Hampshire: Two pale green cups with vertical rims and abraded and trailed decoration, from grave 81 dated AD 350–70 and grave 337 dated AD 330–50 in the Lankhills cemetery (Harden 1979a, 213 nos 62, 385 fig 27).

York: Rim and body, two yellow/green cups one mould-blown with hexagonal honeycomb pattern, one with abraded decoration, in 4th century contexts at the Minster site (Price 1995b, 355 no 14 fig 142, 358 no 35 fig 143). Rim and body, yellow/green with abraded lines and blue blob, from residual context at Fishergate (Hunter and Jackson 1993, 1332 no 4635 fig 644).

Further reading
Isings 1957, form 96. For discussion of these and other 4th–early 5th century vessels in Britain, see Cool 1995b. For discussion in connection with finds from Colchester, see Cool and Price 1995, 88–90.

Hemispherical bowl with figured cutting

Characteristics
Form
Vertical rim, edge cracked-off and ground smooth, convex body, small flat base.

Colours
Colourless.

Decoration
Horizontal wheel-cut lines below rim. Figured scenes in either massed shallow cutting with short, narrow cutting for details such as hair and eyes, or in outline wheel-cutting with pointillé infill.

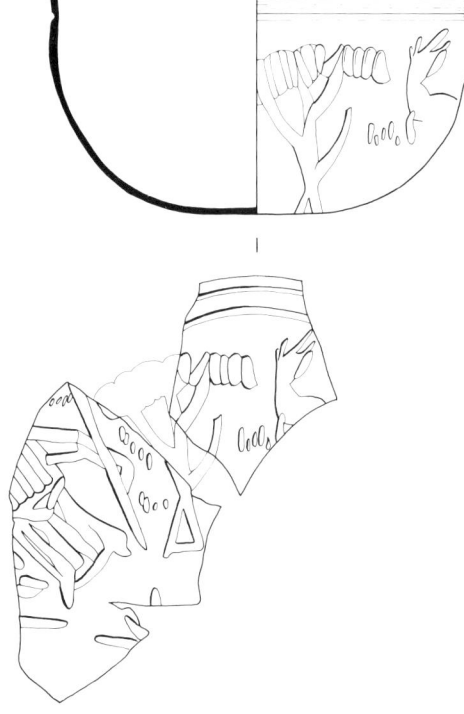

Fig 49   Scale 1:2

Other features
These bowls were generally carefully finished. They were made in good quality glass with few bubbles or impurities.

Range of measurements
Rim diameters *c* 100–200mm, heights *c* 50–90mm.

Distribution
Not common. Generally recognised from small body fragments. Not recorded in burials.

Date range
Second and third quarters of 4th century AD.

Illustrated example (Figure 49)
Lullingstone villa, Kent: Fragmentary small bowl, parts of two figures and a tree, perhaps a Biblical scene, produced in massed wheel-cuts, from pit dated AD 330–50 (Cool and Price 1987a, 129 no 338 fig 54).

Other finds

Chesters, Northumberland: Rim and body with head of figure and foliage in short narrow wheel-cuts (Charlesworth 1959c, 46 fig 7 no 2).

Dorchester, Dorset: Fragmentary large bowl with dancing figures, perhaps a Bacchic scene, in wheel-cuts and pointillé infill, from the upper fill of 4th century rubbish pit at Colliton Park (Toynbee 1962, 185 no 141 pl 159; Harden 1969, 64 fig 8).

Frocester Court villa, Gloucestershire: Rim and body, small bowl with hunting scene in massed wheel cuts (information from Eddie Price).

Lullingstone villa, Kent: Rim, body and base fragments, two small bowls with unidentified scenes in massed wheel-cuts and wheel-cuts and abraded patches (Cool and Price 1987a, 129–30 nos 339–40 figs 53–4).

Traprain Law, Lothian: Rim and body with head of figure in wheel-cuts and pointillé infill (Charlesworth 1959c, 46 pl 1 no 5).

Winterton villa, Lincolnshire: Rim and body with curved area of short narrow wheel-cuts (Charlesworth 1976a, 249 no 23 fig 134).

York: Body with eight-point star in massed wheel-cuts, from Bishophill (Charlesworth 1978b, 56 no 171 fig 30). Rim and body with curved area of short narrow wheel-cuts, from late 4th century post-Roman context at Blake Street (Cool 1995a, 1659 no 6186 fig 744). Two small body fragments, one with short wheel-cuts, one with pointillé infill, from the Minster site (Price 1995b, 357 nos 18–9 fig 142). Body fragments with massed wheelcuts from the Coppergate and Wellington Row sites (information from Hilary Cool).

Further reading

For a survey of 4th century tablewares with figured cutting in Britain, see Price 1995c. See also discussion in connection with the finds from Lullingstone (Cool and Price 1987a, 113–8).

Conical beaker with straight or curved rim

Characteristics

Form

Rim edge cracked-off and usually left unworked, tall straight side tapering in, small concave base, occasionally with open pushed-in base ring.

Colours

Greenish/colourless, pale green, yellow/green, colourless.

Decoration

Light horizontal bands of abrasion almost always present, below the rim and on the upper and lower body. In addition coloured blobs occur on some beakers. Indents and trails, and facet- and figured-cutting are also known. A few mould-blown beakers have arcading and hexagonal honeycomb patterns.

Other features

The glass is generally bubbly with small specks, but beakers with figured cutting were made in good quality glass, and the rim edges of these were carefully ground. The

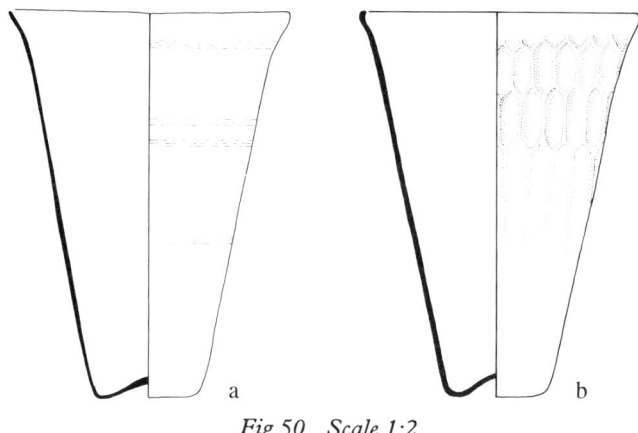

Fig 50   Scale 1:2

combination of straight side and horizontal bands of abrasion together with the colours and quality of the glass makes this form easy to identify from body fragments.

Range of measurements
Rim diameters *c* 70–90mm, heights *c* 90–110mm.

Distribution
Very common. Sometimes found in burials.

Date range
4th century. Some found in last years of 3rd century. Mould-blown examples probably belong to second half of 4th century.

Illustrated examples (Figure 50)
a) *Banwell, Wint Hill, Somerset*: Fragmentary greenish beaker with curved rim and horizontal abraded bands (Harden 1960a, 51–2, figs 8–9).
b) *Winchester, Hampshire*: Greenish mould-blown beaker with hexagonal honeycomb pattern below the rim and vertical ridges on the body, from 5th century context at Brook Street (Price and Cottam 1995, 242 fig 21.4 no 2).

Other finds
Barnsley Park villa, Gloucestershire: Body and base fragments, at least four pale green and colourless beakers, one with abraded decoration from a 5th century context, three with purple and dark green blobs; from contexts dated *c* AD 360–75 and later (Price 1982a, 175, 177 nos 2, 13 fig 59).
Birdoswald, Cumbria: Fragments, at least two pale green and greenish colourless beakers with abraded bands, from late 4th century and post-Roman contexts (Price and Cottam 1997a, 352–3 nos 72–4 fig 249).
Caister-on-Sea, Norfolk: Fragments, at least eleven greenish colourless and yellow/green beakers with abraded bands (Price and Cool 193, 145, 147 nos 78–98, 103–4 fig 131.
Cirencester, Gloucestershire: Rim, body and base fragments, greenish colourless beakers

with abraded decoration and colourless beaker with long diagonal facets (Shepherd 1986, 121 nos 625, 632, 638 figs 86–7).

Colchester, Essex: Fragments, colourless and greenish colourless beakers with facet-cutting, horizontal wheel-cutting and bands of abrasion, from late 3rd–4th century and post-Roman contexts (Cool and Price 1995, 90, 92 nos 570–73, 576–88 fig 5.16).

Dorchester, Dorset: Fragments, four greenish colourless beakers with abraded bands, from Greyhound Yard (Cool and Price 1993, 166 nos 141–4 fig 87).

Frocester Court villa, Gloucestershire: Rim, body and base fragments, at least four beakers. One colourless with four human figures formed from massed wheel-cuts, from a mid 4th century context, three pale blue/green with abraded bands, from mid 4th century or later and unstratified contexts (Price 1979, 41 nos 4, 9–11 fig 16).

Gloucester: Rim and body fragments, at least two colourless beakers, one with abraded bands, one with human figures formed from massed wheel-cuts, from New Market Hall (Charlesworth 1974c, 76 nos 13,18 fig 29). Rim and body, colourless beaker with wheel-cut lines, from Kingsholm (Price and Cool 1985, 54 no 89 fig 20). Fragments, at least seven greenish and yellow/green beakers with abraded bands, from 4th century and later contexts, from Berkeley Street.

Lullingstone villa, Kent: Rim, body and base fragments, at least three beakers, one colourless with figured decoration, two greenish colourless with abraded bands, the latter probably from pit dated AD 330–50 (Cool and Price 1987a, 130, 135 nos 341, 369–72 fig 55).

Portchester, Hampshire: Fragments, colourless and yellow/green beakers, one from well filling with coin dated AD 317–26 (Harden 1975, 371 nos 11–12 & 14 fig 198).

Richborough, Kent : Rim and body, horizontal band of blue blobs (Roach Smith 1850, 77–8 fig 6).

Silchester, Hampshire: Complete profile, greenish beaker with abraded bands (Boon 1974a, 230 no 8 fig 36).

Shakenoak villa, Oxfordshire: Fragments, at least three greenish and pale blue/green beakers, from late 3rd–late 4th century deposits (Harden 1973,103–4 nos 221–6 fig 52).

Towcester, Northamptonshire: Fragments, several greenish colourless beakers with abraded bands, from contexts dated AD 330–70+ in Alchester Road suburb (Price and Cool 1983, 120–2 nos 30–5 fig 47).

Uley, Gloucestershire: Fragments , at least seven colourless and yellow/green beakers with abraded bands or no decoration, from late 3rd–early 4th, late 4th and 5th century contexts (Price 1993b, 214 nos 12–17 fig 158).

Welford on Avon, Warwickshire: Five or six pale green beakers with abraded bands, from inhumation in lead coffin (Cool and Price 1993/4, 45–7 no 2 fig 6).

Winchester, Hampshire: Seven pale green, colourless and greenish blue beakers, four with abraded bands, one with indents, one with looped trails, one with indents and spiral trail, from Graves 63, 347, 351, 369, 396, 398 dated AD 370–410 at Lankhills cemetery (Harden 1979a, 214–5 nos 382, 391, 530, 634, 51, 506, 633 fig 27).

York: Greenish colourless beaker with abraded bands, from inhumation in stone coffin on the Mount (Harden 1962, 140 HG 144 pl 66). Fragments, at least six yellow/green and greenish colourless beakers with abraded bands and one with indents, from late 4th century and post-Roman contexts at the Minster site (Price 1995b, 360–1 nos 36–8, 42 fig 143).

Further reading
Isings 1957, form 106. For discussion of these and other 4th–early 5th century vessels in Britain, see Cool 1995b. For discussion in connection with finds from Colchester, see Cool and Price 1995, 88–92.

Shallow convex bowl

Characteristics

Form
Curved or inturned rim edge cracked-off and either unworked or lightly smoothed, wide shallow convex body tapering in, convex base.

Colours
Colourless, greenish colourless, pale green, yellow/green.

Decoration
Horizontal bands of abrasion are common. Other types of decoration include wheel and facet-cutting, and free-hand incised and abraded designs. Mould-blown decoration is rare.

Other features
Sometimes known as segmental bowls. The glass quality varies considerably; many bowls are thin-walled and bubbly, but some were produced in thicker, less bubbly glass. Small fragments of rim and upper body may also come from indented bowls (see Figure 53).

Range of measurements
Rim diameters c 125–200mm, heights c 35–60mm.

Distribution
Common. Not recorded in burials.

Date range
4th century.

Illustrated examples (Figure 51)
a) *Banwell, Wint Hill, Somerset* : Almost complete, colourless, curved rim with smoothed edge, with free-hand incised hunting scene and inscription in retrograde (Harden 1960a, 47–51 figs 2, 4–7).
b) *Shakenoak villa, Oxfordshire*: Fifty-two fragments, greenish, inturned rim with smoothed edge, from undated deposit (Harden 1968a, 78–9 no 24 fig 26 no 9).
c) *Lullingstone villa, Kent*: Rim and upper body, greenish colourless, curved rim with smoothed edge, three abraded bands (Cool and Price 1987a, 135 no 373 fig 55).

Other finds
Bath, Avon: Rim and upper body, greenish colourless, no decoration, from mid–late 4th century deposit (Shepherd 1985, 163 no 17 fig 92).
Beadlam villa, North Yorkshire: Fragments, three shallow yellow/green mould-blown bowls with arcading, interlocking hexagons, rosettes and curving gadroons (Price and Cottam 1995, 235–7).
Caister-on-Sea, Norfolk: Rim and body, colourless, free-hand incised scene with dog (Price and Cool 1993, 141, 144 no 48 fig 130).
Canterbury, Kent: Rim and upper body, yellow/green, with abraded band, from Canterbury Lane (Charlesworth and Price 1987, 228 no 53 fig 91).

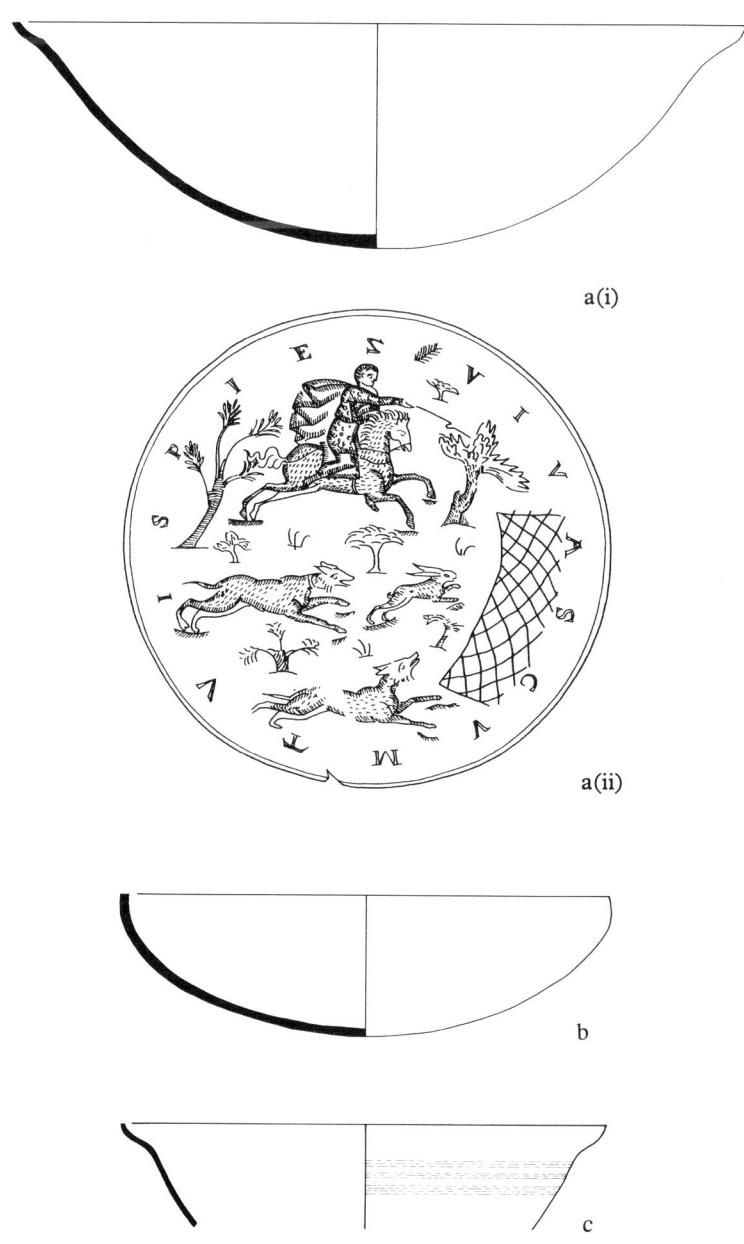

a(i)

a(ii)

b

c

Fig 51   Scale 1:2 (Illustrated scene a(ii) 1:3)

125

Chilgrove villa 2, near Chichester, West Sussex: Rim and body, greenish colourless with free-hand incised and facet-cut mythological scene and inscription (Down 1979, 163 no 7 fig 56).

Cirencester, Gloucestershire: Fragments, at least two greenish colourless bowls with abraded bands (Shepherd 1986, 121 nos 642–4 fig 87).

Colchester, Essex: Fragments, three yellow/green and greenish colourless bowls with abraded bands and without decoration, from 3rd–4th century and later contexts (Cool and Price 1995, 105 nos 729–31 fig 6.8).

Dorchester, Dorset: Fragments, two greenish colourless bowls with abraded bands and wheel-cutting, from Greyhound Yard (Cool and Price 1993, 166 nos 145–6 fig 87). Fragmentary pale green mould-blown bowl with arcading and rosettes and polychrome cane insets, from Charles Street/Acland Road (Cool and Henderson 1993).

Frocester Court villa, Gloucestershire: Fragments, at least two pale green and greenish colourless bowls with abraded bands (Price 1979, 42 nos 12–3 fig 16).

Ilchester, Somerset: Fragments, two yellow/green and colourless bowls with abraded bands and wheel-cut lines (Price 1982b, 230–1 nos 21, 32 fig 112).

Lullingstone villa, Kent: Fragment, yellow/green bowl with abraded bands (Cool and Price 1987a, 135 no 374 fig 55).

Milton Keynes, Bancroft villa, Buckinghamshire: Fragments, at least four colourless and light green bowls with linear and geometric cutting and abraded bands (Price 1987d, 149, 151 nos 216–7, 220, 222–4 fig 48; Allen 1994, 357 no 362 fig 181).

Portchester, Hampshire: Fragments, three greenish colourless bowls, with abraded bands and facet-cutting (Harden 1975, 369 nos 1–3 fig 197).

Richborough, Kent: Fragment, pale green bowl, incised scene with two figures (Bushe-Fox 1932, 86 no 65 pl 17).

Shakenoak villa, Oxfordshire: Fragments, at least six colourless and greenish bowls with abraded bands, wheel-cut lines, free-hand incised figured scenes and without decoration, from late 3rd/4th to late 4th century contexts (Harden 1968, 79 no 24; 1973, 102–3 nos 209–213 fig 52).

Further reading
Isings 1957, form 116. For discussion of these and other 4th–early 5th century vessels in Britain, see Cool 1995b. For discussions of bowls with figured cutting, see Price 1995c, and mould-blown bowls, see Price and Cottam 1995.

Convex bowl with thick walls

Characteristics
Form
Curved rim, edge cracked-off and left unworked, thick convex body, concave base.

Colours
Usually strong yellow/green. Also pale green, pale yellow/green and greenish colourless.

Decoration
Usually horizontal abraded bands. Some bowls have coloured blobs, and some have no decoration.

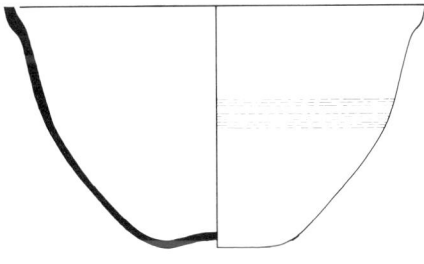

Fig 52   Scale 1:2

Other features
The thick walls and strong colour of these vessels distinguish them from the thinner-walled convex cups discussed above (see Figure 48). The full profile seldom survives.

Range of measurements
Rim diameters generally *c* 80–120mm, heights *c* 50–70mm.

Distribution
Quite common. Not recorded in burials.

Date range
Uncertain. In use in second half of 4th century AD.

Illustrated example (Figure 52)
Sandy, Bedfordshire: Yellow/green, rim, body and base, with horizontal abraded bands, from predominantly late 4th century assemblage.

Other finds
Beadlam villa, North Yorkshire: Fragments, at least seven bowls, four yellow/green, two yellow/brown, one dark yellow/green, with abraded bands and undecorated (Price and Cottam 1996b, 104–5 nos 29–30, 37, 39, 40–1, 48 figs 55–6).
Burgh Castle, Norfolk: Rim and body, two pale green bowls without decoration (Plate 5.3), from late 4th-early 5th century hoard of glass vessels (Harden 1983, 81, 83 nos 83–4 fig 37).
Cirencester, Gloucestershire: Rim and upper body, three greenish colourless bowls with abraded bands (Shepherd 1986, 120 nos 626, 629, 633 fig 86).
Colchester, Essex: Rim and body, two pale yellow/green bowls with abraded bands, from contexts dated to AD 225–400+ and 5th century (Cool and Price 1995, 90 nos 561–2 fig 5.16).
Corbridge, Northumberland: Rim and body, yellow/green cup with dark blue blobs (Charlesworth 1959c, 50 fig 8 no 2).
Portchester, Hampshire: Fragments, at least two yellow/green and dark yellow/green bowls (Harden 1975, 371, nos 9, 10a, figs 97–8).
Sandy, Bedfordshire: At least four more yellow/green bowls.
Winchester, Hampshire: Fragments, several yellow/green bowls, with abraded bands and undecorated.
York: Rim fragment, yellow/green, from post-Roman context at Blake Street (Cool 1995a, 1659–60 no 6202 fig 774).

Further reading
For discussion in connection with the finds from Beadlam, see Price and Cottam 1996b, 99.

Convex bowl with indents

Characteristics
Form
Curved rim, edge cracked-off and left unworked, slightly convex body, small concave base.

Colours
Greenish colourless, pale green, yellow/green.

Decoration
Oval indents on body. Many also have horizontal abraded bands below rim.

Other features
These vessels are often described as truncated conical bowls. The rim and upper body above the indents is very similar to some shallow convex bowls (see Figure 51c).

Range of measurements
Rim diameters *c* 110–140 mm, heights *c* 60–70mm.

Distribution
Quite common. Sometimes found in 5th-century burials (Harden 1951, 262, 266 I(j) fig 5; 1956, 136, 158 Adi Pl 15f).

Date range
Uncertain. In use in second half of 4th century AD. Some in 5th century contexts.

Illustrated example (Figure 53)
Hucclecote villa, Gloucestershire: Pale green bowl with horizontal abraded band and seven oval indents on body (Clifford 1933, 334 fig 10).

Other finds
Abingdon, Barton Court Farm, Oxfordshire: Fragments, pale yellow/green bowl with abraded band (Price 1986a, MF6: A9 no 3 fig 117).
Barnsley Park villa, Gloucestershire: Body and base fragments, greenish colourless, from 5th century context (Price 1982a, 178 no 19).
Birdoswald, Cumbria: Rim and body, yellow/green bowl with abraded bands, from context dated *c* AD 290–350 (Price and Cottam 1997a, 352 no 71 fig 248).
Colchester, Essex: Fragments, at least six greenish colourless and pale green bowls, from 4th century and post-Roman contexts (Cool and Price 1995, 104 nos 720–728 fig 6.8).
Frocester Court villa, Gloucestershire: Rim and body, colourless bowl with abraded band (Price 1979, 42 no 15 fig 16).
Gloucester: Rim and upper body, greenish bowl, from late 4th century or later context at

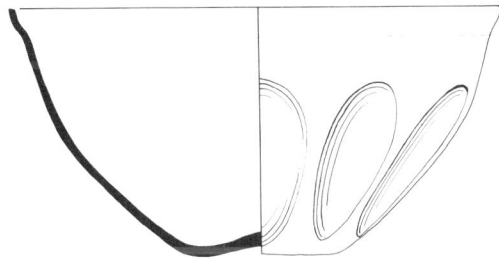

Fig 53   Scale 1:2

New Market Hall (Charlesworth 1974c, 76 no 14 fig 29). At least four yellow/green bowls with abraded bands, two from pits containing coins of last decade of 4th century at Berkeley Street.

Ilchester, Somerset: Fragment, greenish colourless with abraded band (Price 1982b, 231 no 29 fig 112).

Lullingstone villa, Kent: Fragments, two greenish colourless bowls, one with abraded band (Cool and Price 1987a, 137 nos 375–6 fig 56).

Milton Keynes, Bancroft villa, Buckinghamshire: Rim and body, yellow/green bowl with abraded band (Price 1987d, 152 no 230 fig 48).

Shakenoak villa, Oxfordshire: Rim and body, yellow/green, from 3rd–late 4th century deposit; body fragment, greenish colourless, from late 4th century deposit (Harden 1968 79 no 27; 1973, 103 no 220).

Vindolanda, Northumberland: Rim and body, yellow/green bowl with horizontal abraded band (Price 1985c, 210 no 34).

Winchester: Rim and body, yellow/green with abraded band, from post-Roman context.

York: Fragments, at least two light green and yellow/green bowls with abraded bands, from late 4th century to post-Roman contexts at Blake Street (Cool 1995a, 1660 nos 6213–4, 6215–9 fig 744). Fragments, at least five greenish colourless, pale green and yellow/green bowls, three with abraded bands, from 4th century and post-Roman contexts at the Minster site (Price 1995b, 360–1 nos 40–41 fig 143).

Further reading
Isings 1957, form 117. For discussion of these and other 4th–early 5th century vessels in Britain, see Cool 1995b. For discussion in connection with finds from Lullingstone and Colchester, see Cool and Price 1987a, 118–9 and Cool and Price 1995, 104–5.

Beaker with fire-rounded rim

Characteristics
Form
Out-turned rim, edge fire-rounded, straight or very slightly convex body tapering in, small concave base or out-turned tubular base ring and concave base.

Colours
Pale green, yellow/green.

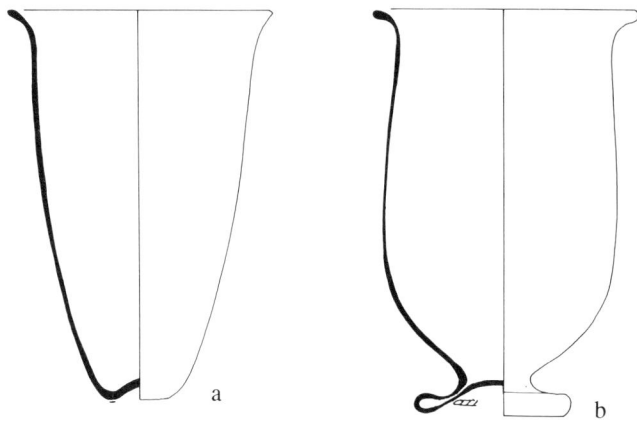

Fig 54   Scale 1:2

Decoration
Usually undecorated. Trails occur very occasionally.

Other features
Pontil mark present on base. These beakers are often recognised from rim fragments and concave bases with pontil marks. Similar tubular base rings occur on other vessels.

Range of measurements
Rim diameters *c* 70mm, heights *c* 100–110mm.

Distribution
Fairly common. Occasionally found in burials.

Date range
Mid 4th–early 5th century AD.

Illustrated examples (Figure 54 Plate 5.4)
a) *Burgh Castle, Norfolk*: Complete green beaker with concave base, from late 4th-early 5th century hoard of glass vessels (Harden 1983, 83 no 85, fig 37).
b) *Burgh Castle, Norfolk*: Complete pale green beaker with tubular base ring, from same hoard (Harden 1983, 83 no 89 fig 37).

Other finds
Abingdon, Barton Court Farm, Oxfordshire: Rim fragment, greenish (Price 1986a, MF 6: A11 fig 117).
Bath, Avon: Four greenish colourless rims, in 4th century contexts (Shepherd 1985, 163 nos 18–21 fig 92).
Burgh Castle, Norfolk: Three beakers, green and pale green, two with concave bases, one with tubular base, from same hoard as Figure 54a–b (Harden 1983, 83 nos 86–88 fig 37).
Canterbury, Kent: Rim fragments, two yellow/green and greenish beakers, from contexts

dated *c* 300–400 at Simon Langton Yard (Charlesworth and Price 1987, 228 nos 54–5 fig 91). Rim and body fragments, three greenish colourless beakers, one in context dated *c* AD 300/20–350, at Marlowe Car Park (Shepherd 1995a, 1248–9 nos 495–7 fig 549).

Carlisle, Cumbria: Rim fragment, pale green, from Lewthwaites Lane.

Cirencester, Gloucestershire: Rim and body fragments, greenish colourless beakers (Shepherd 1986, 120 nos 635–7 fig 87).

Colchester, Essex: Rim and base fragments, at east eight pale green and greenish colourless beakers, from 4th–early 5th and later contexts (Cool and Price 1995, 93 nos 620–9 fig 5.17).

Leicester: Complete pale green beaker with concave base, looped trails on body, from burial at Gallowtree Gate (Dore 1927–8, 39, pl 3 no 2).

Lincoln: Rim and base fragments, several pale green and yellow/green beakers.

Milton Keynes, Bancroft villa, Buckinghamshire: Rim fragments, five yellow/green and greenish beakers, from 5th century or later contexts (Price 1987d, 152, 154 nos 235–8 fig 49; Allen 1994, 358 no 367 fig 182).

Rainham, Essex: Complete greenish beaker with tubular base ring, from inhumation burial in stone coffin (Hull 1930, 28 fig 1 no 1).

Sandy, Bedfordshire: Rim, body and concave base fragments, at least seven yellow/green beakers.

Towcester, Northamptonshire: Rim and body fragments, at least four greenish colourless, pale green and yellow/green beakers, from contexts dated *c* A D 330–70+ in Alchester Road suburb (Price and Cool 1983, 122 nos 40–44 fig 47).

Uley, Gloucestershire: Fragments three greenish colourless and yellow/green beakers, one with concave base, from early 5th century and later contexts (Price 1993b, nos 22–4 fig 158).

Winchester, Hampshire: Rim and body fragments, at least eleven pale green and yellow/green beakers.

York: Rim fragments, three light green and greenish colourless beakers, from late 3rd, late 4th and post-Roman contexts at Blake Street (Cool 1995a, 1660 nos 6227–9 fig 744).

Further reading
For discussion of these and other 4th–early 5th century vessels in Britain, see Cool 1995b. For discussion in connection with finds from Colchester, see Cool and Price 1995, 92–3.

Deep tubular rimmed bowl with tubular base ring

Characteristics
Form
Vertical or slightly flared tubular rim, edge bent out and down, convex or cylindrical upper body, lower body tapering in, out-turned tubular base ring and concave base.

Colours
Greenish/colourless, pale green, yellow/green, occasionally blue/green.

Decoration
The upper body sometimes has diagonal optic-blown ribs, or, less commonly, spiral trails.

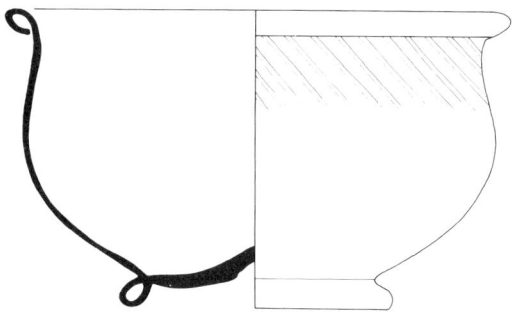

Fig 55   Scale 1:2

Other features
Rim edge occasionally rolled-in before being bent out and down. Pontil mark on base. Bubbly glass with specks. These bowls are distinguishable from earlier tubular rimmed bowls on the basis of the colour and quality of glass, but they are often difficult to recognise from small fragments.

Range of measurements
Rim diameters *c* 90–140mm, heights *c* 70–80mm.

Distribution
Not very common. Not noted in Roman period burials, but one is known from a 5th century burial at High Down, Worthing, Sussex (Harden 1951, 263, 266 I(h) fig 9).

Date range
Uncertain. In use in second half of 4th century AD, perhaps continuing into 5th century.

Illustrated example (Figure 55 and Plate 5.5)
Burgh Castle, Norfolk: Complete colourless bowl with shallow diagonal optic-blown ribs on upper body, from late 4th-early 5th century hoard of glass vessels (Harden 1983, 81 no 81 fig 37).

Other finds
Abingdon, Barton Court Farm, Oxfordshire: Rim and body, greenish bowl, tubular rim, diagonal optic-blown ribs below the rim, colourless (Price 1986a, MF 6:A10–11 nos 4, 7 fig 117).
Bath, Avon: Rim, greenish colourless small bowl or beaker (Shepherd 1985, 163 no 22 fig 92).
Burgh Castle, Norfolk: Pale green bowl without decoration, from same hoard as Figure 55 (Harden 1983, 81 no 82 fig 37).
Colchester, Essex: Rim fragment, small light green bowl, from post-Roman context (Cool and Price 1995, 99 no 692 fig 6.2).
Dorchester on Thames, Oxfordshire: Body and base, green cylindrical bowl with optic-blown ribs, from pit dated *c* AD 390–410 (Charlesworth 1984b, 155 no 1 fig 39).

132

Ilchester, Somerset: Rim, small greenish bowl (Price 1982b, 230 no 25 fig 112).
Overton Down, Wiltshire: Rim and body, pale green bowl, diagonal optic-blown ribs.
Portchester, Hampshire: Rim, yellow bowl (Harden 1975, 369 no 8 fig 197).
Uley, Gloucestershire: Rim and body fragments, blue/green bowl with spiral trail, from mid 4th century context (Price 1993b, 214 no 25 fig 158).

Further reading
Isings 1957, form 115. For discussion of these and other 4th–early 5th century vessels in Britain, see Cool 1995b. For discussion of these and other tubular-rimmed bowls in connection with finds from Colchester, see Cool and Price 1995, 94–99.

Convex cup with tubular rim and handle

Characteristics
Form
Vertical tubular rim, edge bent out and down, or sometimes in and down, convex body tapering in, narrow trailed base ring, slightly concave base. Vertical curved rod or ribbon handle, applied to lower body and attached to rim or upper body.

Colours
Yellow/green, pale green.

Other features
Pontil mark on base noted on one cup. The form is difficult to recognise unless the the rim and handle survive together.

Range of measurements
Rim diameters *c* 55–65mm, heights *c* 60–65mm.

Distribution
Rare. Only recorded in southern Britain; four examples are known from south Hampshire/West Sussex.

Date range
Uncertain. In use in later 4th century. Sometimes in burials.

Illustrated example (Figure 56)
Winchester, Hampshire: Pale green cup, from Grave 390 dated AD 370–410 in Lankhills cemetery (Harden 1979a, 216 no 508 fig 27).

Other finds
Chichester, West Sussex: Rim, body and handle, yellow/green cup, from East Pallant House (Price and Cool 1989, 135 & 140, EP15 fig 19.4).
Chilgrove villa 1, near Chichester, West Sussex: Rim, body and ribbed handle, in mid 4th century or later context (Down 1979, 163 no 2 fig 56).
Colchester, Essex: Fragmentary green cup, from Grave Group 96 dated to mid 2nd–mid 3rd century (May 1930, 280 Grave 96/36 no 214 pl 87.96).

Fig 56   Scale 1:2

Milton Keynes, Bancroft villa, Buckinghamshire: Rim, pale green cup or beaker, from 5th century or later context (Allen 1994, 358 no 366 fig 182).

Winchester, Hampshire: Pale green cup, from Grave 136 dated AD 340–70/90 in Lankhills cemetery (Harden 1979a, 216 no 117 fig 27).

Further reading

For brief notes on these vessels see Price and Cool 1989, 135, and Cool 1995b, 13–4.

Jars

Square jar

Characteristics

Form

Vertical or slightly out-turned tubular rim, edge usually rolled in, then bent out and down to form double fold (occasionally the rim edge is folded inwards), wide neck, shoulder expanding out, straight four-sided body, slightly concave base. Body and base blown into square-sectioned mould or flattened on marver.

Colours

Blue/green.

Decoration

The raised basal designs on the mould-blown examples are similar to those on square bottles (see Figure 89). Motifs include circles, squares and crosses.

Other features

The rim is sometimes called a collar rim. A pontil mark occurs on some bases. These jars are not easy to recognise on settlements, as the body and base fragments are identical with those of prismatic bottles, and the rims are often similar to the rims on globular jars, although they are usually made in thicker glass (see Figure 58).

Range of measurements

Rim diameters *c* 50–120mm, heights *c* 100–260mm.

Distribution

Not very common. Some come from burials.

Date range

Uncertain. In use in 1st–2nd century AD.

Illustrated example (Figure 57)

Cirencester, Gloucestershire: Complete large jar with five raised circles on the base, from burial at Kingsmead (Lysons 1792, 131 pl 11 fig 1; Thorpe 1935, 5 pl 2c).

Other finds

Carlisle, Cumbria: Fragment, rim, shoulder and body, from Annetwell Street.

Chichester, West Sussex: Complete jar from Flavian burial (Burial Group 79) in St Pancras cemetery (Down and Rule 1971, 99 fig 5.22/79e).

Cirencester, Gloucestershire: Complete jar, rim edge folded in, from burial 357 (Charlesworth 1982, 132 fig 81).

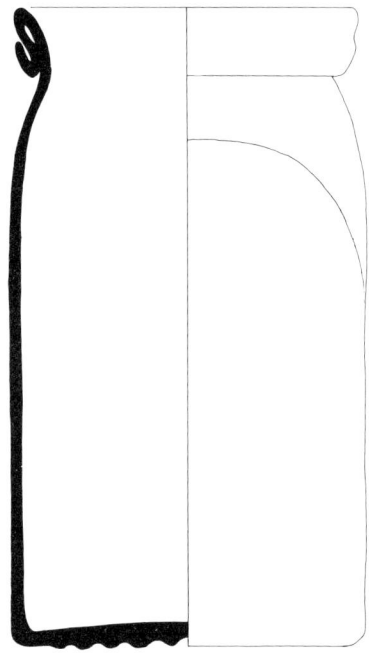

Fig 57   Scale 1:3

Colchester, Essex: Fragments, several thick-walled rims, which may come from square jars, in residual contexts (Cool and Price 1995, 107 nos 742–4 fig 7.2).

Lincoln: Fragmentary jar, found with inhumation burial in east cemetery (Carter 1796, 108 pl 13 no 1).

Mancetter, Warwickshire: Complete jar with flattened sides, from cremation dated to first half of 2nd century (Price 1982c, 134 no 1 fig 2).

Richborough, Kent: Two, from pit dated *c* AD 75–100 (Bushe-Fox 1949, 159 no 377 pl 69).

Thornborough, Buckinghamshire: Complete jar, sides flattened to produce squarish body, from cremation burial 3 dated *c* A D 65–75 (Price 1975, 20–1 no 2 fig 10).

Verulamium, St Stephen's cemetery, Hertfordshire: Complete jar in cremation burial (Davies & Saunders 1986, 28 fig).

Usk, Gwent: Thick-walled rim fragment, from Flavian or later context (Price 1995a, 184 no 121 fig 48).

Further reading
Isings 1957, form 62. For discussion of the problems of recognising square jars, in connection with finds at Colchester and Usk, see Cool and Price 1995, 106, 185, and Price 1995a, 184.

Convex jar with collar rim

Characteristics

Form
Vertical or slightly out-turned tubular rim, edge often rolled in, then bent out and down to form double fold, wide globular or ovoid body, open pushed-in base ring, concave base.

Colours
Polychrome rare, strongly coloured monochrome (dark blue, yellow/brown, yellow/green) found quite frequently, blue/green most common.

Decoration
Narrow vertical or slightly diagonal ribs are found on many jars. Marvered opaque white splashes occur on a few jars.

Other features
The rim formation is easily recognised, although a thicker version, always in blue/green, is also found on square jars (see Figure 57). The body and base fragments are identical with those of convex jugs (see Figure 66).

Range of measurements
Rim diameters *c* 80–130, heights *c* 120–180mm.

Distribution
Very common. Sometimes present in burials.

Date range
Third quarter of 1st century -early/mid 2nd century.

Illustrated example (Figure 58)
Richborough, Kent: Fragmentary pale blue/green ribbed jar, from pit dated AD 80–120 (Bushe-Fox 1932, 84 no 57 pl 15).

Other finds
Baginton, The Lunt, Warwickshire: Fragmentary blue/green jar, lacking rim, from contexts dated *c* AD 60–140 (Charlesworth 1975c, 39 no 5 pl 10a).
Caerleon, Gwent: Fragments, two dark blue and yellow/green jars, in Flavian-Trajanic contexts in barrack 12, Prysg Field (Price 1995d, 84 fig 9 nos 5 & 9). Fragments, two blue/green jars, from late 1st–mid 2nd century and later contexts at Roman Gates (Allen 1992, 180 nos 9–9a+fig).
Colchester, Essex: Intact yellow/brown jar, from burial (Colchester Museum 1869, 22 no 301 pl 4 no 2). Fragments, around 28 polychrome, dark blue, yellow/brown, yellow/green, pale green and blue/green jars, from mid 1st–early/mid 2nd century and later contexts (Cool and Price 1995, 107 109 nos 732–41, 745–64 fig.7.2).
Exeter, Devon: Fragmentary undecorated jar, from late Neronian context, and blue/green rim fragment, from context dated *c* AD 80–100 (Charlesworth 1979a, 227 nos 23–4 fig 70).

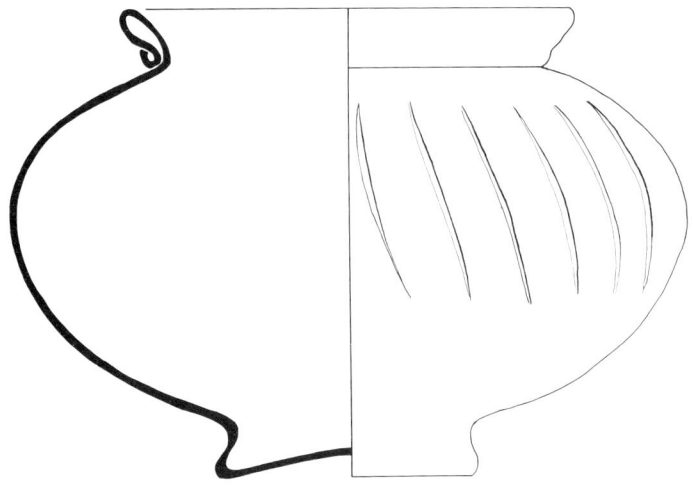

Fig 58   Scale 1:2

Shefford, Bedfordshire: Almost complete yellow/brown ribbed jar from cremation burial (Kennett 1970, 201–2).

Towcester, Northamptonshire: Yellow/brown body and base fragments, probably from a ribbed jar, in pit dated to AD 155–65 in Park Street (Price 1980a, 66 no 10 fig 16).

Thornborough, Buckinghamshire: Blue/green ribbed jar used as cinerary urn, from cremation group 7, not closely dated within second half of 1st century (Price 1975, 21 no 3 fig 10).

Usk, Gwent: Fragments, at least sixteen polychrome, dark blue, yellow/brown, yellow/green, blue/green jars in Neronian-early Flavian and later contexts in legionary fortress (Price 1995a, 157 no 30, 170–71 nos 71–5 figs 44–5).

Verulamium, Hertfordshire: Two fragmentary dark blue and blue/green jars from contexts dated AD 60–75 and *c* AD 105, and rim fragments of five other blue/green jars from late 1st-mid 2nd century contexts in insula 14; one complete blue/green jar and six blue, yellow/brown, yellow/green and blue/green rim fragments, from 1st-mid 2nd century and later contexts in insulas 27 and 28 (Charlesworth 1972, 204 fig 76 nos 25–26; 1984, 166 nos 246–252 fig 67 nos 105–6). Rim fragments, at least three blue/green jars, from King Harry Lane (Price 1989a, 44 nos 295–7 fig 26).

Further reading
Isings 1957, form 67*c* For discussion in connection with finds at Colchester and Usk, see Cool and Price 1995, 106–9, and Price 1995a, 169–71.

Large convex jar with handles

Characteristics
Form
Horizontal out-turned rim, either with rounded edge and tubular fold on underside, or folded up and in. Wide neck expanding out, wide convex upper body, rounded change

of angle, slightly convex lower body tapering in, open base ring and concave base. Two handles, formed in several ways:-

i. Thick M-shaped rod handles on upper body, applied horizontally from left to right with tooled loop at centre pulled down to join body.

ii. Thick curved rod handles on upper body, applied horizontally from left to right, sometimes with pinched projections.

iii. Vertical angular ribbon handles with ribs.

Colours
Blue/green, pale green

Other features
These vessels were often used as cinerary urns and may have been produced for this purpose. The very thin walls would probably have been impractical for storage vessels.

Range of measurements
Rim diameters *c* 140–170mm, heights *c* 300–370mm.

Distribution
Not common. Generally found in burials in the south and east of England.

Date range
Uncertain. In use in 1st–2nd centuries AD.

Illustrated example (Figure 59)
Southfleet, Kent: Intact blue/green jar with M-shaped handles, containing cremated bones, found in stone cist (Rashleigh 1803, pl 38 no 4; Harden *et al* 1987, 96 no 38).

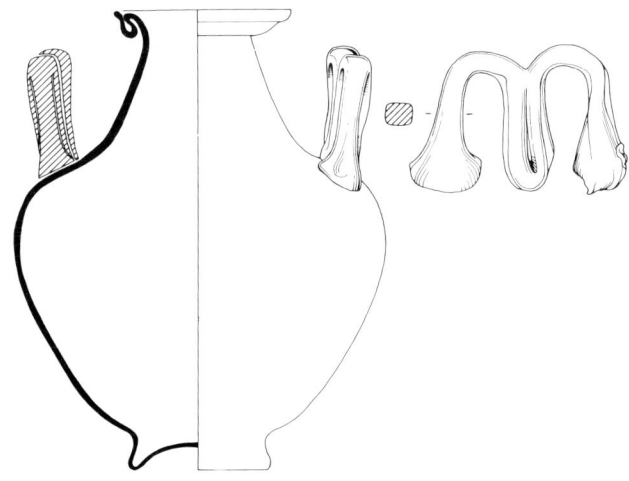

Fig 59   Scale 1:3

Other finds

Colchester, Essex: Pale green jar with M-shaped handles (Price 1888, 3 group 7 no 30)

Geldestone, Norfolk: Blue/green jar with vertical angular ribbon handles, containing cremated bones, in burial with Hadrianic coin (Yates 1849, 110–1 and fig).

London: Blue/green jar with M-shaped handles, from All Hallows Barking, Tower Street (Guildhall Museum 1908, 75 X no 1 pl 7). Blue/green jar with curved rod handles with pinched projections, containing cremated bones, found with lid in lead container in Warwick Square (RCHM London 1928, 154 pl 56).

Lower Walmer, Kent: Pale green jar with angular ribbed handles (Woodruff 1902, 8 no 2 and pl).

Old Newton, Suffolk: Blue/green jar with M-shaped handles and lid (Low 1907/9 256 pl A).

Rougham, Suffolk: Blue/green jar with angular ribbed handles, containing cremated bone (Henslow 1843, 264–5 and fig).

Stebbing, Essex: Fragmentary blue/green jar with curved rod handles with pinched projections, containing cremated bone, from Flavian burial (information from Chris Going).

Upchurch, Kent: Blue/green jar with M-shaped handles (Saffron Walden Museum, Essex).

Further reading

Isings 1957, forms 63–65.

Large convex jar with horizontal rim

Characteristics

Form

Horizontal rim, edge either rolled up and in or rolled-in and then bent out and down to form a double fold, wide globular or ovoid body, concave base.

Colours

Blue/green, very occasionally pale green or dark green.

Other features

Rim fragments are known from occupation sites; larger jars often used as cinerary urns. There is some overlap between these jars and a range of smaller jars with similar rims (see Figure 62).

Range of measurements

Rim diameters of jars used as cinerary urns *c* 140–200mm, heights *c* 200–250+mm.

Distribution

Fairly common. Frequently found in burials.

Date range

Uncertain. In use in 1st–late 2nd centuries AD.

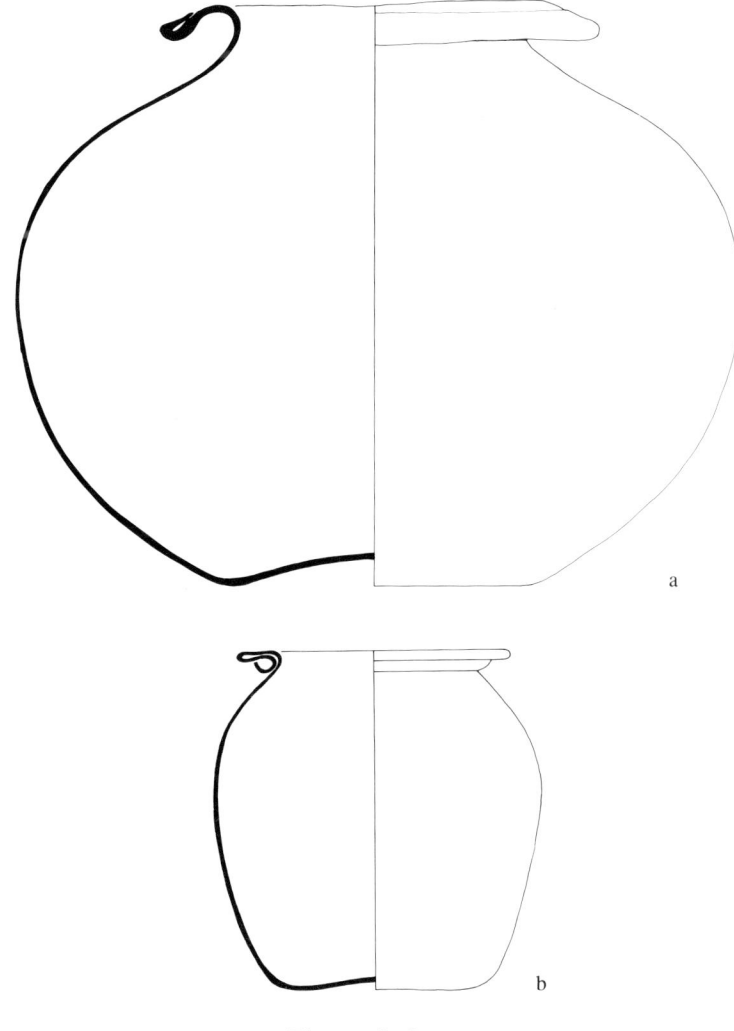

Fig 60   Scale 1:3

Illustrated examples (Figure 60)

a) *Boxmoor, Hertfordshire*: Dark green jar containing cremation, from cist grave (Girton 1838, 434 no 1 fig; Charlesworth 1974/6c, 102 (B) fig 59).

b) *York*: Blue/green ovoid jar with lid, containing cremation, from Clifton (Harden 1962, 136–7 YM 1948.3.1 fig 89).

Other finds

Colchester: Rims, large jars, from residual contexts (Cool and Price 1995, 110 nos 776, 778 fig 7.4). Ovoid jar, from burial, findspot unknown (Colchester Museum 1869, 22 no 304 pl 4 no 1). Globular jar, lacking rim, from cremation burial dated *c* AD 50–100

(May 1930, 264–5 Grave 42/23, pl 80). Jar containing cremation, from Abbey Field (Colchester and Essex Museum no 5211.26).

London: Blue/green jar containing cremation, from Bishopsgate. Blue/green jar with lid containing cremation, from Southwark (RCHM London 1928, 159 fig 65 no 32, 169 fig 69 no 63).

Mersea Island, Essex: Blue/green jar from cremation burial in lead box (Hazzledine Warren 1915, 130–1 pl E).

Southfleet, Kent: Blue/green jar containing cremated bone, found in stone cist (Rashleigh 1803, pl 38 no 3).

Towcester, Northamptonshire: Rim and upper body, blue/green ovoid jar, from pit dated *c* AD 155–65 in Park Street (Price 1980a, 66 no 12 fig 16).

West Mersea, Essex: Pale green jar from late 1st–early 2nd century cremation (Montagu-Benton 1926, 129 and pl).

Further reading

Isings 1957, form 67a. See discussion of jars with tubular and rolled rims in connection with finds from Colchester (Cool and Price 1995, 109–112).

Lid

Form

Wide conical body with stepped, fire-rounded edge, and central globular or flattened knob.

Colours

Blue/green.

Other features

Virtually always found in association with large jars used as cinerary urns (see Figures 59–60).

Range of measurements

Diameters *c* 130–40mm, heights *c* 60–70mm.

Distribution

Not common. Principally from burials.

Date range

Uncertain. In use in 1st–2nd centuries AD.

Illustrated example (Figure 61)

York, Clifton: Complete blue/green lid found with ovoid jar illustrated in Figure 60b (Harden 1962, 136–7 YM 1948.3.1 fig 89).

Other finds

Aldborough, North Yorkshire: Fragment from edge of blue/green lid.

Colchester, Essex: Pale green lid, found with jar with M-shaped handles (Price 1888, 3 group 7 no 31). Blue/green lid with knob, found with biconical long-necked jar from cremation burial dated *c* AD 117–38 (May 1930, 276 grave 83/79 pl 85).

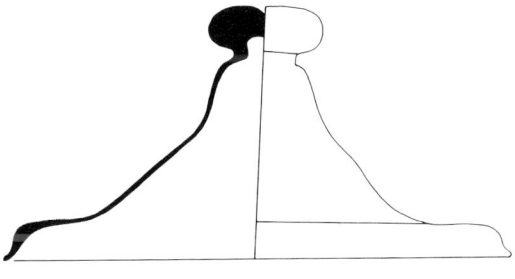

Fig 61   Scale 1:2

London: Blue/green lid, found in Warwick Square with jar with curved handles containing cremation. Almost complete blue/green lid with flattened knob, found in Southwark with jar containing cremation (RCHM London 1928, 154 pl 56, 169 fig 69 no 63).

Old Newton, Suffolk: Blue/green lid found with jar with M-shaped handles containing cremation (Low 1907/9, 256 pl A).

Further reading
Isings 1957, form 66.

Convex jar with out-turned rim

Characteristics
Form
Out-turned rim, edge either rolled-in or fire-rounded, funnel mouth, convex body, concave base, sometimes with open base ring.

Colours
Yellow/brown, pale green and yellow/green. Most frequently blue/green.

Decoration
Oval indents in body of some jars.

Other features
Complete profiles are rare. Pontil mark on base of jars with fire-rounded rims and some with rolled-in rims. These jars are usually identified from rim and body fragments. There is some overlap between these jars and a range of larger and smaller jars with similar rims (see Figures 60, 63). Rim fragments found with evidence for glass working at Mancetter, Warwickshire are likely to have been produced at the site (Price and Cool 1991, 26 fig 2 no 10).

Range of measurements
Rim diameters *c* 55–90mm, heights *c* 80–160mm.

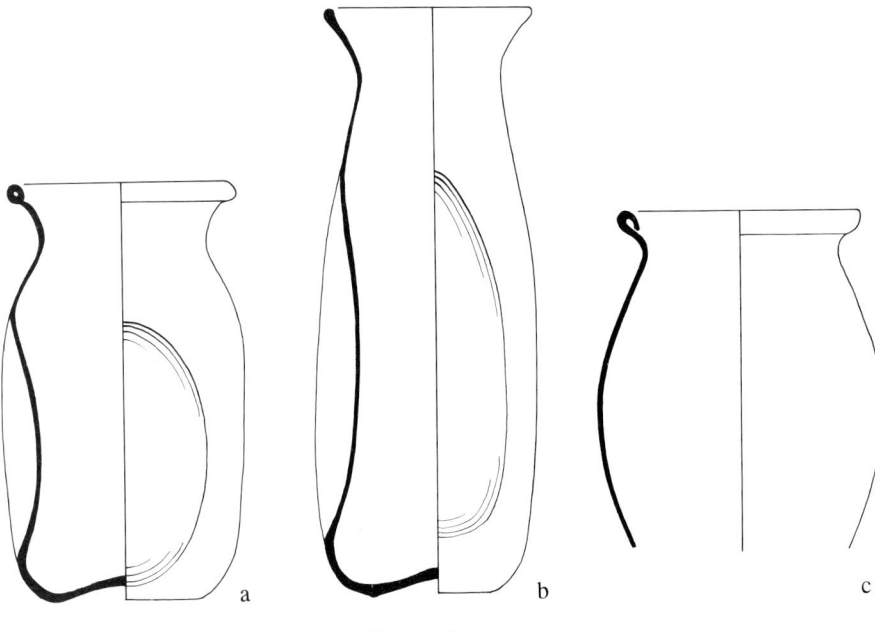

Fig 62   Scale 1:2

Distribution
Quite common. Occasionally found in burials.

Date range
Uncertain. In use in later 1st–2nd century AD.

Illustrated examples (Figure 62 and Plate 3.5)
a) *Harlow, Felmongers, Essex*: Blue/green jar with rolled-in rim, ovoid indented body and pontil mark on the base, from pit dated *c* A D 160–70 (Price 1987a, 205 no 24 fig 3).
b) *Harlow, Felmongers, Essex*: Tall blue/green jar with fire-rounded rim, ovoid indented body and pontil mark on base, from same pit group (Price 1987a, 205 no 25 fig 3).
c) *Harlow, Felmongers, Essex*: Tall yellow/brown jar with rolled-in rim and ovoid convex body (base missing), from same pit group (Price 1987a, 205 no 23 fig 3).

Other finds
Bourton-on-the Water, Gloucestershire: Fragments, blue/green jar with fire-rounded rim, convex body, open base ring and concave base (Renfrew nd, 28 no 7 fig 13).
Castleford, West Yorkshire: Rim and body, blue/green jar with fire-rounded rim and convex body, from mid 2nd century context in vicus (Cool and Price 1998, 170 no 244 fig 59).
Colchester, Essex: Fragmentary blue/green globular jar with pontil mark, from mid 2nd-mid 3rd century context; rims, yellow/brown, pale green and blue/green jars from 2nd century and later contexts (Cool and Price 1995, 110, 112–113 nos 772, 781–98, 807–827, 114–5 nos 844–848 figs 7.6- 7.7).
Lenham, Lower Runhams, Kent: Rim, body and base, pale green indented jar from Hadrianic burial (Monckton 1979, 120 g fig 2).

144

Manchester: Rim, body and base, blue/green jar, from deposit containing later 1st century pottery (Petch 1954, 193 no 22 fig 10).

Usk, Gwent: Fragments, fire-rounded rims, blue/green jars, from Neronian, early Flavian and later deposits (Price 1995a, 171 nos 79–80 fig 45).

Verulamium, Hertfordshire: Fire-rounded and rolled-in rims, two blue/green jars, from contexts dated AD155/60 and later, in insula 14; rolled-in rims, two blue/green jars, from unstratified context in insula 28 (Charlesworth 1972, 205(x) nos 2, 4 fig 76 nos 28, 30; 1984a, 167 nos 262–3 fig 67 nos 116–7).

Further reading
For discussion in connection with finds from Felmongers, Harlow and Colchester, see Price 1987a, 195–6, and Cool and Price 1995, 112–5.

Small jar with out-turned rim

Characteristics
Form
Out-turned rim, edge rolled-in or bent up, in and flattened, straight side expanding out, or convex side, flat or concave base.

Colours
Blue/green, pale green.

Other features
Pontil scar sometimes present on the base. A wide range of jars is included in this group, including some very small examples which have a distinctive wide rim and hat-shaped profile. There is some overlap between these jars and a range of larger jars with similar rims (see Figure 62).

Range of measurements
Rim diameters c 35–50mm. Smallest jars are 25–30mm high. Larger jars are c 60mm high.

Distribution
Not common. Sometimes found in burials.

Date range
Not closely dated; found in 1st–3rd century contexts.

Illustrated examples (Figure 63)
a) *Colchester, Essex*: Blue/green miniature jar with hat-shaped profile, from context dated A D 225–275/325 at Culver Street (Cool and Price 1995, 116 no 861 fig 7.10).
b) *Housesteads, Northumberland*: Green convex jar, from latrine drain deposit containing 2nd century material (Charlesworth 1971a, 35 no 10 and fig; 1975, 24).

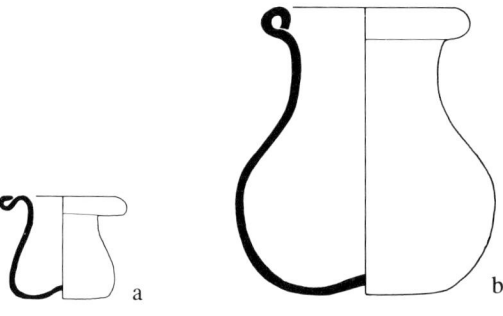

Fig 63   Scale 1:2

Other finds

Billericay, Essex: Four blue/green and greenish miniature hat-shaped jars with wide flattened rims, from burial.

Brighton, Sussex: Complete small hat-shaped jar with wide rim, from burial containing later 2nd century pottery at Springfield Road (Dudley 1981, 86 fig 9 no 5).

Canterbury, Kent: Body and base, small blue/green hat-shaped jar, from context dated AD 170–220, St George's Street (Charlesworth and Price 1987, 225 no 26 fig 89).

Carlisle, Cumbria: Rim and upper body, small blue/green jar, from Annetwell Street.

Colchester, Essex: Fragment, small blue/green jar, from late 3rd–4th century context at Balkerne Lane (Cool and Price 1995, 115 no 859 fig 7.8).

Corbridge, Northumberland: Complete small blue/green jar with horizontal rolled-in rim (Allen 1988, 289 no 11 fig 131).

London: Very small globular jar, from cremation dated AD 120–80 at West Tenter Street in the east cemetery (Jones 1986, 91 fig 38 no 4).

Verulamium, Hertfordshire: Rim and upper body, small hat-shaped green jar, from context dated AD 70–110 in insula 28 (Charlesworth 1984a, 167 no 254 fig 67 no 108).

York: Small hat-shaped jar with wide flattened rim, from stone coffin in the Railway cemetery (Harden 1962, 140 H.G.2 fig 89).

Further reading

Isings 1957, form 68. For discussion of small jars in connection with finds from Colchester, see Cool and Price 1995, 115–6.

Jugs

Convex jug with two handles (amphorisk)

Characteristics

Form

Out-turned folded rim, edge bent out, down and up to form collar, or rolled-in, wide cylindrical neck, expanding to tall ovoid body, open base ring, concave base. Two curved ribbon handles with three ribs, applied to upper body and attached at neck and rim edge.

Colours

Strong colours, particularly dark blue. Blue/green.

Other features

Handles often have three-pronged claw attachments, and the central projection is sometimes extended and decorated with tooled projections. The glass is often very thin in the body and base.

Range of measurements

Rim diameters *c* 60mm, heights *c* 220–300mm.

Distribution

Not very common. Found on early sites in southern Britain.

Date range

AD 43–*c* AD 65/70.

Illustrated example (Figure 64)

Colchester, Sheepen, Essex: Fragmentary dark blue amphorisk, from early Neronian pit (Charlesworth 1985a, MF3:F8 no 54 fig 81).

Other finds

Brandon Camp, Herefordshire: Three or four amphorisks, dark blue, yellow/green and blue/green, from military site occupied *c* AD 55–60 (Price 1987c, 74–6 nos 4–7 fig 15 nos 2–3).

Chichester, West Sussex: Rim, neck and handle, blue/green miniature amphorisk with curved rod handles (Price and Cool 1989, 138 no CM26 fig 19.2).

Colchester, Sheepen, Essex: At least six further amphorisks, four dark blue, one yellow/brown and one blue/green, from early Neronian pit and other Neronian contexts (Charlesworth 1985a, MF 3:F8–9 nos 55–64, 85 figs 82–3).

Colchester, Essex: Handle fragments, at least three dark blue, yellow/brown and blue/green amphorisks, from Claudian-early Neronian and later contexts (Cool and Price 1995, 148–9 no 1167 fig 9.1).

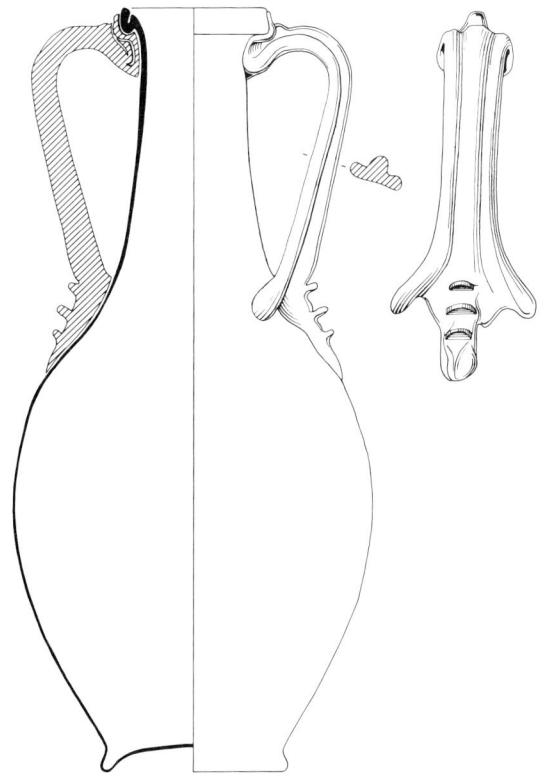

Fig 64   Scale 1:3

Exeter, Devon: Dark blue amphorisk with plain ribbon handles, early Flavian context (Charlesworth 1979a, 228 no 30 fig 71).

Fishbourne Palace, West Sussex: Neck with handle scars, body and base fragments, blue/green amphorisk (Price and Cottam 1996a, 180 no 84 fig 6.29).

Gloucester: Fragments, at least two blue/green and yellow/green amphorisks, from Neronian military site at Kingsholm (Price and Cool 1985, 48 & 50 nos 36, 54–5 figs 18–9).

London: Rim, neck and handle, dark blue, pre-Flavian context at 201–211 Borough High Street, Southwark (Townend and Hinton 1978b, 151 no 11 fig 60).

Usk, Gwent: Rim with handle scar, neck, body, blue/green amphorisk with rolled-in rim, handles missing, pre-Flavian context in legionary fortress (Price 1995a, 182 no 115 fig 47).

Further reading
Isings 1957, form 15. For discussion in connection with finds from Colchester and Fishbourne, see Cool and Price 1995, 148–9, and Price and Cottam 1996, 167.

Convex thin-walled jug

Characteristics

Form
Small diagonal folded rim, edge bent out, up and in, narrow cylindrical neck, wide globular or discoid body, concave base, sometimes with open base ring. Angular ribbon handle with edge ribs, or narrow central ribs, applied to upper body and attached to neck below rim.

Colours
Occasionally polychrome. Strong colours, including dark blue. Blue/green.

Other features
Carefully formed in very thin glass, especially in body and base (see also amphorisks, Figure 64). The form is not easy to recognise unless large fragments survive.

Range of measurements
Rim diameters *c* 30mm, heights *c* 160mm.

Distribution
Not common.

Date range
Uncertain. AD 43–3rd quarter of 1st century.

Illustrated example (Figure 65)
Usk, Gwent: Blue/green jug, rim missing and broken edge of neck reworked, from pre-Flavian pit in legionary fortress (Price 1995a, 182 no 114 fig 47).

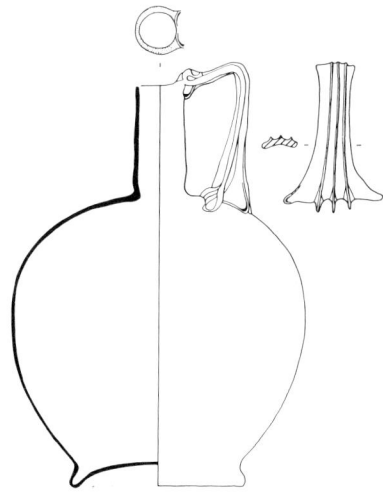

Fig 65   Scale 1:3

149

Other finds

Cadbury Castle, Somerset: Blue convex body fragment, opaque white handle, from Claudian-early Neronian military occupation.

Colchester, Essex: Blue globular jug with open base ring (Thorpe 1935, 25 pl 3a).

Elginhaugh, Lothian: Blue/green handle fragment, from mid-Flavian military site.

London: Blue/green jug with discoid body, from pit containing mid Flavian pottery at St Swithins House, Middle Walbrook Valley (Price 1991a, 159 no 616 fig 114).

Ower, Dorset: Dark blue convex body and handle fragments, from late 1st century and post-Roman contexts (Price 1987e, 103–4 no 251 fig 55).

Wimborne, Lake Farm, Dorset: Blue convex body fragment, opaque white handle; blue/green convex body and handle fragment, from Claudian-early Neronian military occupation.

Further reading

Isings 1957, forms 14, 52a. See discussion in connection with the finds from St Swithins House, Walbrook (Price 1991a, 164–5) and Usk (Price 1995a, 178–9).

Convex jug with long neck

Characteristics

Form

Horizontal or diagonal folded rim, edge bent out, up, in and flattened, long, narrow cylindrical neck with slight tooled constriction at base, globular or discoid body, open base ring, concave base. Angular ribbon handle with either one prominent central rib or several narrow ribs, applied to upper body and attached to neck and rim edge.

Colours

Strong colours, particularly dark blue and yellow/brown. Blue/green, pale green. Occasionally polychrome.

Decoration

Marvered opaque white splashes occur on a few jugs. Vertical or diagonal ribs on body, sometimes beginning on neck. Some jugs have ribs which change direction, from diagonal on the lower neck and upper body to vertical on the middle of the body.

When the handle has one central rib, the lower terminal is formed as a three-pronged claw attachment, and the central projection is sometimes extended and decorated with tooled projections or ridges.

A few jugs have mask medallions (Bacchus masks) applied to the body below the lower handle attachment (see Figure 4.4).

Other features

The single most diagnostic part of these jugs is the handle with several narrow ribs, as the rim, neck and handle with central rib are generally identical to long necked conical jugs (see Figures 67–8), and small parts of the body and base are indistinguishable from globular jars with collar rims (see Figure 58).

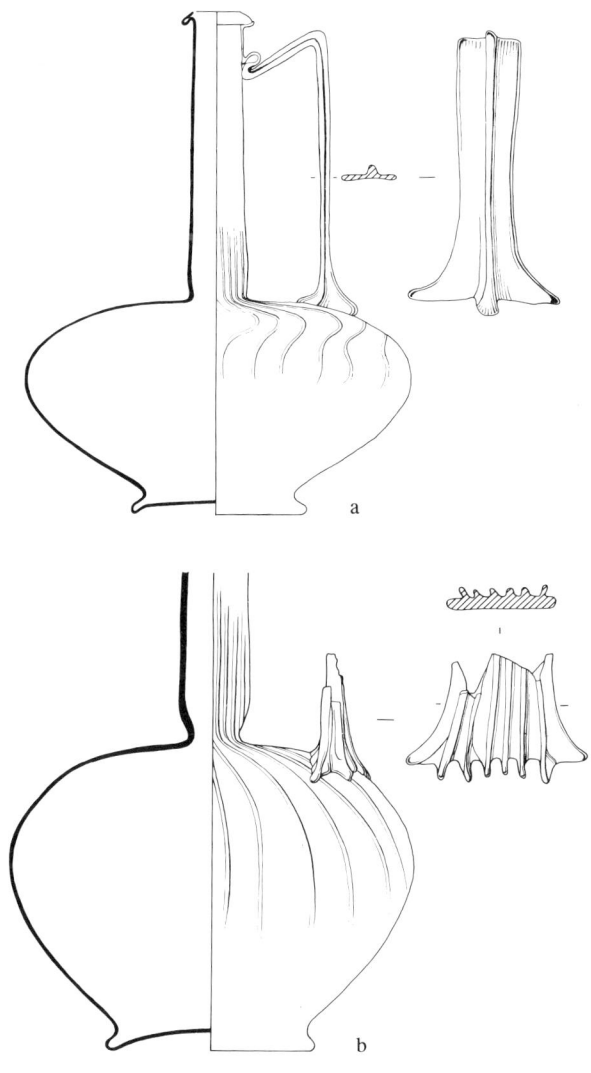

Fig 66   Scale 1:3

Range of measurements
Rim diameters *c* 30–40mm, heights *c* 200mm, body diameters *c* 150–60mm.

Distribution
Common. Sometimes found in burials.

Date range
Third quarter of 1st-early 2nd century.

Illustrated examples (Figure 66 and Plate 2.1)

a) *London*: Fragmentary yellow/brown discoid jug with diagonal ribs on the neck and upper body, which change to vertical on the middle of the body, from pit dated to the early 2nd century AD at Lincoln Road, Enfield (Price 1977, 155 no 2 fig 27 pl 7).

b) *Baldock, Hertfordshire*: Pale yellow/green globular jug with vertical ribs, rim and part of neck and handle missing, from cremation burial no 5, dated *c* AD 65–85 (Price 1986b, 61 no 3 fig 27).

Other finds

'Near Canterbury' or Faversham, Kent: Complete discoid jug with vertical ribs (Goldney 1899/1901, 280 and fig; Ward 1911, 182G fig 52).

Carlisle, Cumbria: Neck and body fragments, dark blue globular jug with vertical ribs and opaque white splashes, from Flavian fort annexe (Cool 1992, 67 no 5 fig 10).

Colchester, Essex: Handle and body fragments, yellow/brown, light green and blue/green globular and discoid jugs, from pre-Boudican, later 1st century and later contexts (Cool and Price 1995, 124 nos 888–90, 904, 907, 915–22 figs 8.3–8.5).

Colchester, Sheepen, Essex: Blue/green rim, neck, body, handle, with mask medallion, Neronian cremation burial (Charlesworth 1985a, MF1:A7 a fig 16).

Dorchester, Dorset: Body fragments, dark blue discoid jug with vertical ribs, from Greyhound Yard (Cool and Price 1993, 158 no 18 fig 84).

Gloucester: Body and handle scar, dark blue globular jug with diagonal ribs, from Berkeley St.

Litlington, Cambridgeshire: Blue/green discoid jug with vertical ribs and mask medallion at base of handle, from burial (Thorpe 1935, 26 pl 3c; Fitzwilliam 1978, 36–7 no 65a and fig).

Old Newton, Suffolk: Yellow/brown globular jug with vertical ribs, from burial (Low 1907/9, 256 pl C).

Further reading

Isings 1957, form 52. See discussion of globular and discoid jugs in connection with the find from Enfield (Price 1977, 155–8), and of mask medallions and globular and conical jugs in connection with finds from Colchester (Cool and Price 1995, 118–30).

Conical jug with long neck and concave base

Characteristics

Form

Horizontal or diagonal folded rim, edge bent out, up, in and flattened, long cylindrical neck, straight side expanding out, concave base. Angular ribbon handle with central rib, applied to body and attached to neck below rim. On some jugs the neck is comparatively short and wide in relation to the body, while others have a long narrow neck which forms about half the height of the vessel.

Colours

Strong colours, particularly dark blue, yellow/brown and yellow/green. Frequently blue/green. Occasionally polychrome.

Decoration
Vertical or spiral ribs are very common. Some jugs have ribs which change direction from spiral to vertical (see discussion in connection with convex jugs, and Figure 66a). Very occasionally ribs nipped together at intervals to produce loose lattice pattern are found, and a few jugs have opaque white marvered splashes. Applied mask medallions (Bacchus masks) are found on some conical jugs (see Figure 4.4). The lower handle terminal is usually formed as a three-pronged claw attachment, and the central projection is often extended and decorated with tooled or pinched projections.

Other features
The variations in neck and body proportions appear to have some chronological significance. Jugs with shorter wider necks and taller narrower bodies generally belong to the 1st century, whereas jugs with longer, narrower necks and shorter, wider bodies often occur in 2nd century contexts. The rim, neck and handle fragments are often comparable with those of the long necked globular jugs. A tooled constriction occurs at the base of the longer, narrower necks.

Range of measurements
Rim diameters *c* 30–40mm, heights *c* 250–300+mm.

Distribution
Very common. Found in some burials.

Date range
Last third of 1st century–third quarter of 2nd century. Dark blue jugs are not often noted after the third quarter of the 1st century. Yellow/green, yellow/brown and blue/green examples continue in use to the third quarter of the 2nd century.

Illustrated example (Figure 67 and Front cover)
Radnage, Buckinghamshire: Yellow/brown jug with narrow vertical ribs, from Flavian cremation burial (Skilbeck 1923, 334–5 pl 35 fig 2c; Harden *et al* 1987, 140 no 68).

Other finds
Barnwell, Cambridgeshire: Blue/green jug, spiral ribs, from burial (Harden *et al* 1968, 59 no 73).
Carlisle, Cumbria: Handle and body, dark blue with opaque white marvered splashes, base form uncertain, from Flavian military context at Annetwell Street.
Colchester, Essex: Small fragments, yellow/brown, yellow/green and light green jugs, from Neronian-Flavian and later contexts (Cool and Price 1995, 123–4 nos 874, 879–80, 898, 900, 911–3 fig 8.3–4).
Faversham, King's Field, Kent: Yellow/brown jug with spiral ribs which change direction to become vertical (Thorpe 1935, 27 pl 4 f).
Gorhambury, St Albans, Hertfordshire: Body, base and handle, blue green jug with vertical ribs (Neal *et al* 1990, 203 no 68 fig 164).
Harlow, Felmongers, Essex: Body and base, yellow/green jug with vertical ribs, from pit containing samian dated *c* AD160–70 (Price 1987a, 204 no 20 fig 3).
Lincoln, Holmes Grainwarehouse: Handle and body, blue/green with opaque white marvered splashes, base form uncertain (Cool and Price 1988, 42–3 no 10 fig 11).

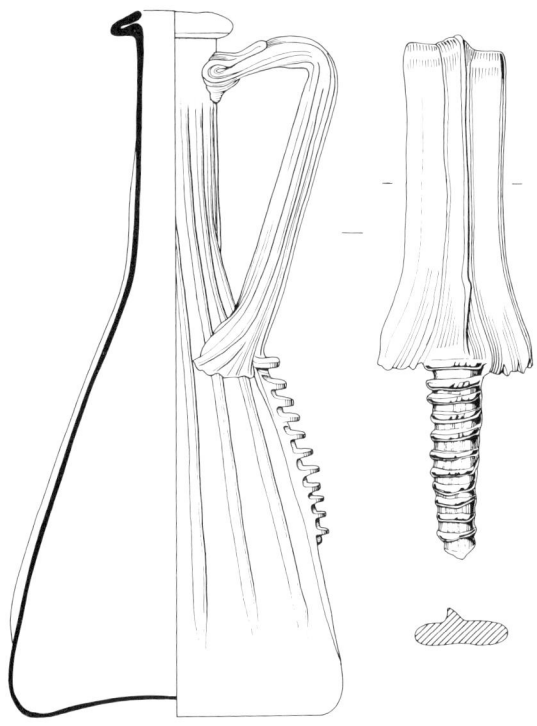

Fig 67   Scale 1:3

Malton, North Yorkshire: Neck, body, base, dark blue jug with vertical ribs (Price and Cottam 1997b, 122 no 2 fig 46).

Milton-next-Sittingbourne, Kent: Pale green jug with vertical ribs and mask medallion on body, found outside inhumation in lead coffin (Payne 1874, 170–1 + pl).

Richborough, Kent: Fragments, two blue/green jugs with ribs and one greenish undecorated jug, from late 1st century or later contexts (Bushe-Fox 1949, 158 nos 367–8, 370 pls 67–8).

Turriff, Grampian: Pale yellow/green jug with diagonal ribs (Thorpe 1933–4).

Usk, Gwent: Very fragmentary yellow/green jug with spiral ribs which change direction to become vertical, and body and base, blue/green with spiral ribs, both from late Neronian/early Flavian contexts in legionary fortress (Price 1995a, 179 nos 100–101 fig 46).

Winchester, Hampshire: Dark blue jug with vertical ribs pinched into lattice pattern, Flavian cremation burial in Grange Road (Harden 1967).

Wroxeter, Shropshire: Dark blue jug with short neck and undecorated body, from pit dated *c* AD60–90 (Atkinson 1942, 233 no 1 pl 63A).

Further reading

Isings 1957, form 55a. See discussion in connection with finds from Grange Road, Winchester (Harden 1967), Colchester, where mask-medallions and forms of convex and conical jugs are considered (Cool and Price 1995, 118–30) and Usk, where mask medallions and conical jug forms are considered (Price 1995a, 177–82).

Conical jug with long neck, open base ring and concave base

Characteristics

Form
Horizontal or diagonal folded rim, edge bent out, up, in and flattened, long, narrow cylindrical neck with tooled constriction at junction with straight or slightly convex body expanding out, change of angle to straight or slightly convex lower body tapering in, open base ring, concave base. Angular ribbon handle with central rib, applied to upper body and attached to neck below rim.

Colours
Strong colours, particularly yellow/brown and yellow/green, and occasionally purple. Frequently blue/green.

Decoration
Vertical or spiral ribs often occur. The lower handle terminal is usually formed as a three-pronged claw attachment, and the central projection is frequently extended and decorated with tooled or pinched projections.

Other features
These jugs are very closely related to jugs with long necks and concave bases (see Figure 67); only the lower body and base is distinctive. The rims, necks and handles are also comparable with some of the long-necked convex jugs (see Figure 66a). Jugs with two handles are found very occasionally. On some jugs the change of angle is rounded, on others it is very sharp, and one or two have a cut-out fold (see Figure 5.4).

Range of measurements
Rim diameters *c* 30–40mm, heights *c* 250–300+mm.

Distribution
Very common. Found in some burials.

Date range
Last quarter of 1st century–3rd quarter of 2nd century AD.

Illustrated example (Figure 68)
Castleford, West Yorkshire: Fragmentary purple jug without decoration, from context dated *c* AD 140–80 in vicus (Cool and Price 1998, 157 no 51 fig 53).

Other finds
Alcester, Warwickshire: Fragmentary yellow/green jug, from pit dated *c* AD150–160, and almost complete yellow/green jug with short neck and curved handle, from pit with mid 2nd-mid 3rd century pottery (Price and Cottam 1994, 224 nos 9–10 fig 104).
Ashdon, Bartlow Hills, Essex: Jug without decoration, from Barrow I (Gage 1834, 5 pl 2 fig 1).
Colchester, Essex: Intact green jug with vertical ribs from Jarmin collection grave 8, dated *c* AD 69–96 (May 1930 288 Grave 8(f) pl 90 no 8).

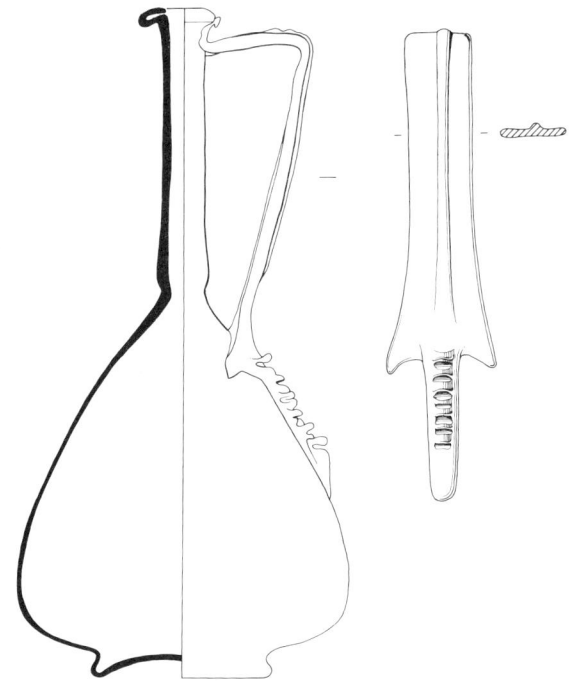

Fig 68   Scale 1:3

Bayford-next-Sittingbourne, Kent: Intact yellow/green jug with vertical ribs and two handles, one of the normal type, the other a short curved rod handle, from cremation burial, grave no 2 (Payne 1886, 2 no 5 and fig; Harden *et al* 1968, 82–3 no 108).

Caerleon, Gwent: Fragments, blue/green jug with vertical ribs, from Flavian-Trajanic context in barrack 12, Prysg Field (Price 1995d, 87 no 5 fig 10 no 6).

Chesterford, Essex: fragmentary green jug without decoration (Neville 1855, 113 and fig).

Huntingdon, Cambridgeshire: Fragmentary pale green jug with cut-out fold, from inhumation burial with coin of Hadrian (Harden 1968b, 308 (a) pl 80a; Fitzwilliam 1978, 37–8 fig).

Lenham, Lower Runhams, Kent: Fragmentary pale green jug without decoration, probably from a Hadrianic burial (Monckton 1979, 120g fig 3).

Litlington, Cambridgeshire: Body, base and handle trail, yellow/brown jug with spiral trails (Kempe 1836, 375 pl 45 no 8).

Murston, East Hall, Kent: Blue/green jug with vertical ribs, from inhumation burial (Payne 1893, 40 pl 4).

Northill, near Shefford, Bedfordshire: Fragmentary purple jug without decoration, from inhumation burial (Roach Smith 1846, 448 fig).

Piercebridge, Co Durham: Body, base and handle, blue/green jug without decoration.

Stonea, Cambridgeshire: Body, base and handle, yellow/brown jug without decoration, from mid–late 2nd or 3rd century context (Price 1996b, 398 no 5 fig 125).

Towcester, Northamptonshire: Fragments, two jugs without decoration, yellow/green (lacking base) and yellow/brown, from pit dated *c* AD155–65 in Park Street (Price 1980a, 66 nos 7, 9 fig 15).

Further reading
Isings 1957, form 55b. See discussion in connection with finds from Enfield (Price 1977, 155–8) and Alcester (Price and Cottam 1994, 225–8).

Globular jug with pinched-in spout

Characteristics
Form
Rim edge either rolled-in or fire-rounded, pinched in two places to form a spout, funnel mouth, short cylindrical neck, wide convex body, concave base, occasionally with base ring. Curved ribbon or rod handle, applied to upper body and attached to rim edge, sometimes with a folded loop or thumb-rest.

Colours
Blue/green or pale green. Strongly coloured and colourless examples are also found.

Decoration
Sometimes with vertical ribs or self coloured trails.

Other features
Some spouts are pinched-in gently, forming a trefoil or clover-leaf mouth. Some are pinched-in more tightly, producing a long, narrow spout with the two sides almost meeting and forming a figure-of-eight mouth. These jugs are usually identified from the rim fragments, but small asymmetrical fragments may not distinguish between pinched-in spouts and pulled-out spouts (see Figure 70).

Range of measurements
Heights *c* 120–200mm.

Distribution
Quite common. Occasionally found in burials.

Date range
Uncertain. The pinched-in spout occurs in the later 1st and the 2nd–early 3rd centuries AD. Jugs with pinched-in spouts appear to be in use earlier than jugs with pulled-out spouts.

Illustrated example (Figure 69)
Braughing, Skeleton Green, Hertfordshire: Greenish jug, from cremation burial 35 with coin of Antoninus Pius (Charlesworth 1981a, 271 B 35b fig 106 no 11).

Other finds
Brading villa, Isle of Wight: Rim fragment, colourless jug (Tomalin 1987, 43 no B6 and fig).
Canterbury, Kent: Rim and neck fragments, blue/green jugs, from contexts dated *c* AD

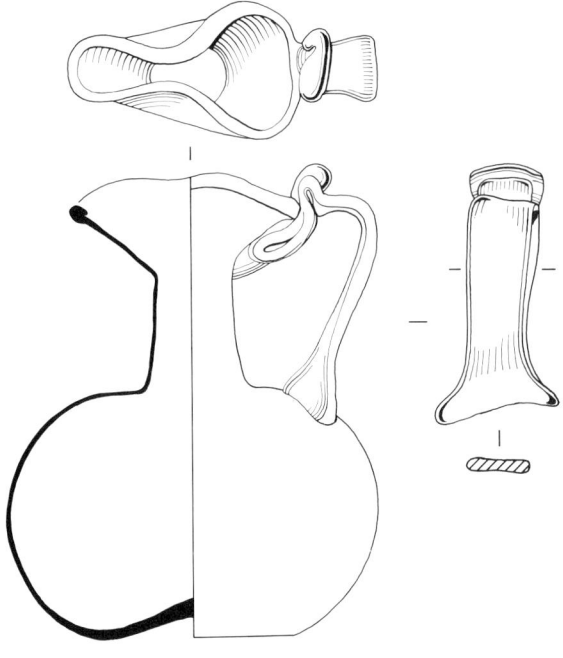

Fig 69   Scale 1:2

175–300/20 and 300/20–350, Marlowe Car Park (Shepherd 1995a, 1245 nos 428–9 fig 548).

Claydon Pike, Gloucestershire: Fragments, blue/green jug with short vertical ribs, rim decorated with pinched trail, from context dated *c* AD 100–50.

Colchester, Essex: Fragments, blue/green jugs, one with vertical ribs, from mid 2nd–late 4th/early 5th and post-Roman contexts (Cool and Price 1995, 141 nos 1037–39 fig 8.9). Blue/green jug with short vertical ribs, rim and handle decorated with pinched trail, from cremation burial (Colchester Museum 1869, 22 no 302 pl 4 no 3; Thorpe 1935, 23 pl 8c).

Lockham, Joy Wood (?), Kent: Three small jugs, perhaps from cremated deposit no 4 (Robertson 1883, 86 fig W).

London: Fragments, three or four blue/green jugs, one with short vertical ribs, from period 2 (*c* AD 65–70+) and late 1st century contexts at Leadenhall Court (Shepherd 1996, 110 nos 145–50 fig 65). Rim, neck and handle fragments, two jugs (Guildhall Museum 1908, 77 nos 76–92 pl 8 nos 5, 10).

Shefford, Bedfordshire: Dark blue jug with vertical ribs, from burial, apparently found with coin of Vespasian (Dryden 1840/46, 13 pl 1 no 1; Fox 1923, 213, 216 pl 26 no 2; Fitzwilliam 1978, 37 no 66a and fig).

Usk, Gwent: Rim, blue/green jug, from late Neronian/early Flavian context in fortress ditch (Price 1995a, 184 no 120 fig 48).

Verulamium, Hertfordshire: Fragmentary blue/green jug with spiral trails, from pit 19 in insula 14, context dated *c* AD 175–275; rim fragment, blue/green, from insula 27 in context dated AD145–150 (Charlesworth 1972, 204 (viii) jugs no 3 fig 76 no 24; 1984a, 165 no 234 fig 67 no 98).

Further reading
Isings 1957 forms 56 & 88a-b. See discussion of spouted jugs in connection with finds from Colchester (Cool and Price 1995, 131–4).

Globular or discoid jug with pulled-out spout

Characteristics
Form
Rim edge rolled-in or fire-rounded, and pulled out and up at one side to form narrow spout, funnel mouth, short cylindrical neck, wide globular or discoid body, concave base, sometimes with tubular base ring. Curved or angular ribbon handle, applied to upper body and attached to the rim edge, sometimes with a tooled loop or thumb-rest.

Colours
Colourless, pale green, blue/green.

Decoration
Sometimes with horizontal or spiral self-coloured trails.

Other features
The mouth is oval in shape with a pointed spout positioned either at 90 degrees to the handle, or opposite the handle. A small tooling mark at the end of the spout shows where pincers have been used to pull the spout out and up. These jugs are usually identified from the rims, but it may not be possible to distinguish between pulled-out spouts and pinched-in spouts (see Figure 69) from small fragments.

Range of measurements
Heights *c* 100–150mm.

Distribution
Quite common. Found in some burials.

Date range
Uncertain. In use in 2nd and 3rd centuries AD.

Illustrated examples (Figure 70)
a) *Caerleon, Gwent*: Fragments, rim, neck, handle, body and base (spout restored), colourless jug, two horizontal trails, from drain deposit in Fortress baths dated *c* AD 160–230 (Allen 1986, 109 no 57 fig 42).
b) *Ham Hill, Bedmore Barn, Somerset*: Rim, neck and handle (one side of rim restored), colourless jug.

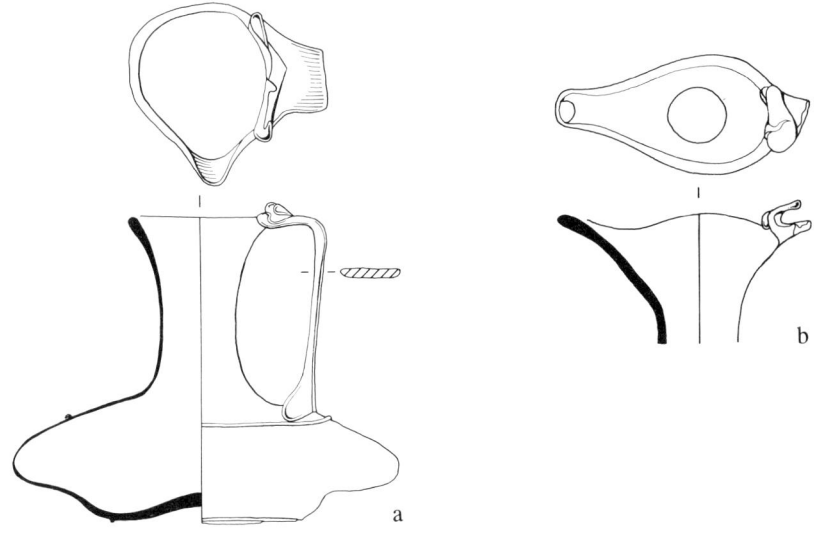

Fig 70   Scale 1:2

Other finds

Aldborough, North Yorkshire: Fragment, rim and neck, colourless jug (Ecroyd Smith 1852, 48 no 5 pl 24).

Bath, Combe Down, Avon: Rim, neck, body and handle fragments, two jugs, one with base ring and spout opposite handle, the other with spout at 90 degrees to handle (Scarth 1864, 96 pl 44).

Colchester, Essex: Fragments, pale green and blue/green jugs, from 2nd–3rd century and later contexts (Cool and Price 1995, 140–41 nos 1005/6, 1040–41 figs 8.8–9). Blue/green discoid jug, spout at 90 degrees to angular handle, tubular base ring, from grave 91/40 (Joslin collection) dated *c* AD 150–200 (May 1930, 278 Grave 91/40 pl 86 no 91; Thorpe 1935, 21 pl 8a).

Eccles villa, Kent: Rim and neck, colourless jug.

Godmanchester, Cambridgeshire: Rim, neck and handle fragments, colourless jug, found with mid–late 2nd century pottery (Frend 1968, 33 no 3 fig 6).

Gorhambury, St Albans, Hertfordshire: Rim, neck and handle, colourless jug with trail on neck (Neal *et al* 1990, 203 no 40 fig 163).

Lincoln: Rim, neck and handle, colourless jug with handle at 90 degrees to spout, from Cottesford Place.

London: Rim, neck and handle fragment (Guildhall Museum 1908, 77 no 76–92 pl 8 no 11).

Ospringe, Kent: Globular jug, found near to inhumation burial 141 (Whiting 1926, 129 no 154 pl 17; 1931, 58 and pl 17 no 154).

Stonea, Cambridgeshire: Fragments, four blue/green jugs, from mid–late 3rd century and later contexts (Price 1996b, 402 nos 49–51 fig 131).

Verulamium, Hertfordshire: Fragments, rim, neck body, base and handle, colourless globular jug with horizontal trail, from building debris over street 14/28, in context dated AD 370–430 (Charlesworth 1984a, 166 no 245, fig.67 no 104).

Wroxeter, Shropshire: Rim, neck and handle, greenish jug (Bushe-Fox 1913, 32 pl 12 fig 1 no 3).

Further reading
Isings 1957, form 88, especially 88*c* See discussion of spouted jugs in connection with finds from Colchester (Cool and Price 1995, 131–4).

Tall convex jug with funnel mouth

Characteristics
Form
Rim edge rolled-in or fire-rounded, short funnel mouth, cylindrical neck expanding out, ovoid or globular body, concave base, applied or tubular base ring. Handle applied to upper body and attached below rim, often with folded loop or thumb-rest.

Colours
Colourless, pale green, blue/green.

Decoration
Horizontal trail or narrow spiral trail below rim and/or on neck, occasionally two horizontal trails pinched together at intervals to form loops. Vertical ribs or trails on body, sometimes pinched into lattice.

Other features
These jugs have a range of rim, body and handle forms. Ribbon handles, sometimes with ribs, and chain handles are found. The most distinctive of the handles is the chain handle, although these also occur on smaller jugs with pouring spouts. The jugs are not easy to identify from small fragments, and the forms probably overlap with the biconical jugs with funnel mouths (see Figure 72).

Range of measurements
Rim diameters *c* 55–70mm, heights *c* 150–250+mm.

Distribution
Quite common. Some found in burials.

Date range
Uncertain. In use in late 2nd–3rd century AD.

Illustrated examples (Figure 71)
a) *Braughing, Skeleton Green, Hertfordshire:* Blue/green jug, ribbon handle with three ribs and applied base ring, from cremation burial 21, dated to late 2nd century (Charlesworth 1981a, 268 B21 fig 106 no 9).
b) *Wimborne, Bucknowle Farm, Dorset:* Fragmentary blue/green jug with trails on neck, vertical ribs, chain handle and applied base ring, from 3rd century deposit.

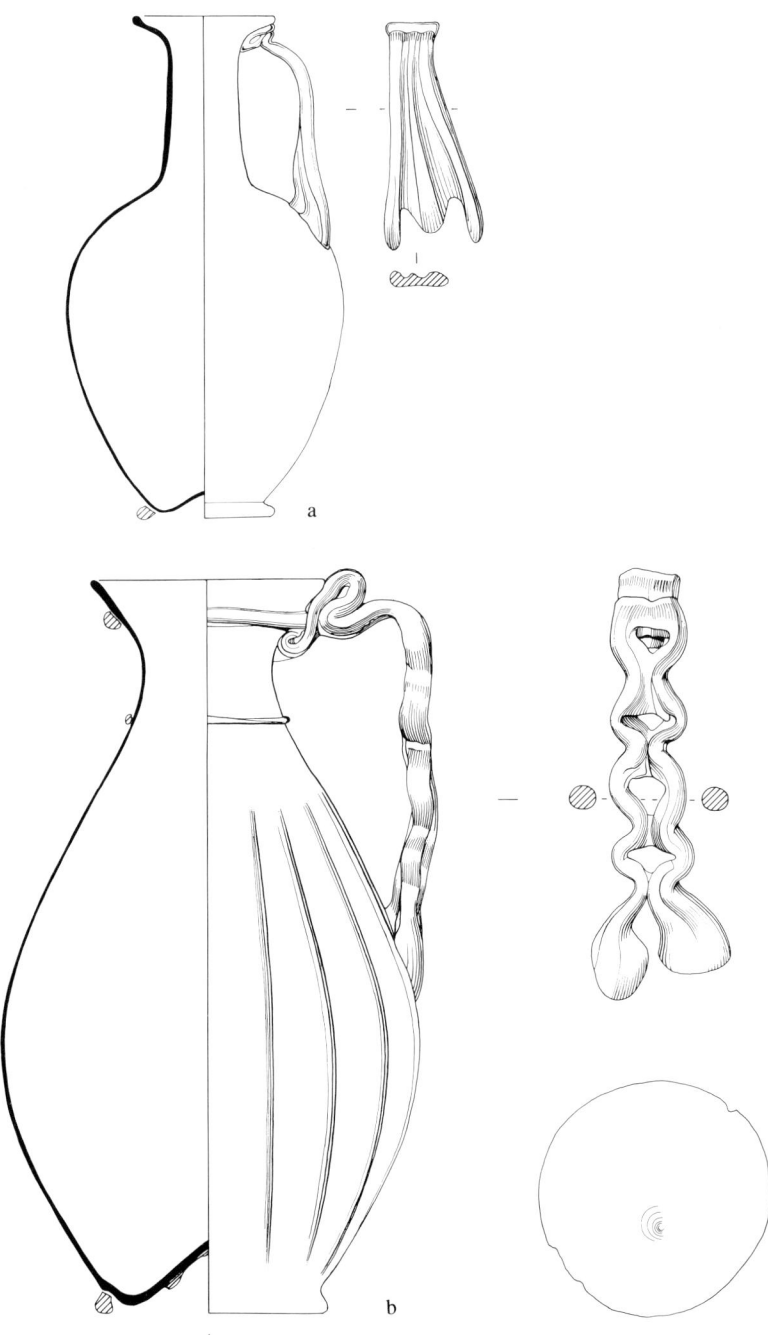

Fig 71   Scale 1:3

Other finds

Caerleon, Gwent: Fragments, rim, neck, body, handle, small colourless jug with spiral trails on neck and body and plain ribbon handle, from drain deposit in Fortress baths dated *c* AD 160–230 (Allen 1986, 109, 111 no 58 fig 42).

Colchester, Essex: Blue/green jug, horizontal trail on neck, vertical trails pinched into lattice on body, chain handle, tubular base ring (Thorpe 1935, 30 pl 6d; Harden *et al* 1968, 84 no 111). Fragmentary colourless jug, spiral trail on neck, vertical ribs, chain handle, applied base ring (Colchester Museum Accession no 467.P). Rim, neck and handle fragments, at least two colourless and blue/green jugs, from 3rd century and post-Roman contexts (Cool and Price 1995, 140–1 figs 8.8–9).

Lincoln: Rim, neck and handle fragments, several colourless jugs.

Ospringe, Kent: Jug, spiral trail on rim and neck, curved ribbon handle with two ribs and folded thumb-rest, from burial group 157 (Whiting *et al* 1931, 69 no 503 pl 42).

Verulamium, Hertfordshire: Fragmentary blue/green jug, spiral and looped trails on neck, single trail on lower body, tubular base ring, ribbon handle with three ribs, from well in building IV, containing 2nd century AD material (Wheeler and Wheeler 1936, 186 no 25 fig 29). Colourless globular jug, spiral trail on neck, chain handle, tubular base, from inhumation burial in stone coffin at Kingsbury (Davies and Saunders 1986, 22, 29, 34).

Winterton villa, north Lincolnshire: Rim, neck and body fragments, two colourless jugs with trails on neck, one from Antonine context (Charlesworth 1976a, 249 nos 25–6, fig 134).

York: Blue/green jug, ribbon handle with two ribs, trailed base ring, from stone coffin in Ebor Street (Harden 1962, 140 HG 44 pl 67).

Further reading

For discussion of a wide range of convex jugs in connection with finds from Colchester, see Cool and Price 1995, 134–7.

Biconical jug with funnel mouth

Characteristics

Form

Rim edge fire-rounded, wide funnel mouth, neck and upper body expanding out, rounded change of angle, lower body tapering in, diagonal tubular base ring and concave base, sometimes with high central kick. Curved handle with edge ribs, applied to upper body and attached to rim edge with folded loop or thumb rest.

Colours

Pale green, yellow/green, greenish colourless. Strong colours, such as dark blue, are rare.

Decoration

Thick horizontal trail below rim, sometimes with narrow spiral trail around neck, and occasionally also on the body. Some jugs have close-set narrow spiral optic-blown ribs on the lower neck and body.

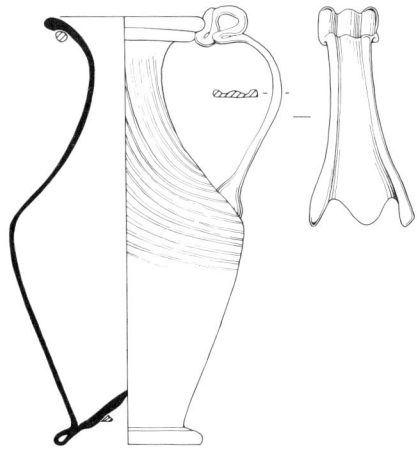

Fig 72   Scale 1:3

Other features
Pontil mark on base. The body is sometimes convex rather than biconical. These jugs are not easy to identify from small fragments; the most diagnostic parts are the rim and handle and the optic-blown ribbing on the body. The rather bubbly quality of the glass also helps to distinguish them from the tall convex jugs with funnel mouth discussed above (see Figure 71).

Range of measurements
Rim diameters *c* 40–60mm, heights *c* 120–200+mm.

Distribution
Quite common. Sometimes found in burials.

Date range
Uncertain. In use in later 4th century.

Illustrated example (Figure 72 and Back cover)
Colchester, Essex: Greenish colourless jug with optic-blown ribs, from grave 180 dated A D 360–80 in Butt Road cemetery (Cool and Price 1995, 147 no 1160 fig 8.11).

Other finds
Claydon Pike, Gloucestershire: Greenish colourless handle and body fragments, two jugs with optic-blown ribs.
Colchester, Essex: Greenish jug, optic-blown ribs and spiral trail on neck (Thorpe 1935, 31 pl 4c). Rim, body and handle fragments, convex jug with single trail below rim and spiral trail on body, from post-Roman context in Butt Road cemetery (Cool and Price 1995, 147 no 1161 fig 8.11).
Dorchester-on-Thames, Oxfordshire: Yellow/green jug, optic-blown ribs, from deposit of late 3rd–4th century glass, pottery and metal vessels (Harden 1939, 293). Fragments,

convex body with spiral trail and handle, possibly from this form of jug, from pit dated *c* AD 395–410 (Charlesworth 1984b, 155 no 13 fig 39).

Frocester Court villa, Gloucestershire: Greenish colourless handle and body fragment, jug with optic-blown ribs, from context dated *c* AD 340 or later (Price 1979, 44 no 39 fig 17).

Milton-next-Sittingbourne, Kent: Small light blue jug with single trail below rim and plain body, from inhumation burial in lead-lined wooden coffin (Roach Smith 1868, 263 no 4 fig).

Winchester, Hampshire: Greenish jug with spiral trail on neck and plain body, from grave 333 dated AD 390–410 in the Lankhills cemetery (Harden 1979a, 217 no 310 fig 27).

York: Small dark blue jug, from 4th century burial in stone coffin in Sycamore Terrace (Harden 1962, 140–1 H.12 fig 58 pl 67).

Further reading
Isings 1957, form 120a, 121. For general discussion of these and other 4th-early 5th century vessels in Britain, see Cool 1995b. For discussion of these and other jugs in connection with finds from Colchester, see Cool and Price 1995, 134–6.

Small globular jug

Characteristics
Form
Slightly out-turned rim, edge rolled-in or fire-rounded, cylindrical neck, wide convex body, concave base. Narrow rod handle applied to upper body and attached to neck or rim edge.

Colours
Yellow/green, pale green, greenish colourless.

Decoration
Lower handle terminal sometimes has pinched extension or folds on the body.

Other features
Bubbly glass. Pontil scar on base. Rarely noted in other parts of north-western provinces, perhaps produced in Britain.

Range of measurements
Rim diameters *c* 30mm, heights *c* 100–125mm.

Distribution
Not very common. Sometimes found in burials.

Date range
Uncertain. In use in mid–late 4th century AD.

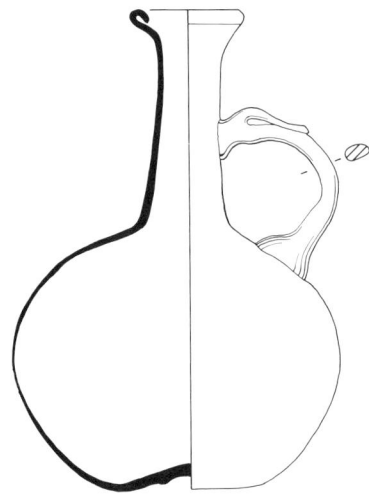

Fig 73   Scale 1:2

Illustrated example (Figure 73 and Plate 5.6)

Burgh Castle, Norfolk: Complete pale green jug, from late 4th–early 5th century hoard of glass vessels (Harden 1983, 81 no 80 fig 37).

Other finds

Burgh Castle, Norfolk: Complete green jug, from late 4th–early 5th century hoard of glass vessels (Harden 1983, 81 no 79 fig 37).

Colchester, Essex: Fragmentary greenish colourless jug, extended lower handle terminal with S-shaped folds, from grave 15, dated to last quarter of 4th century in Butt Road cemetery (Cool and Price 1995, 147 no 1164, fig 8.12). Fragments, three jugs (Cool and Price 1995, 137; Colchester Museums Accession nos 235, 702.04, 76.41).

Icklingham, Suffolk: Complete pale green jug (British Museum, Department of Prehistoric and Romano-British Antiquities; 1900.6–14.2).

Lincoln: Fragments, five pale green, yellow/green and greenish colourless jugs.

London: Two pale green jugs with pinched or folded handle extensions, from burials 269/270 and 309/310, dated to mid 4th century at West Tenter Street in the east cemetery (Jones 1986, 87 nos 28, 31 fig 40 nos 10–11). Yellow/green jug from burial at Mansell Street in east cemetery (information from John Shepherd).

Richborough, Kent: Yellow/green jug, from 4th century pit (Bushe-Fox 1932, 85 no 62 pl 15).

Winchester, Hampshire: Three jugs, two green, one yellow/green, from graves 385, 472, dated AD 370–410, and rescue-observation in the Lankhills cemetery (Harden 1979a, 28 nos 472, 551 & 632 fig 27).

Further reading

See discussion in connection with finds from Burgh Castle (Harden 1983, 123) and Colchester (Cool and Price 1995, 137).

Globular jug with two handles

Characteristics
Form
Out-turned rim, edge bent in and flattened or fire-rounded, cylindrical neck, usually with horizontal trail pinched into projecting ring, constriction at base, wide convex body, tubular or applied base ring, concave base. Two curved ribbon handles, applied to upper body and attached to neck or neck-ring.

Colours
Pale green, yellow/green. Very occasionally blue/green or polychrome.

Decoration
Handles often have vertical ribs and looped fold or pinched thumb-rest. Spiral un-marvered trail occasionally found on lower body.

Other features
Bubbly glass. Pontil mark sometimes on base. The most diagnostic part is the neck with horizontal ring. Rarely noted in other parts of north-western provinces, perhaps produced in Britain.

Range of measurements
Rim diameters *c* 20–30mm, heights *c* 90 –250mm.

Distribution
Not very common. Occasionally found in burials, including one without a neck-ring from a Saxon grave at Mitcham, Surrey (Harden 1956, 158 A:f.1 pl 15k).

Date range
Uncertain. In use in later 4th century AD.

Illustrated example (Figure 74)
Winchester, Hampshire: Nearly complete green jug with rod handles, from grave 322 dated A D 370–90 in Lankhills cemetery (Harden 1979a, 219 no 450 fig 27).

Other finds
Canterbury, Kent: Pale green jug without neck-ring, broad ribbon handles with four ribs and looped folds (Plate 5.1), in burial with coin dated A D 287–93 at Bourne Park (Thorpe 1935, 22 pl 5b).
Colchester, Essex: Complete jug with spiral trail on lower body (Colchester Museums Accession no 84.14). Fragment, curved ribbon handle with five ribs and folded loop, perhaps from this jug form, from modern context in Butt Road cemetery (Cool and Price 1995, 147 no 1162 fig 8.11).
Frocester Court villa, Gloucestershire: Neck, neck-ring and handle fragments, three green-ish jugs (Price 1979, 44 nos 43–5 fig 18).
Great Staughton villa, Rutlandshire: Fragment, greenish neck with dark blue neck-ring without handle scars (Charlesworth 1994, 102 no 37 fig).

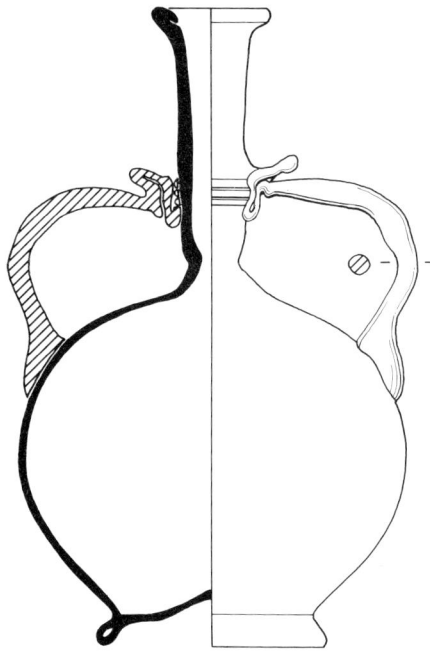

Fig 74   Scale 1:2

Ifold/Painswick villa, Gloucestershire: Fragment, rim, neck, neck-ring and handle (Baddeley 1904, 168 fig 1 no 1).

Mucking, Essex: Fragment, rim, neck, neck-ring, handle scar and body, yellow/green jug.

Sandy, Bedfordshire: Rim, neck, neck-ring, ribbed ribbon handles with folded loops and body, pale green jug, from late 3rd –4th century context (Johnston 1974, 46 no 1 fig 10).

Winchester, Hampshire: Intact small pale green jug with ribbon handles with edge ribs and applied base ring, from grave 236 dated AD 340–370/90 in Lankhills cemetery (Harden 1979a, 219 no 270 fig 27).

York: Neck and neck-ring fragment, blue/green, from post-Roman context in Swinegate (Cool 1995a, 1669 no 6454 fig 766).

Further reading

Isings 1957, form 129 is generally similar in shape, but it has a cracked-off rim. For discussion of these and other 4th–early 5th century vessels in Britain, see Cool 1995b. For discussion in connection with finds from Lankhills cemetery, Winchester, see Harden 1979a, 218–9.

Flasks, unguent bottles and bath-flasks

Tubular unguent bottle

Characteristics

Form

Out-turned rim, edge sheared unevenly, or very occasionally rolled-in, cylindrical neck, tooled constriction, straight body expanding out, convex lower body, small flattened area on base.

Colours

Generally blue/green. A few are strongly coloured or pale yellow/green.

Other features

Body and base fragments most diagnostic. Pontil mark occasionally present on base fragments, probably indicating that the unguent bottle had a rolled-in rim.

Range of measurements

Rim diameters *c* 20–25mm, heights *c* 60–120mm.

Distribution

Common in settlements and burials. Sometimes found in bath-houses. Melted examples sometimes found with cremations.

Date range

Unguent bottles with sheared rims, *c* AD 43–75/80. Unguent bottles with rolled rims, used in third quarter of 1st century AD, probably also in use in later 2nd–early 3rd century AD.

Illustrated example (Figure 75)

York: Light blue unguent bottle with sheared rim, from burial in tomb made of tiles with VIth Legion stamps (ie early 2nd century), in the Railway Station cemetery (Harden 1962, 137 H.G 32 fig 89).

Other finds

Caerleon, Gwent: Rim, body and base fragments, blue/green, from contexts in the legionary bath-house drain dated *c* AD 75–100/110 and AD 160–230 (Allen 1986, 99, 101, 105 nos 1, 8–10, 30 fig 40–1).
Carlisle, Cumbria: Fragments, three blue/green unguent bottles, one with pointed base and another with pontil scar from Castle Street (Cool and Price 1991, 173 nos 656–8 fig 153). At least two blue/green unguent bottles with sheared rims, from Annetwell Street.
Colchester, Essex: Fragments, at least twenty-six blue/green unguent bottles, from Claudian-early Neronian, Neronian-Flavian and later contexts (Cool and Price 1995,

Fig 75   Scale 1:2

160 nos 1210–1242 fig 9.11). Many examples from burials, for example, Joslin Collection Grave 7/43 dated AD 40–70, Graves 29/37, 32/52, 35/64, 42/23, 44/26, 45/34 dated AD 50–100, Grave 48/16 dated AD 69–96, Graves 56/29, 57/116 dated AD 90–100, Graves 72/8, 75/42 dated AD 100–150 , Taylor collection Grave 5/20 dated AD 69–96, and others (May 1930, 254, 260–2, 264–5, 267, 269, 273–4, 291 pls 76, 79–82, 84, 91; Brailsford 1958, 44 no 16 pl 12).

Colchester, Sheepen, Essex: Fragments, at least three blue/green unguent bottles, from Claudian- early Neronian contexts (Harden 1947, 305 nos 85–8 pl 88).

Fishbourne Palace, West Sussex: Fragments, at least ten unguent bottles, some in Claudian-early Flavian contexts (Harden and Price 1971, 357–8 nos 83–4 fig 141; Price and Cottam 1996a, 182 nos 116–24 fig 6.30).

Gloucester: Fragments, at least eighteen unguent bottles, sixteen blue/green, two yellow/green, from Neronian military site at Kingsholm (Price and Cool 1985, 48, 52–4 nos 39, 69–83 figs 19–20).

Lincoln: Two complete vessels, one with sheared rim, one with rolled-in rim, plus many fragments, some melted, from 1st century cremation cemetery at Monson Street.

London: Fragments, blue/green unguent bottles, from Southwark Street (Shepherd 1995b, 130 nos 147, 171–2 fig 39). Complete blue/green unguent bottles, from mid 1st century and Neronian-early Flavian cremation burials at Great Alie Street and Bishopsgate (RCHM London 1928, 159 fig 65 nos 24, 32).

Usk, Gwent: Fragments, numerous blue/green unguent bottles with sheared rims, from late Neronian-early Flavian and later contexts in legionary fortress (Price 1995a, 175 nos 84–90 fig 45).

Verulamium, Hertfordshire: Fragments, at least five unguent bottles from contexts dated *c* AD 44–58, *c* AD 75–115 in insulas 14, 17 and 21 (Charlesworth 1972, 205 (xi) nos 3, 9, 10 fig 77 no 34; 1984a, 167 nos 265–6 fig 68 nos 119–20).

Winchester, Hampshire: Unguent bottle in burial dated AD 55–65 at Winnall housing estate (Charlesworth 1978c, 85, fig 30 no 20). Unguent bottle from burial dated AD 75–100 at Milland (Price 1978, 102 fig 40 no 49).

York: Complete unguent bottle with rolled-in rim, with cremation burial in Railway

170

Station cemetery (Harden 1962, 137 H.G.231 fig 89). Numerous similar unguent bottles with sheared rims, in dark blue, light green and blue/green glass (information from Hilary Cool).

Further reading
Isings 1957, form 8. See discussion in connection with finds from Colchester (Cool and Price 1995, 159–60, and Usk (Price 1995a, 172–4).

Convex flask

Characteristics
Form
Narrow diagonal folded rim, edge bent out, up, in and flattened, wide cylindrical neck, tooled at base, ovoid or globular body, concave base.

Colours
Blue/green.

Decoration
Horizontal bands of abrasion very occasionally present on body.

Range of measurements
Rim diameters *c* 35–50mm, heights *c* 150–220mm.

Distribution
Fairly common. Sometimes in burials.

Date range
AD 43–*c* AD 70.

Illustrated example (Figure 76 and Plate 3.2)
Usk, Gwent: Fragmentary ovoid flask, from late Neronian-early Flavian pit in legionary fortress (Price 1995a, 177 no 96 fig 45).

Other finds
Colchester, Essex: Two nearly complete ovoid flasks from Joslin collection Grave 3/124, dated AD 40–50, and one from Grave 39/10 (Marcus Favonius Facilis), dated AD 50—100 (May 1930, 252 nos 1139–40 pl 75 no 3a, and 264 no 48).
Colchester, Sheepen, Essex: Fragmentary ovoid flask from Claudian/Neronian pit (Harden 1947, 304 no 83 pl 88); two ovoid flasks with horizontal abraded bands from cremation group 4, Neronian burial (Charlesworth 1985a, MF 1:A8 b & c fig 17).
Fishbourne Palace, West Sussex: Fragments, at least ovoid three flasks (Price and Cottam 1996a, 180 nos 101–4 fig 6.29).
London: Ovoid flask, from St Martin's-le-Grand (Guildhall Museum 1908, 76 no 27 pl 8 no 15).
Verulamium, Hertfordshire: Rim, neck and body fragments, globular flask from King

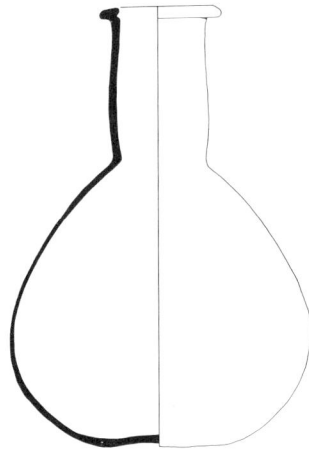

Fig 76   Scale 1:3

Harry Lane (Price 1989a, 45, nos 313–4 fig 27); Complete convex flask from Flavian burial south west of Silchester Gate (Niblett and Reeves 1990, 444 no 15 pl 59).
Wroxeter, Shropshire: Ovoid flask from burial in east cemetery (Haverfield and Taylor 1908, 240 fig 32).
York: Globular flask, from Railway Station cemetery (Harden 1962, 137 HG 49 fig 89).

Further reading
Isings 1957, form 16. See discussion in connection with finds from Usk (Price 1995a, 174–5) and Fishbourne (Price and Cottam 1996a, 167–8).

Conical unguent bottle

Characteristics
Form
Out-turned rim, edge sheared or occasionally rolled-in, long cylindrical neck, short conical body, flat or slightly concave base.

Colours
Blue/green.

Other features
Conical body sometimes has slight constriction. Body and base often quite thick. Pontil mark on a few bases, probably indicating that the unguent bottle had a rolled-in rim.

Range of measurements
Heights *c* 90mm to *c* 130mm.

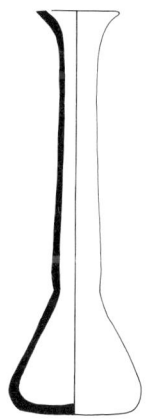

Fig 77   Scale 1:2

Distribution
Quite common. Sometimes in burials.

Date range
Last quarter of 1st century-first quarter of 2nd century.

Illustrated example (Figure 77)
York: Complete unguent bottle, from Railway Station cemetery (Harden 1962, 137 H G 36.1 pl 66).

Other finds
Caerleon, Gwent: Body and base fragments, two unguent bottles, in contexts in the legionary bath-house drain dated AD80–100/110 and 160–230 (Allen 1986, 101, 105 nos 9, 31 figs 40–41).

Carlisle, Cumbria: Body and base fragment, blue/green unguent bottle from Castle Street (Cool and Price 1991, 173 no 659 fig 153).

Chichester, West Sussex: Complete unguent bottle, from burial group 6 in St Pancras cemetery, dated to later 1st–2nd century (Down and Rule 1971, 92 burial group 26I fig 5.20).

Colchester, Essex: Body and base fragments, at least two unguent bottles, from post-Roman/modern contexts (Cool and Price 1995, 162 nos 243, 247 fig 9.12). Body fragments, two unguent bottles from Jarmin Collection cremation grave 10 dated *c* AD 100 (May 1930, 288 grave 10 pl 90).

Derby: Neck, body and base with pontil mark (Allen 1985, 135 no 7 fig 53).

Dorchester, Dorset: Body and base fragment, from Greyhound Yard (Cool and Price 1993, 164 no 113 fig 87).

Park Street villa, near St Albans, Hertfordshire: Neck, body and base, dark green ungent bottle, from pit dated to late 1st century (Harden 1945, 72 no 22 fig 11).

Usk, Gwent: Fragment, neck and body, from 2nd century context (Price 1995a, 176 no 91 fig 45).

Verulamium, Hertfordshire: Fragments, at least five unguent bottles, from contexts dated

AD 85–105, 150–155/60, and 3rd and late 4th century, in insulas 14, 21 and 27 (Charlesworth 1972, 205 (xi) nos 4, 11, 12 fig 77 no 35; 1984a, 167 nos 267–8 fig 68 nos 121–2).

Welwyn, Hertfordshire: Complete unguent bottle, from cremation burial (Kindersley 1922, 22 pl 5 fig 1).

Wroxeter, Shropshire: Almost complete unguent bottle, from context dated AD 80–120 (Bushe-Fox 1914, 20 fig 11).

York: Complete unguent bottle from the Railway Station cemetery (Harden 1962, 137 HG 36.2 pl 66).

Further reading
Isings 1957, form 82b. See brief discussion in connection with finds from Usk (Price 1995a, 174).

Globular wheel-cut flask with funnel mouth

Characteristics
Form
Flared rim, edge cracked-off and ground smooth, funnel mouth, narrow cylindrical neck, wide convex body, slightly concave base.

Colours
Strong colours, colourless.

Decoration
Groups of close-set horizontal wheel-cut lines on mouth and body.

Other features
Difficult to identify unless rim and neck survive, as body and base fragments are not diagnostic. The glass in the body and base is often very thin.

Range of measurements
Rim diameters *c* 45–55mm, heights *c* 100–170mm.

Distribution
Not common.

Date range
Uncertain. In use in early–mid 2nd century.

Illustrated example (Figure 78 and Plate 4.3)
Stansted, Essex: Fragmentary colourless flask, from cremation burial 247 at the Duck-end Carpark site, dated to first quarter of 2nd century.

Other finds
Baldock, Hertfordshire: Rim, body and base fragments, colourless flask, from cremation group 10, dated *c* AD 120–40 (Westell 1931, 257 pl 5).

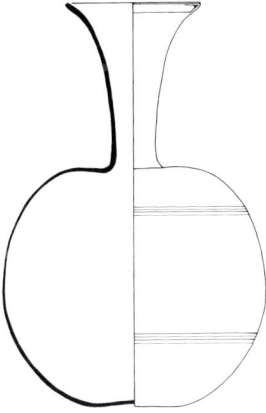

Fig 78   Scale 1:3

Castleford, West Yorkshire: Fragments, one or two pale yellow/green flasks, one with long neck, and one colourless flask, from mid 2nd century contexts in the vicus (Cool and Price 1998, 159 nos 74–5, 162 no 128 fig 54).
Flint, Pentre Farm, Clwyd: Rim, neck and body fragments, strong green/blue (peacock blue) flask with short neck, from 3rd century context (Price 1989b, 81 no 2 fig 29).

Further reading
Isings 1957, form 92.

Tall discoid unguent bottle

Characteristics
Form
Out-turned rim, edge rolled-in, long cylindrical neck, low, slightly convex body, wide flat or slightly concave base. A small group have short wide necks.

Colours
Blue/green, pale green, colourless.

Decoration
Base sometimes impressed with stamp, usually consisting of a ring of letters surrounding a central letter or figure.

Other features
The thickness of the body and base varies considerably.

Range of measurements
Rim diameters *c* 45–55mm, heights *c* 100–*c* 200+mm.

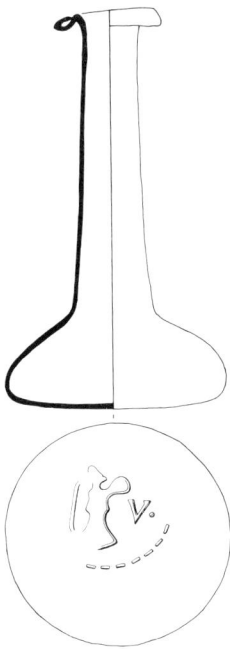

Fig 79   Scale 1:3

Distribution
Quite common. Sometimes found in burials.

Date range
Uncertain. In use in second and third quarters of 2nd century.

Illustrated example (Figure 79)
York: Complete pale blue/green unguent bottle with base stamp (Harden 1962 137 HG 16 fig 89; RIB II, 2, no 2419.156).

Other finds
Bignor villa, west Sussex: Neck, body and base, pale blue/green unguent bottle (information from Brenda Compton).
Canterbury, Kent: Neck and body fragments, colourless unguent bottle, from cremation burial 46, dated mid 2nd–early 3rd century, at Cranmer House, London Road (Tatton-Brown 1987, 280).
Chester: Unguent bottle with short wide neck and base stamp, from grave 26, a burial containing a coin of Antoninus Pius (Newstead 1914, 148 fig 10; RIB II, 2, no 2419.154).
Chichester, West Sussex: Unguent bottle with short wide neck and base stamp, from burial group 247 containing late 1st century pottery in St Pancras cemetery (Down and Rule 1971, 116 247H fig 5.26; RIB II, 2, no 2419.87).

Colchester, Essex: Nearly complete unguent bottle from grave 302 in area of pottery kilns, dated *c* AD 190 (Hull 1963, 146 fig 79 no 7). Blue/green unguent bottle, from Joslin collection burial 93/125, dated AD 150–200 (May 1930, 279 no 1181 pl 86 no 93). Unguent bottles with base stamps (RIB II, 2, no 2419.103, 155).

Harlow, Felmongers, Essex: At least five colourless and blue/green unguent bottles, two with base stamps (Plate 3.5), from pit dated *c* AD160–70 (Price 1987a, 205–6 nos 27–32 fig.4; RIB II, 2, no 2419.105, 109).

London: Blue/green unguent bottle from Ewer Street, Southwark (Brailsford 1958, 44 no 13 pl 12).

Lullingstone villa, Kent: Body fragment, blue/green (Cool and Price 1987a, 134 no 364 fig 55).

Shakenoak, Oxfordshire: Greenish unguent bottle, from context not later than *c* AD 140 (Harden 1971, 98 no 53 fig 43 no 31).

Verulamium, Hertfordshire: Body and base fragment and fragmentary unguent bottle, both blue/green, from contexts dated AD 275–80 and AD 160–80 in insulas 14 and 28 (Charlesworth 1972, 205 (xi) no 8 fig 77 no 39; 1984a, 167 no 273 fig 68 no 126).

York: Nearly complete pale green unguent bottle with short wide neck and base stamp, from Railway Station cemetery (Harden 1962, 137 HG 217 fig 89; RIB II, 2, no 2419.131).

Further reading
Isings 1957, form 82B2. See discussion in connection with finds from Felmongers, Harlow (Price 1987a, 196–7) and Colchester (Cool and Price 1995, 161–2). Bases with inscriptions are recorded in RIB II, 2.

Unguent bottle with indents

Characteristics
Form
Slightly out-turned narrow rim, edge either sheared or bent out, up, in and flattened, cylindrical neck, long body, either straight and tapering in or slightly convex, small concave base.

Colours
Blue/green, pale green, greenish colourless.

Decoration
Four (or occasionally more) long oval indents on body.

Other features
Sometimes has funnel mouth. Pontil mark on base. The variation in body shapes is shown in Figure 80. The body and base are the most diagnostic parts of this form.

Range of measurements
Rim diameters *c* 20–30mm, heights *c* 135–160mm.

Distribution
Fairly common. Found in burials.

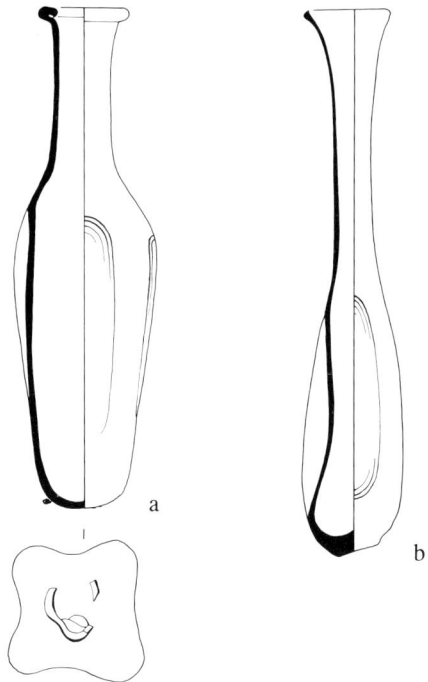

Fig 80   Scale 1:2

Date range
In use in late 2nd–3rd century AD.

Illustrated examples (Figure 80)
a) *Colchester, Essex*: Complete greenish colourless unguent bottle from 3rd–4th century inhumation burial at Maldon Road (Cool and Price 1995, 162–3 no 1252 fig 9.13).
b) *York*: Complete greenish colourless unguent bottle from burial in Railway Station cemetery (Harden 1962, 140 HG 9 fig 89).

Other finds
Brougham, Cumbria: Colourless unguent bottle, from burial in cemetery dated to A D 220/30–260/70.
Canterbury, Kent: Neck and body, colourless unguent bottle, from cremation burial 48, dated to late 2nd–4th century, at Cranmer House, London Road (Tatton-Brown 1987, 281 burial 48 fig 105 no 48a).
Colchester, Essex: Fragments, blue/green and greenish unguent bottles, from unstratified or modern contexts (Cool and Price 1995, 162–3 nos 1251, 1253 fig 9.13). Green unguent bottle, from Joslin collection Grave 100/71 dated AD 200–250 (May 1930, 281 410 pl 87 no 100). Colourless unguent bottle from inhumation burial in lead coffin (Brailsford 1958, 44 no 15 pl 12).
London: Unguent bottle, from cremation burial in Mansell Street in the east cemetery

(RCHM London 1928, 157 fig 64 no 20). Unguent bottle (Guildhall Museum 1908, 77 no 146 pl 7 no 7).

Lullingstone villa, Kent: Body and base, blue/green unguent bottle (Cool and Price 1987a, 134 no 363 fig 55).

Ospringe, Kent: Greenish unguent bottle from inhumation burial 94, dated to first half of 3rd century (Whiting *et al* 1931, 31 no 321 pl 31).

Piercebridge, Co.Durham: Lower body fragment, blue/green.

South Shields, Tyne and Wear: Neck and body fragment, colourless.

Swainswick, near Bath, Avon: Unguent bottle with more than four indents, from inhumation burial in stone coffin (Scarth 1864, 96 pl 45).

York: Complete small blue/green unguent bottle with cracked-off rim (probably secondary repair–information from Hilary Cool) and pontil scar, from inhumation in Railway Station cemetery (Harden 1962, 140 no H 324.5 fig 88). Fragments, five other greenish colourless and blue/green unguent bottles (information from Hilary Cool).

Further reading
Isings 1957, form 83. See discussion in connection with finds from Colchester (Cool and Price 1995, 162–3).

Flask with square body (Mercury flask)

Characteristics
Form
Broad, horizontal folded rim, edge bent out, up, in and flattened, long narrow cylindrical neck, square (rarely hexagonal) body with straight sides, flat base.

Colours
Usually colourless, greenish colourless. Sometimes pale green, blue/green.

Decoration
The base is either plain or decorated with raised motifs. Raised designs on the body are rare in Britain.

Other features
The body and base are blown into a mould. These vessels are often called Mercury flasks as the base designs sometimes include a representation of this deity. The colour and the thickness of the wall are distinguishing features.

Range of measurements
Uncertain. Rim diameters *c* 25–45mm, heights *c* 100–200+mm.

Distribution
Not common. Some in burials.

Date range
Uncertain. In use in second half of 2nd century AD.

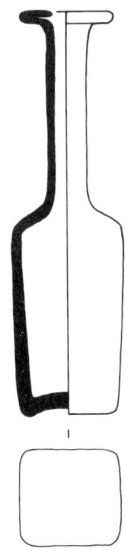

Fig 81   Scale 1:2

Illustrated example (Figure 81)
Ospringe, Kent: From cremation burial 43 (Whiting 1926, 127 no 151 pl 17; Whiting *et al* 1931, pl 17 no 151).

Other finds
Benwell, Northumberland; Body and base fragments, greenish colourless.
Caerleon, Gwent: Colourless body with hexagonal section, from contexts in the legionary bath-house drain dated AD160–230 (Allen 1986, 113 no 77 fig 43).
Milton Keynes, Caldecotte, Buckinghamshire: Colourless body, from ditch containing late 2nd–3rd century and earlier material at Berrystead Close (Price 1994, 136 no 161).
Chester: Fragmentary colourless flask, from mid–late 2nd century inhumation burial at Infirmary Field (Newstead 1914, 128 pl 31 fig 2).
Colchester, Essex: Pale green and colourless, small body and base fragments, one with raised design on body, from post-Roman contexts (Cool and Price 1995, 153 nos 1182–3 fig 9.6).
Fishbourne Palace, West Sussex: Greenish colourless rim and neck, from unstratified context (Harden and Price 1971, 358 no 87 fig 142).
London: Greenish colourless thin-walled flask, pontil mark on base, and thick-walled body and base, raised design on base, from Mansell Street in the east cemetery (information from John Shepherd).
Ospringe, Kent: melted fragments, from cremation burial 43, apparently similar to Figure 81 (Whiting 1926, 127).
Stonea, Cambridgeshire: Body fragment, colourless, from topsoil (Price 1996b, 403 no 60 fig 132).
Witcombe villa, Gloucestershire: Greenish colourless body fragment (Price and Cottam 1998, 75–6, 80 no 25).

York: Blue/green base with raised dot, and colourless hexagonal lower body and base, from Church Street sewer (Charlesworth 1976b, 17 nos 44–6 fig 13). Pale green and colourless body fragments, from late 2nd–late 3rd and later contexts at Blake Street (Cool 1995a, 1652, 1656 nos 5909–3, 6029 fig 748).

Further reading
Isings 1957, form 84; Stern 1977, 64–72 form 18. For discussion in connection with finds from Colchester, see Cool and Price 1995, 152–3.

Globular flask with cylindrical neck

Characteristics
Form
Vertical rim, edge cracked-off and ground smooth, narrow cylindrical neck, sometimes with constriction at base, wide convex body, concave base.

Colours
Colourless, greenish colourless. Very occasionally blue/green.

Decoration
Horizontal abraded or wheel-cut lines are very common. More complex wheel-cutting and ribs are rare.

Other features
The rim and neck are easily recognised, but these also occur on other forms. Not easy to identify from small body fragments.

Range of measurements
Rim diameters *c* 15–25mm, heights *c* 140–250+mm.

Distribution
Not very common. Occasionally found in burials.

Date range
Uncertain. In use in mid/late 3rd century AD.

Illustrated example (Figure 82)
Complete greenish flask from Kölnstrasse/Ecke Kaiser-Karl-Ring, Bonn (Follmann-Schulz 1988, 38 no 87, taf 8), shows the typical profile and decoration.

Other finds
Colchester, Essex: Rim and neck fragments, at least four blue/green and greenish colourless flasks, from contexts dated c AD 250–300 and later (Cool and Price 1995, 154–155 nos 1184–7 fig 9.7). Blue/green flask without decoration (Price 1888, 73 no 940).
Dorchester, Dorset: Rim and neck fragment, blue/green flask from Greyhound Yard (Cool and Price 1993, 164 no 107 fig 86). Complete colourless flask with slightly diagonal ribs, from inhumation burial 3664 at Alington Avenue.

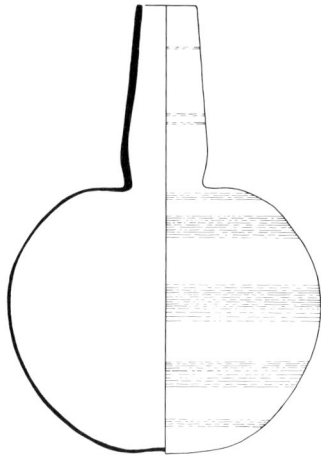

Fig 82   Scale 1:3

St Albans, Hertfordshire: Complete flask with horizontal wheel-cut lines, from inhumation burial in stone coffin at Kingsbury.

Wimborne, Bucknowle Farm, Dorset: Body and base, large colourless flask with horizontal wheel-cutting, from 3rd century AD context.

Witcombe villa, Gloucestershire: Body, colourless flask with concentric wheel-cut circles and horizontal lines (Price and Cottam 1998, 75, 78–80 nos 17–18 fig 22).

York: Complete colourless flask, with horizontal wheel-cut lines (Harden 1962, 141 H G 33 pl 67).

Further reading

Isings 1957, form 103. See discussion in connection with finds from Colchester (Cool and Price 1995, 153–4).

Convex flask with funnel mouth

Characteristics

Form

Flared rim, edge cracked-off and ground, or sometimes fire-rounded, funnel mouth, convex body, concave base, sometimes with trailed base ring.

Colours

Colourless, greenish colourless.

Decoration

Horizontal bands of abrasion on neck and body. Some also have indents on the body.

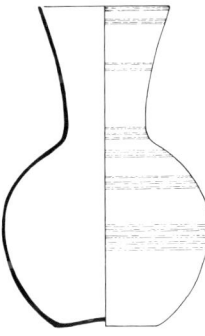

Fig 83   Scale 1:3

Other features
The rim and funnel mouth are often the most diagnostic parts. The poorer quality of the glass and the rim finish distinguish these flasks from the earlier globular flasks (see Figure 78).

Range of measurements
Rim diameters *c* 50–70mm, heights *c* 130mm–160mm.

Distribution
Not common. Occasionally found in burials.

Date range
Uncertain. In use at various periods in the 3rd–early 4th centuries AD.

Illustrated example (Figure 83)
London: Colourless flask, from burial thought to be 3rd century AD, at the Minories in the east cemetery (Harden and Green 1978, 163–4 figs 1, 3).

Other finds
Binchester, Co Durham: Fragment, indented body and trailed base, greenish colourless.
Chilgrove, near Chichester, West Sussex: Flask, from inhumation burial (Harcourt 1846, 312–314 pl 9).
Colchester, Essex: Fragmentary colourless flask with abraded bands, indents and trailed base, from burial dated AD280–300/320 in Butt Road cemetery (Cool and Price 1995, 155 no 1188 fig 9.8). Rim, body and base fragments, colourless flask with indents and trailed base, from 4th century context (Cool and Price 1995, 155 no 1189 fig 9.8)
Lincoln: Fragment, indented body and trailed base, greenish colourless, from St Paul in the Bail.
London: Fragments, neck and body, colourless flask without abraded lines, from West Tenter Street, in context dated early-mid 3rd century AD; and another example, from Shadwell (Jones 1986, 86–8 no 26). Indented body and trailed base fragment, greenish colourless, from Shadwell.
Witcombe villa, Gloucestershire: Fragments, two colourless flasks (Price and Cottam 1998, 75, 78 nos 15–16 fig 22).

York: Fragments, indented body and trailed base, greenish colourless, from Rougier Street.

Further reading
Isings 1957, form 104. See discussion in connection with finds from the Minories, London (Harden and Green 1978) and Colchester (Cool and Price 1995, 155).

Cylindrical flask with funnel mouth

Characteristics
Form
Flared rim, edge fire-rounded, funnel mouth, cylindrical neck, narrow shoulder, straight side, tapering in slightly, concave base.

Colours
Colourless, greenish colourless.

Decoration
Thick horizontal trail on funnel mouth. Horizontal bands of wheel-cut or abraded lines on body.

Other features
All parts of these flasks also occur on other 3rd–4th century forms, so they are difficult to identify from small fragments. A form sometimes found in association with these flasks has an identical body and base with a hole-mouth rim (Harden 1962, 140 HG146.1–2 fig 90).

Range of measurements
Rim diameters *c* 50–55mm, heights *c* 120–150mm.

Distribution
Not very common. Some in burials.

Date range
Uncertain. In use in first half of 4th century AD.

Illustrated example (Figure 84)
York: Greenish colourless flask, from inhumation burial in lead coffin in North Midland Railway cemetery (Harden 1962, 140 no H.G.146.4 fig 90).

Other finds
Cambridge: Three greenish colourless flasks with funnel mouths, found in stone coffin at Gravel Hill Farm (Liversidge 1977, 16 pl 2; Fitzwilliam 1978 41 no 80 and fig).
Cirencester, Gloucestershire: Fragments, rim, neck body and base (Buckman and Newmarsh 1850, 97 fig 29b).
Gestingthorpe, Essex: Rim, neck and shoulder, greenish flask with funnel mouth (Charlesworth 1985b, 66 no 313 fig 30).

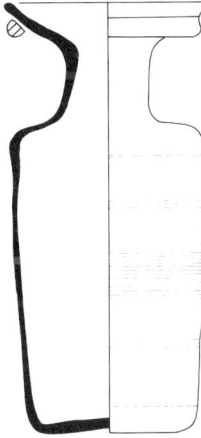

Fig 84   Scale 1:2

London: Neck and upper body, colourless flask with abraded lines, originally with funnel mouth, but reworked after breakage, from Mansell Street in east cemetery (information from John Shepherd).

York: Greenish colourless flask, from same inhumation burial in the North Midland Railway cemetery Figure 84 (Harden 1962, 140 no.HG 146.3 fig 90 pl 67). Rim and upper body of flask, from inhumation burial in the Railway Station cemetery containing coin of AD 317–26 (Harden 1962, 140 fig 89 H 15). At least five further flasks (information from Hilary Cool).

Further reading
Isings 1957, form 102. For general discussion of these and other 4th-early 5th century vessels in Britain see Cool 1995b.

Ovoid flask

Characteristics
Form
Wide horizontal folded rim, edge bent out and up, and rolled-in or flattened, cylindrical neck, constricted at base, convex body, concave base, occasionally with high kick.

Colours
Colourless, greenish colourless.

Other features
Sometimes has pontil mark on base. Small fragments are not very diagnostic. The colour and quality of the glass distinguishes these from other convex flasks (for example, see Figure 76).

Range of measurements
Rim diameters *c* 35–60mm, heights *c* 150–220mm.

Distribution
Not very common. Some in burials.

Date range
Uncertain. In use in late 2nd and 3rd centuries AD.

Illustrated example (Figure 85)
Cirencester, Gloucestershire: Greenish flask from inhumation burial 356 in stone coffin (Charlesworth 1982, MF 2.D14, 132 burial 356 fig 81).

Other finds
Colchester, Essex: Greenish colourless flask (Plate 4.6), from 3rd – 4th century inhumation burial at Maldon Road (Cool and Price 1995, 151 no 1176 fig 9.4).
Chester: Colourless flask with kicked base, from grave 1 in the Infirmary Field (Newstead 1914, 126 pl 31 fig 1).
London: Greenish colourless flask in burial with mid/late 2nd century pottery at St Clare Street; greenish colourless flask from burial at Mansell Street, both from the east cemetery (information from John Shepherd).

Further reading
See discussion in connection with finds from Colchester (Cool and Price 1995, 150).

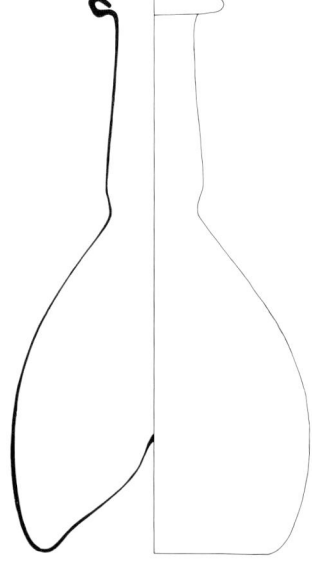

Fig 85   Scale 1:3

Long narrow unguent bottle (pipette-shaped)

Characteristics

Form
Rim edge rolled-in or folded out, up and in, sometimes forming a funnel mouth with narrow aperture, long straight neck and upper body expanding out, convex change of angle, lower body tapering in, convex base.

Colours
Pale green, greenish colourless, blue/green.

Other features
Bubbly glass with black specks. Pontil mark on base. Lower body and base often very thick.

Range of measurements
Rim diameters *c* 25–50mm, heights 150–370+mm.

Distribution
Not very common. Usually found in burials.

Date range
Uncertain, in use in 4th century.

Illustrated example (Figure 86)
York: Greenish colourless unguent bottle, from the Mount (Harden 1962, 140 H G 6 fig 89).

Other finds
Milton-next-Sittingbourne, Kent: Short light blue unguent bottle, from inhumation burial in lead-lined wooden coffin (Roach Smith 1868, 263 no 3 fig). Similar unguent bottle, from burial in lead coffin (Payne 1874, 166).
Caerleon, Gwent: Short greenish colourless unguent bottle with wide body, from burial in stone coffin on line of Monmouthshire branch of South Wales Railway (Lee 1862, 49 pl 27 no 4; Boon 1972, 110 fig 77).
Exeter, Devon: Fragments, unguent bottle, from the Valiant Soldier site (Charlesworth 1979a, 229 no 39 fig 71).
Park Street villa, near St Albans, Hertfordshire: Very long unguent bottle and fragments of a second, from inhumation burial in lead-lined stone coffin (Saunders 1961, 117 pl 6B; Davies and Saunders 1986, 28 and fig).
York: Greenish colourless long unguent bottle, from lead-lined wooden coffin in Railway Station cemetery (Harden 1962, 140 H G 7). Six similar unguent bottles (information from Hilary Cool). Colourless rim and neck, from post-Roman context at the Minster site (Price 1995b, 364 no 65 fig 145).

Further reading
Isings 1957, form 105.

Fig 86   Scale 1:3

Small globular flask with two looped handles (bath flask)

Characteristics

Form

Folded rim, edge bent out, up and in, short cylindrical neck, horizontal shoulder, wide globular body, small flattened or slightly concave base. Two small looped handles ('dolphin' handles) applied to shoulder and neck.

Colours

Blue/green, occasionally colourless or greenish/colourless. Polychrome examples are rare.

Decoration

Unmarvered spiral trails on the neck, body and base of some flasks. A few have horizontal wheel-cut lines. Facet-cutting and opaque white marvered blobs are rare.

Other features

Long-lived vessel form. Some features appear to be chronologically significant. First century flasks often have small folded rims with triangular profiles, and handles applied to the shoulder, folded to form a small ring and attached to neck (Figure 87a), while 2nd and 3rd century handles are generally applied to shoulder, trailed up the neck and bent out and down (Figure 87 b-c). The thickness of the handles also varies considerably, and bath flasks with thin handles tend to belong to the 2nd and early 3rd centuries. Some flasks have copper alloy loops or chains attached to the handles. Pontil mark often present on base. Some unusual body shapes are known.

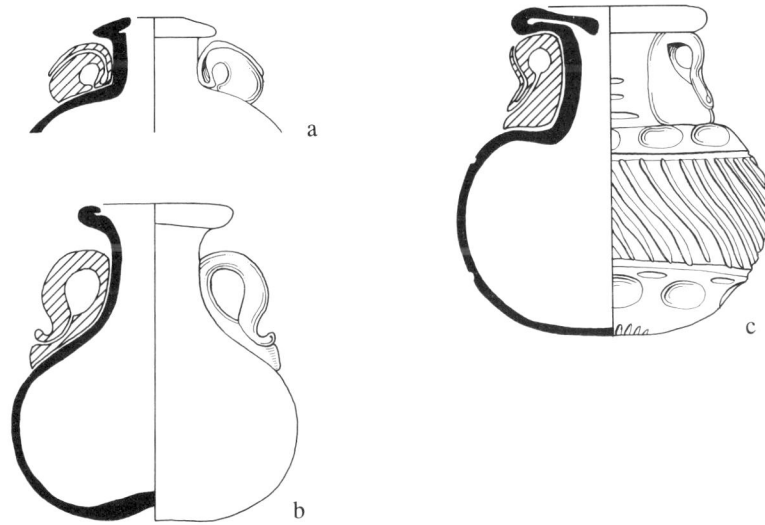

Fig 87   Scale 1:2

Range of measurements
Rim diameters of *c* 30–40mm, heights of *c* 50–100mm.

Distribution
Quite common. Found in bath houses, and occasionally in burials.

Date range
Third quarter of 1st century AD–mid 3rd century AD.

Illustrated examples (Figure 87)
a) *Usk, Gwent*: Rim, neck, body and handles, blue/green flask, from late Neronian–early Flavian pit in legionary fortress (Price 1995a, 172 no 81 fig 45).
b) *Silchester, Hampshire*: Blue/green flask (Boon 1974a, 230 fig 36 no 9).
c) *Caerleon, Gwent*: Colourless flask with narrow aperture at rim, facet-cutting on neck and body; from legionary bath house in context dated *c* AD160–230 (Allen 1986, 109 no 52 fig 42).

Other finds
Aldborough, North Yorkshire: Rim, neck and handles, blue/green (Ecroyd Smith 1852, 48 pl 24 no 19).
Caerleon, Gwent: Fragments, large number of colourless and blue/green undecorated, wheel-cut and trailed flasks, from dated deposits in legionary bath house drain (Allen 1986, 105, 107 nos 32–42, 52–56 figs 41–2).
Carrawburgh, Northumberland: Blue/green, with trails (Charlesworth 1959c, 56 fig 10 no 11).

Colchester, Essex: Fragments, at least fifteen blue/green flasks, from late 2nd century and later contexts (Cool and Price 1995, 158–9 nos 1190–1209 fig 9.9).

Sheepen: Blue/green flask with narrow rim, from cremation group 5, Neronian burial (Charlesworth 1985a, MF1:A9 c, fig 18 no 3).

Corbridge, Northumberland: Complete blue/green flask, copper alloy chain attached to handles, Antonine pit (Richmond and Gillam 1952, 259–60 no 11 pl 8).

London: Blue/green flask with triangular rim (Plate 3.3), probably from Southwark (Wheeler 1930, 121 no 4 pl 53). Flask with copper alloy handle, handle fragments with copper alloy chain (Guildhall Museum 1908, 76 pl 8 nos 1, 4).

Ospringe, Kent: Two bath flasks, one with trailed decoration, from cremation burials 40 and 42 (Whiting 1926, 125 no 141 and 126 no 146 pl 16; Whiting *et al* 1931, pl 16 nos 141 and 146).

near Richborough, Kent: Complete dark blue bath flask with opaque white marvered blobs, probably in later 1st century context (Harden *et al* 1968, 58 no 70).

York: Fragments, at least five blue/green and colourless flasks, from legionary bath house drain in Church Street (Charlesworth 1976b, 15–6 nos 32–42 fig 12). Fragmentary flask with ring-shaped body, from inhumation burial in Railway Station cemetery; and handle fragment, find spot unknown (Harden 1962, 140–1 H 324.6, H G 227 fig 88).

Further reading
Isings 1957, form 61. See discussion in connection with finds from Caerleon (Allen 1986, 104–5, 107–8), Colchester (Cool and Price 1995, 156–8) and Usk (Price 1995a, 172).

Bottles

Cylindrical bottle

Characteristics
Form
Folded rim with horizontal or diagonal profile, edge bent out, up, in and flattened, cylindrical neck with tooling marks at base, horizontal shoulder, vertical side, often with a slight bulge at the top of the body, slightly concave base. Angular ribbon handle applied to edge of shoulder and attached to neck below rim. Lower part of handle usually has narrow close-set vertical ribs (reeding), pulled into points on top of body. Handles with two broad ridges, or ribs in high relief, or plain ribbon handles, are also found.

Colours
Blue/green. Occasionally pale yellow/green for bottles with wheel-cut decoration.

Decoration
A few bottles have horizontal bands of wheel-cutting or abrasion on the body.

Other features
There is wide variation in the size and capacity of these bottles, which held up to *c* 8 litres, and in the diameter of the neck and the dimensions of the body, which may be tall or short, and wide or narrow. Horizontal scratches are often present on the neck, marking the attachment point of the stopper, and vertical scratches are almost always present on the body, showing that the bottle was lifted in and out of a close-fitting wood or basketry container. The edges of the rim and base, and the widest point of the shoulder or upper body are sometimes very heavily worn. The lower surface of the base is almost always slightly dimpled The rims, necks, shoulders and handles are identical to those of one-handled prismatic bottles (see Figures 89–90).

Range of measurements
Rim diameters *c* 40–160mm+, heights *c* 150–400mm+, body diameters *c* 80–*c* 250mm+.

Distribution
Very common. Found in virtually all late 1st century settlements, and in some burials. Large examples sometimes re-used as cinerary urns.

Date range
AD 43 –110+ Particularly common in last quarter of 1st century, and went out of use rapidly in the early 2nd century.

Illustrated examples (Figure 88 and Plate 3.4)

a) *Stansted, Essex*: Fragmentary tall bottle with wide neck and body, from cremation burial 247 at the Duckend Carpark site, dated to first quarter of 2nd century.

b) *Stansted, Essex*: Fragmentary bottle with narrow neck and body, from the same cremation burial as a).

c) *Flint, Pentre Farm, Clwyd*: Short bottle, lacking rim and part of neck, with wide neck and body, horizontal wheel-cut and abraded bands on body (Price 1989b, 82 no 24 fig 30).

Other finds

Ashdon, Bartlow Hills, Essex: Two short, wide-necked bottles, one containing cremated bone and a coin of Hadrian, from Barrow 2 (Gage 1834, 7 pl 3 figs 5, 7).

Bayford-next-Sittingbourne, Kent: Short bottle with narrow neck and wide body, from cremation burial 4 (Payne 1893, 48 no 4 pl 12).

Caerleon, Gwent: Two almost complete bottles, one tall with narrow neck, one short with wide neck (Lee 1862, 48–9 pl 27 nos 1–2; Boon 1967, 95 fig 1).

Carlisle, Cumbria: Body, base and handle, short bottle with wide body, and numerous fragments, from Blackfriars Street (Price 1990a, 175, MF2: 76–7 nos 59a–d fig 163). At least two bottles with wide bodies, from Castle Street (Cool and Price 1991, 175–6 nos 681–2 fig 155).

Colchester, Essex: Short bottle with wide neck and body, from Taylor collection Grave 9/8, cremation burial dated AD 50–100 (May 1930, 292 pl 92). Fragments, at least three cylindrical bottles, including tall bottle with narrow neck, from late 1st century and later contexts; three body fragments, yellow/green with horizontal abraded bands, from contexts dated AD 60–80 and later (Cool and Price 1995, 191, 199 nos 1835, 2231–2, 2240 figs 11.7, 12–13).

Fishbourne Palace, West Sussex: Fragments, cylindrical bottles in 1st–3rd century contexts, the largest group dating from *c* AD 43–75 (Harden and Price 1971, 363 table II). Fragments, two bottles with wide bodies and horizontal wheel-cut lines, one from context containing Augustan-Flavian pottery (Price and Cottam 1996a, 184 nos 143–4 fig 6.31).

Inchtuthil, Tayside: Fragments, tall bottle with narrow neck and wide body, and fragments of five other bottles, from legionary fortress occupied *c* AD 83–6 (Price 1985a, 312 no 11 fig 94).

Newstead, Borders: Nearly complete tall bottle, from Flavian pit, and fragments (Curle 1911, 271–2 fig 36).

Old Newton, Suffolk: Short bottle with wide neck and body, containing cremation (Low 1907/9, 256 pl B).

Ribchester, Lancashire: Three hundred and forty-eight fragments, blue/green bottles, and part of yellow/green bottle with wide body and horizontal abraded bands, in 1st–early 2nd century contexts.

Richborough, Kent: Tall bottle with narrow neck, from pit filled before AD 85 (Bushe-Fox 1949, 158 no 371 pl 68).

Usk, Gwent: More than eighty fragments, blue/green bottles, and one yellow/green bottle with horizontal wheel-cut and abraded lines, from late Neronian/early Flavian deposits in legionary fortress and later contexts (Price 1995a, 185 nos 122–3 fig 48).

Verulamium, Hertfordshire: Two short bottles, one large with wide neck, one small with narrow neck, from Flavian cremation burial southwest of Silchester gate (Niblett and Reeves 1990, 443–4 fig 3 pl 59).

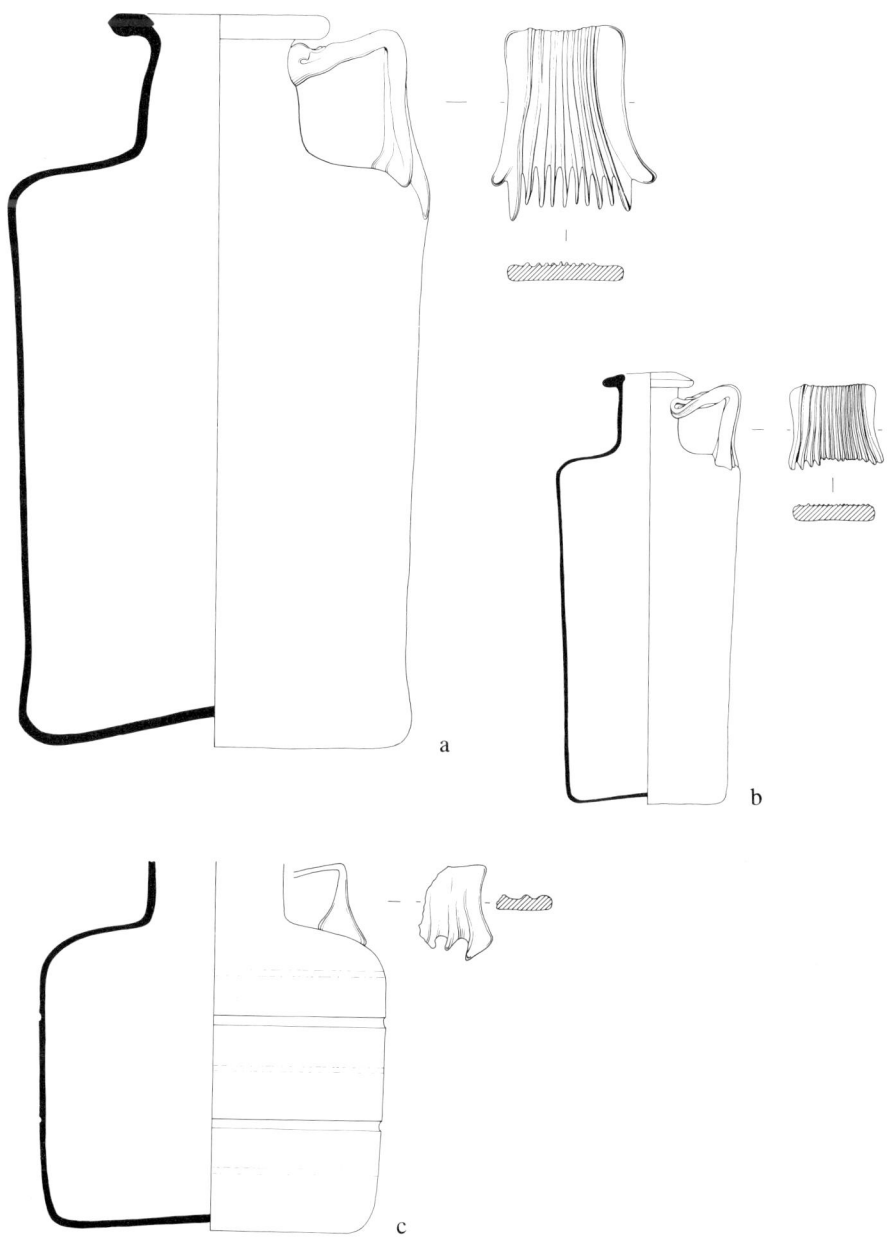

a

b

c

Fig 88   Scale 1:4

York: Large short bottle with wide neck, containing cremation, found on the Mount (Harden 1962, 136 H.G.53 pl 66).

Further reading
Isings 1957, form 51. See discussion in connection with Inchtuthil (Price 1985a, 307), and discussion of cylindrical and prismatic bottles in connection with finds from Colchester (Cool and Price 1995, 179–200).

Square bottle

Characteristics
Form
Folded rim, with horizontal or diagonal profile, edge bent out, up, in and flattened, cylindrical neck with tooling marks at base, horizontal shoulder, straight, square-sectioned body, flat or concave base. Angular ribbon handle applied to edge of shoulder and attached to neck below rim. Lower part of handle usually has narrow close-set vertical ribs (reeding), pulled into points on top of body. Handles with two broad ridges, or ribs in high relief, or plain ribbon handles, are also found.

Colours
Blue/green.

Decoration
Designs in relief are found on most bases. Concentric circles or other geometric motifs are very common, sometimes with lettering. Pictorial motifs are rare.

Other features
These bottles are generally made in good quality glass. Very bubbly, thin-walled bottles sometimes occur in 2nd century contexts. Wide variation occurs in the size and capacity of the body and in the diameter of the neck. The height of body to width of base ratio ranges from 1:1 to 3:1.
The body and base are almost always blown into a multi-part body mould with separate base piece. The rims, necks, shoulders and handles are identical to those of cylindrical and other prismatic bottles (see Figures 88, 90). The precise form of prismatic bottles is often very difficult to identify from small body or base fragments. The rims of Claudian/Neronian bottles are often narrow and triangular in section, and these early bottles sometimes have handles with two broad vertical ridges. Horizontal scratches are often present on the neck, marking the attachment of the stopper, and vertical scratches are almost always present on the body, showing that the bottle was lifted in and out of a close-fitting wood or basketry container. The edges of the rim and base and the widest point of shoulder are sometimes very heavily worn. An irregular indented area is sometimes found at the centre of each side on the lower body. Faint diagonal lines (presumably guidelines for planning the design) are sometimes visible on the base. A pontil mark is present on some bottles.

Range of measurements
Rim diameters 40–160+mm, heights 120–350+mm, body widths 50–150+mm.

Distribution

Very common. Fragments are found in virtually all later 1st and 2nd century settlements, often accounting for 30%–50% of glass assemblages in this period. The bottles are also found in burials; large examples were sometimes re-used as cinerary urns.

Date range

Long-lived form. *c* AD 43–end 2nd century. Very common from last quarter of the 1st century onwards

Illustrated examples (Figure 89 and Plate 3.4)

a) *London*: Fragmentary bottle with ten concentric circles on base, from pit containing mid Flavian pottery at St Swithins House, Middle Walbrook Valley (Price 1991a, 159 no 617 fig 115).

b) *Godmanchester, Cambridgeshire*: Fragmentary bottle with circle enclosing M A P on base, from cremation burial.

c) *Carrawburgh, Coventina's Well, Northumberland*: Tall narrow bottle with CCPC and two concentric circles on base (Allason-Jones and McKay 1985, 38 no 131 fig).

d) Bases from Aldborough, Carlisle, Catterick, Corbridge and Dover illustrate some further designs found in Britain.

Other finds

Alcester, Warwickshire: Nearly complete bottle with SAI and L-shaped corner supports, from pit dated AD150–160 (Price and Cottam 1994, 225 no 25, fig 105; RIB II,2 no 2419.144).

Ashdon, Bartlow Hills, Essex: Nine bottles in five barrows. Small bottle with narrow neck in Barrow 1. Large bottle with wide mouth containing cremation and two small bottles with narrow necks in Barrow 3. Large bottle with wide neck containing cremation and tall narrow bottle in Barrow 4. Large bottle with wide neck containing cremation and broken small bottle with narrow neck in Barrow 5. Large bottle with wide rim containing cremation in Barrow 7 (Gage 1834, 5, 8 pl 2 figs 2, 8–9; 1836, 305–6 pl 32 figs 1, 5; 1840, 2–3 nos 1, 6; Gage Rokewode 1842, 2–3 no 1; RIB II,2 no 2419.98).

Baldock, Hertfordshire: Bottle from cremation burial dated *c* AD 150 (Westell 1931, 279 group 102 no 6; Charlesworth 1966, 36 fig 1; RIB II,2 no 2419.125).

Barrow-on-Soar, Leicestershire: Large bottle containing cremation, mouth covered with lead sheet and contained in limestone cist, and two other bottles (Ellis 1874, 224–5 pl 2 fig 4).

Carlisle: Large bottle containing cremation, from Grey Street (Charlesworth 1959a, 37 no 1a pl 1b; RIB II,2 no 2419.124). Fragments, square/other prismatic bottles, from Blackfriars Street (Price 1990a, 175–7 fig 163 nos 60–67 MF2: 77–9). Fragments, square/other prismatic bottles, from Castle Street (Cool and Price 1991, 173–5 nos 669–79 figs 154–5).

Colchester, Essex: Fragments, many square/prismatic bottles, in 1st–2nd century and later contexts (Cool and Price 1995, 194,198–9 nos 2144–2220 figs 11.8–12).

Faversham, Kent: Bottle with narrow neck (Harden *et al* 1968, 56 no 67; RIB II,2 no 2419.127).

Harlow, Felmongers, Essex: Fragments, three bottles, including two small, thin-walled bubbly examples (Plate 3.5) from pit containing samian dated to *c* AD 160–70 (Price 1987a, 206 nos 33–4 fig 4; RIB II,2 no 2419.79).

London: Small bottle, handle with two ridges, from late 1st century cremation at Bishopgate (RCHM London 1928, 159 fig 65 no 32). Large bottles with wide necks,

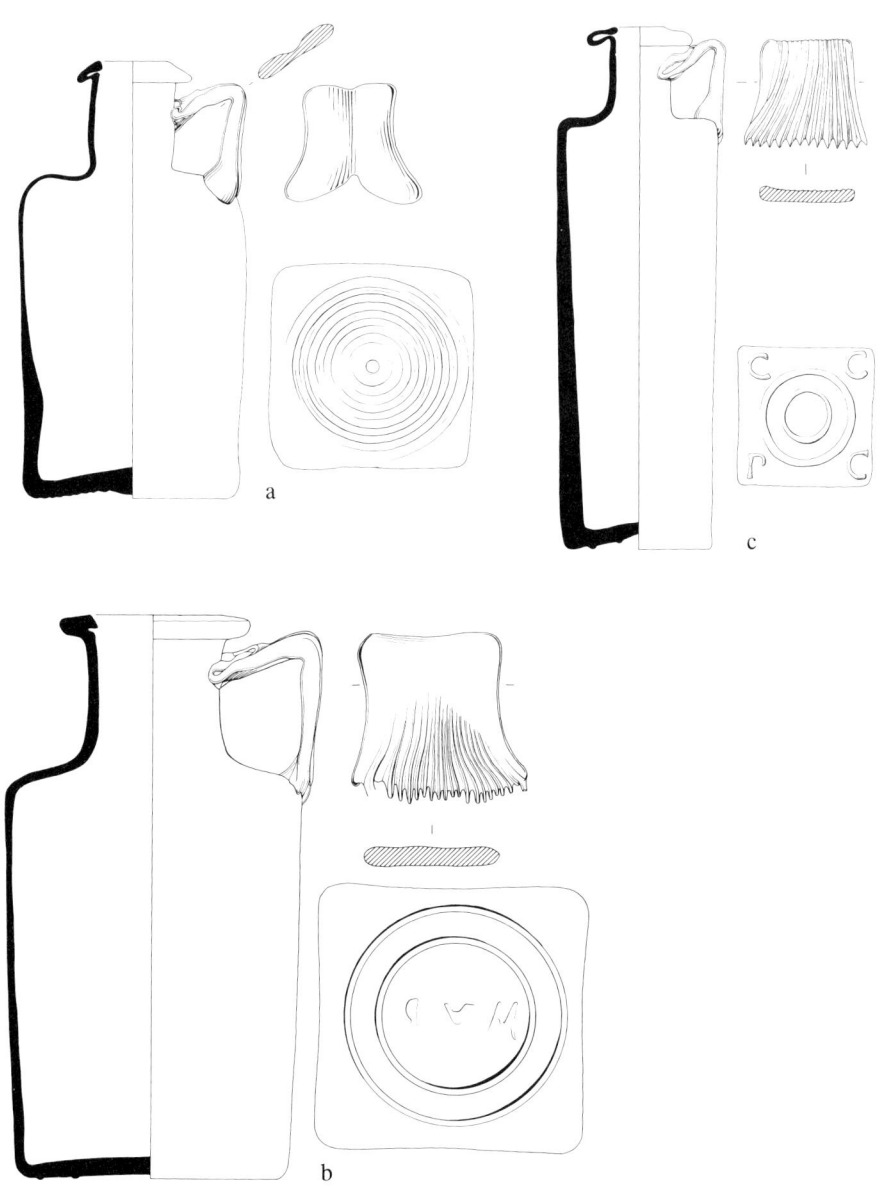

Fig 89 a–c   Scale 1:4

d

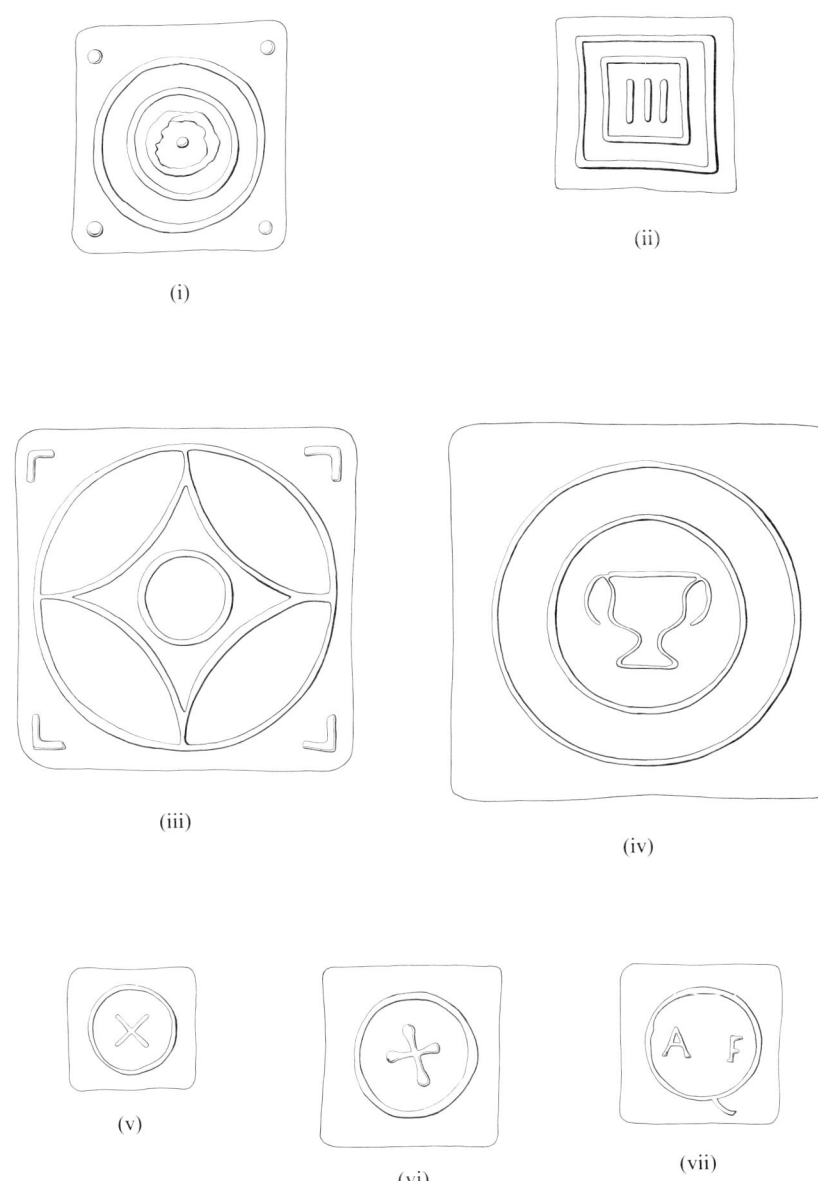

(i)

(ii)

(iii)

(iv)

(v)

(vi)

(vii)

Fig 89 d   Scale 1:3

197

from Moorfields, ? Blomfield Street and Milk Street, small bottles, one free-blown with flattened sides, without find spots, and fragments (Guildhall Museum 1908, 75–6 nos 22, 4–16 pl 7 nos 8, 10 pl 8 nos 8, 18-9; RIB II,2 no 2419.80).

Braughing, Skeleton Green, Hertfordshire: Fragmentary large bottle, lacking rim, neck and handle, and lower body and base of small bottle, from cremation burial 33 dated to mid-late 2nd century (Charlesworth 1981a, 270 B 33k-l figs 104 no 1 105 no 8).

Towcester, Northamptonshire: Fragmentary bottle, from pit dated *c* AD 155–65 at Park Street (Price 1980, 66, 68 no 16 fig 16; RIB II,2 no 2419.145).

Usk, Gwent: Fragments, small bottles (Plate 3.2), in late Neronian-early Flavian deposits in legionary fortress, and later contexts (Price 1995a, 185–91 nos 124–135 figs 48–9; RIB II,2 no 2419. 101, 146).

York: Tall, narrow bottle, from Trentholme Drive cemetery (Harden 1968c, 92 no 1 fig 35; RIB II, 2 no 2419.147).

Further reading
Isings 1957, form 50. Charlesworth 1966. See discussion of 1st–2nd century square, other prismatic and cylindrical bottles in connection with finds from Colchester (Cool and Price 1995, 179–199). Bases with inscriptions are recorded in RIB II, 2.

Hexagonal bottle

Characteristics
Form
Folded rim, with horizontal or diagonal profile, edge bent out, up, in and flattened, cylindrical neck with tooling marks at base, horizontal shoulder, straight, six-sided body, flat or concave base. Angular ribbon handle applied to edge of shoulder and attached to neck below rim. Lower part of handle usually has narrow close-set vertical ribs (reeding), pulled into points on top of body. Handles with two broad ridges, or ribs in high relief, or plain ribbon handles, are also found.

Colours
Blue/green.

Decoration
Designs in relief are found on most bases. Concentric circles or other geometric motifs are very common, sometimes with lettering. A few bottles have plain bases.

Other features
The body and base are almost always blown into a multi-part body mould with separate base piece. The rims, necks, shoulders and handles are identical to those of cylindrical and other prismatic bottles (see Figures 88, 89). The precise form of prismatic bottle is often very difficult to identify from small body or base fragments. Horizontal scratches are often present on the neck, marking the attachment point of the stopper, and vertical scratches are almost always present on the body, showing that the bottle was lifted in and out of a close-fitting wood or basketry container. The edges of the rim and base, and the widest point of the shoulder or upper body are sometimes very heavily worn.

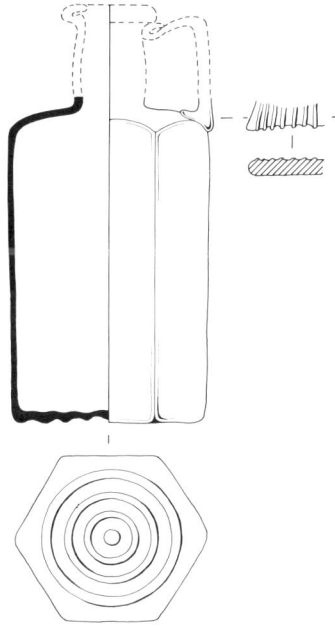

Fig 90   Scale 1:3

These bottles were generally made in good quality glass. Some small, bubbly, thin walled bottles are known.

Range of measurements
Rim diameters *c* 40–120+mm, heights *c* 100–275+mm.

Distribution
Quite common on settlements and in burials, though never as numerous as cylindrical and square bottles. Large bottles were sometimes re-used as cinerary urns.

Date range
Uncertain. In use from third quarter of 1st century–third quarter of 2nd century.

Illustrated example (Figure 90)
Corbridge, Northumberland: Fragmentary bottle, lacking rim, neck and part of handle, from pit in temple 3 area (information from Georgina Plowright).

Other finds
Alcester, Warwickshire: Almost complete base with letters in ring (RIB II, 2 no 2419.128). Base with three concentric circles and central dot, from pit dated *c* AD 150–60 (Price and Cottam 1994, 225 no 28 fig 105).

Barrow-on-Soar, Leicestershire: Large bottle, mouth covered with lead sheet, containing cremation (Ellis 1874, 224 pl 2 fig 1).

Cambridge: Bottle containing cremation, Roman cremation burial 2, dated to the second or third quarter of 2nd century in Girton College cemetery, (Liversidge 1977, 17 pl 3).

Castleford, West Yorkshire: Body and base fragments, large bottle with plain base, from late 1st–2nd century context in fort (Cool and Price 1998, 174 no 286 fig 61).

Colchester, Essex: Base fragments, three small bottles, from context dated late 1st–4th century (Cool and Price 1995, 194 nos 2141–3 fig 11.8). Large bottle containing cremation, inscription in ring on base (RIB II, 2 no 2419.86).

Huntingdon: Bottle with narrow neck, from inhumation burial containing coin of Hadrian at Three Nuns Bridge (Fitzwilliam 1978, 38 no 67c and fig).

London: Small bottle with circle and six triangular bosses on base, from burial in Mansell Street in the east cemetery (information from John Shepherd).

Ospringe, Kent: Small bottle, from inhumation burial 41 with late 2nd-early 3rd century pottery (Whiting 1926, 125 no 144 pl 16; Whiting *et al* 1931, pl 16 no 144).

Ribchester, Lancashire: Fragments, at least nine bottles, including one with undecorated base, from late 1st -early 2nd century contexts.

Stansted, Essex: Body and base with four concentric circles and central dot, from cremation burial 249 at the Duckend Carpark site, dated to second quarter of 2nd century.

Usk, Gwent: Fragments, bottles from late Neronian-early Flavian deposits in the legionary fortress, and later contexts (Price 1995a, 190 no 136 fig 49).

Verulamium, Hertfordshire: Bottle with narrow neck and circles on base, from Flavian cremation burial southwest of Silchester gate (Niblett and Reeves 1990, 444 fig 3 pl 59).

Walton-le-Dale, Lancashire: Body and base fragment, small, bubbly bottle, two circles on base (information from Chris Howard-Davis).

York: Small bottle with circle and six triangular bosses on base, from cremation burial in the Railway Cemetery dated to late 3rd–early 4th century, probably old when buried (Harden 1962, 137 H34c fig 88 pl 67).

Further reading
See discussion of 1st–2nd century prismatic and cylindrical bottles in connection with examples from Colchester (Cool and Price 1995, 179–199). Bases with inscriptions are recorded in RIB II, 2.

Rectangular bottle

Characteristics
Form
Horizontal folded rim, edge bent out, up, in and flattened, cylindrical upper neck, becoming oval towards shoulder, horizontal shoulder, straight, rectangular sectioned body (two long and two short sides), flat or concave base. Two angular ribbon handles, with reeding or broad ribs, applied to shoulder above the short sides and attached to neck below rim.

Colours
Blue/green.

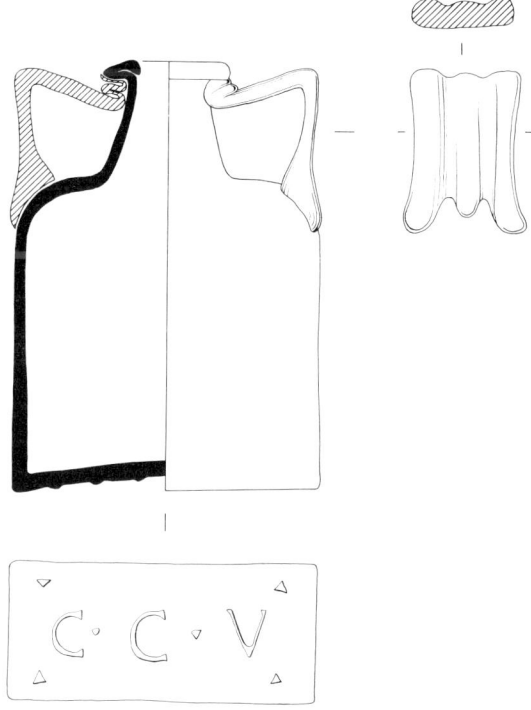

Fig 91   Scale 1:3

Decoration
Base designs include geometric and other motifs and lettering.

Other features
The body and base are blown into multi-piece mould. The rims, shoulders and handles are often identical to those of cylindrical and other prismatic bottles (see Figures 88–90). Some rectangular bottles have softer body angles than square bottles, but small fragments with 90 degree angles cannot be reliably allocated to a specific prismatic form. Patterns of scratching and wear are similar to cylindrical and other prismatic bottles.

Range of measurements
Rim diameters *c* 45–*c* 90+mm, heights *c* 150–250+mm, length of longest side *c* 80–*c* 200+mm

Distribution
Not very common. Found in some burials.

Date range
Uncertain. In use in second and third quarters of 2nd century.

Illustrated examples (Figure 91)

Colchester, Essex: Almost complete bottle, handles with three ribs, C C V and six triangular bosses on base, probably from West Lodge (Anon 1927, 65 pl 17; Thorpe 1935, pl 2a; RIB II,2 no 2419.96).

Other finds

Ashdon, Bartlow Hills, Essex: Two bottles. One from Barrow 4 has handles with three ribs, and two tulip-shaped motifs within rectangle on base. One from Barrow 5 has two reeded handles, and C and F flanking circle on base, both from burials dated to second–third quarters of 2nd century (Gage 1836, 306 no 11, pl 32 fig 4; Gage 1840, 3 no 5; RIB II, 2 no 2419.100).

Baldock, Hertfordshire: Bottle with reeded handles and cross on base, from cremation burial dated *c* AD150 (Westell 1931, 274 no 4818 fig 6).

Bearsden, Strathclyde: Body and base, bottle with rounded angles, and CN ASINI... MARTIAL.. in two lines on base, from Antonine Wall fort, occupied *c*AD 142–58 (RIB II, 2 no 2419.106).

Carlisle, Cumbria: Base fragment, with ∧∧ or VV within rectangle, from Blackfriars Street (Price 1990A, 177, MF 2: 78 no 68 fig 163; RIB II, 2 no 2419.142).

Carpow, Tayside: Body fragment; from late 2nd-early 3rd century pit.

Leicester: Body and base, bottle with C C V and triangular stops from Braunstone Gate (RIB II,2 no 2419.97).

London: Complete bottle with reeded handles, CCPC in corners, central circle and pontil mark on base, probably from Southwark (Wheeler 1930, 121 no 1 pl 53; Charlesworth 1966, 34 fig 15; RIB II,2 no 2419.95).

Further reading

Isings 1957, form 90. For discussion of 1st–2nd century prismatic and cylindrical bottles in connection with examples from Colchester, see Cool and Price 1995, 179–99.

Cylindrical bottle with funnel mouth and wheel-cutting

Characteristics

Form

Out-turned rim, narrow folded edge bent down, out and up, small funnel mouth, narrow cylindrical neck, horizontal shoulder, tall straight side tapering in slightly, flat or slightly concave base. Angular ribbon handle, either plain or reeded, applied to shoulder and attached to neck below rim.

Colours

Colourless, greenish colourless.

Decoration

Horizontal wheel-cut lines in bands on body. Ring of wheel-cut lines sometimes on underside of base.

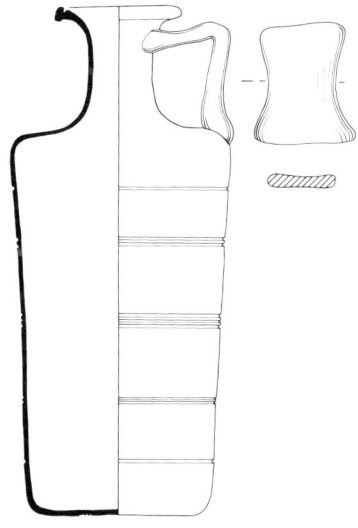

Fig 92   Scale 1:3

Other features
The good quality of the glass and the decoration distinguishes these from most other bottles and suggests that they were intended as table-ware. The bottles are often recognised by the rim and handle fragments. Small body fragments are often very similar to colourless cylindrical wheel-cut cups (for example, see Figure 34).

Range of measurements
Rim diameters *c* 50–*c* 75+mm, base diameters *c* 70–*c* 135mm, heights *c* 200mm.

Distribution
Quite common. At least one probably from burial.

Date range
Uncertain. In use in late 2nd -early 3rd century.

Illustrated example (Figure 92)
Hauxton, Cambridgeshire: Complete bottle, probably from cemetery in use in later 2nd to 3rd centuries (Harden 1958b, 12 no 2 fig 6 pl 3b).

Other finds
Caerwent, Gwent: Rim, body and base (Boon 1972/3, 112 no 3 fig 1).
Carlisle, Cumbria: Rim, neck, handle and upper body fragments, two bottles, one with plain, one with reeded handle (Charlesworth 1959a, 37 nos 2a-b figs 4–5).
Colchester, Essex: Rims, two bottles, from 2nd-late 4th century and post-Roman contexts (Cool and Price 1995, 200, nos 2243–4 fig 11.14).
Corbridge, Northumberland: Upper part of bottle, reeded handle (Charlesworth 1959c, 54 fig 10 no 1).

Fishbourne Palace, West Sussex: Shoulder, body and base fragments (Price and Cottam 1996a, 176 no 64 fig 6.28).

Leicester, Opera House Pit: Upper part of bottle, reeded handle.

Lullingstone villa, Kent: Fragments, at least two bottles (Cool and Price 1987a, 121, 132–4 nos 356–9 fig 55).

Snettisham, Norfolk: Fragments, shoulder, body and base, from site abandoned after 3rd century.

Winterton villa, Lincolnshire: Fragments, at least two bottles, one from 2nd century context (Charlesworth 1976a, 249 nos 14 & 28 fig 133–34).

Further reading
For discussion in connection with finds from Colchester, see Cool and Price 1995, 200.

Tall cylindrical bottle with funnel mouth and one or two handles

Characteristics
Form
Out-turned rim, edge fire-rounded or rolled-in, funnel mouth, cylindrical neck, horizontal or sloping shoulder, straight side tapering in slightly, concave base. One or two angular ribbon handles, applied to shoulder and attached to neck below rim. The handles are reeded or ribbed, or undecorated.

Colours
Greenish colourless, colourless, yellow/green, blue/green.

Decoration
Thick horizontal trail below rim edge. Some bottles have horizontal abraded bands on the body; at least one has unmarvered spiral trails.

Other features
Pontil mark on base. Small fragments are not very diagnostic Funnel mouths with trails are also found on late Roman jugs and flasks (see Figures 71–2, 84).

Range of measurements
Rim diameters *c* 50–80mm, heights *c* 150–250mm.

Distribution
Not very common. Some found in burials.

Date range
Uncertain. In use in late 3rd–4th centuries.

Illustrated example (Figure 93 and Back cover)
Colchester, Essex: Greenish colourless bottle with one handle, from grave 132 dated to second half of 4th century, probably *c* AD360–80 in Butt Road cemetery, (Cool and Price 1995, 203 no 2257 fig 11.15).

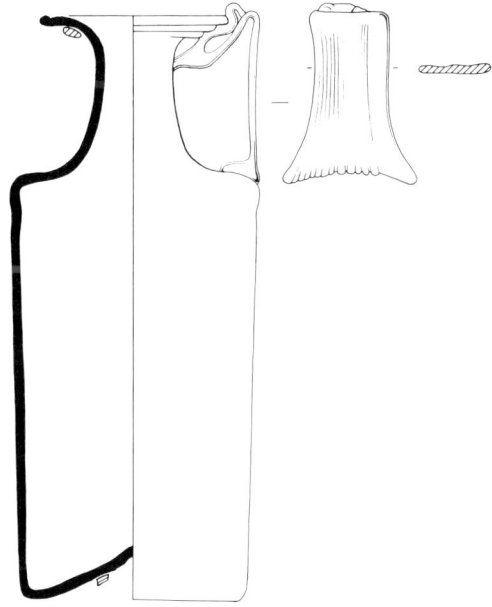

Fig 93   Scale 1:3

Other finds

Beadlam villa, north Yorkshire: Fragments, neck, shoulder, body, base, yellow/green bottle (Price & Cottam 1996, 106 no 60 fig 56).

Colchester, Essex: Fragments, colourless and blue/green bottles, from contexts dated AD150–50 and later (Cool and Price 1995, 201, 203 nos 2245, 2248, 2254–5 fig 11.15).

Dorchester-on-Thames, Oxfordshire: Two small yellow/green bottles with two handles, one with spiral trails on the upper and lower body, from deposit of glass, pottery and metal vessels dated to late 3rd–4th century (Harden 1939, 293; British Museum, Department of Prehistoric and Romano-British Antiquities; 67.7–25.1).

London: Lower body and base fragments, yellow/green bottle with horizontal abraded lines, from Mansell Street in the east cemetery (information from John Shepherd).

Sandy, Bedfordshire: Neck and handle fragments, yellow/green bottle with two handles.

Shakenoak villa, Oxfordshire: Fragments, colourless bottle with two reeded handles (Harden 1968a, 76 no 8 fig 26 no 6).

Winchester, Hampshire: Blue/green bottle with two handles from the fill of grave 398, dated *c* AD 370–90, in Lankhills cemetery (Harden 1979a, 219 no 549 fig 27).

Further reading

Isings 1957, form 126–127. For general discussion of these and other 4th–early 5th century vessels in Britain, see Cool 1995b. For discussion in connection with finds from Colchester, see Cool and Price 1995, 201–3.

Cylindrical bottle with two looped handles

Characteristics
Form
Vertical rim, edge cracked-off and ground, cylindrical neck, sometimes with constriction at base, horizontal or sloping shoulder, straight side tapering in, concave base. Two looped, dolphin-shaped, handles, applied to shoulder and neck.

Colours
Greenish colourless, colourless, yellow/green

Decoration
Horizontal abraded bands on neck and body.

Other features
Small fragments are not diagnostic, as many features are similar to other late Roman bottles, flasks and jugs. The handles were either applied to the shoulder and neck and then bent out and down to form a thin pointed ridge and a folded 'dolphin beak' on the edge of the shoulder (see Figures 94–5) or applied to the lower neck and shoulder and bent up and in to form a broad ring and a folded 'dolphin beak' at the top of the handle on the neck.

Range of measurements
Rim diameters *c* 15–25mm, heights *c* 160–210+mm.

Distribution
Quite common in settlements. Some from burials.

Date range
Uncertain. In use in later 3rd–third quarter of 4th century.

Illustrated example (Figure 94)
Lullingstone villa, Kent: Pale greenish colourless, almost complete bottle, from the temple-mausoleum, early 4th century (Cool and Price 1987a, 137–8 no 382 fig 56).

Other finds
Barnsley Park villa, Gloucestershire: Partly melted greenish handle, from context dated *c* AD 340–60 (Price 1982a, 182 no 37).
Cambridge: Small colourless bottle with abraded bands, from stone coffin at Gravel Hill Farm (Liversidge 1977, 16 pl 2; Fitzwilliam 1978, 41 no 80b and fig).
Cirencester, Gloucestershire: Upper part of bottle, greenish colourless (Shepherd 1986, 120 no 623 fig 86).
Frocester Court villa, Gloucestershire: Yellow/green, neck, shoulder and handle fragment (Price 1979, 44 no 42 fig 17).

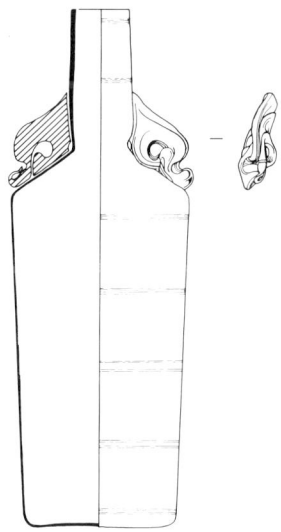

Fig 94   Scale 1:3

London: Two complete greenish colourless bottles, from burials at Haydon Road and West Tenter Street in the east cemetery, (information from John Shepherd).

Lullingstone villa, Kent: Two or three further examples from the temple-mausoleum, now lost (Cool and Price 1987a, 121).

Milton Keynes, Caldecotte, Buckinghamshire: Greenish colourless neck, shoulder and handle fragment, from modern pit fill at Berrystead Close (Price 1994, 135 no 158 fig 76).

Ospringe, Kent: Colourless, almost complete, from inhumation burial 141 (Whiting *et al* 1931, 59 no 448 pl 38).

Piercebridge, Co Durham: Greenish colourless, neck, shoulder and handle fragment.

Shakenoak villa, Oxfordshire: Green, rim, neck, handle and shoulder, and similar greenish and blue/green fragments, some from late 3rd–4th century contexts (Harden 1973, 104, nos 232–8 fig 52).

Thistleton villa, Rutlandshire: Colourless, neck, shoulder and handle fragment.

Winchester, Hampshire: Two complete greenish colourless bottles from graves 35 and 38 dated *c* AD310–50; handle, neck and shoulder, greenish colourless, from grave 337 dated *c* AD330–50, from Lankhills cemetery (Harden 1979a, 220 nos 20–1, 411 figs 27, 91).

York: Light green, almost complete, perhaps from Railway Station cemetery (Harden 1962, 141 H.G.182 fig 89). Fragments of three other light green and greenish colourless bottles (information from Hilary Cool).

Further reading
Isings 1957, form 100. See discussion of bottles with dolphin-handles in connection with finds from Colchester (Cool and Price 1995, 207–8).

Hexagonal bottle with two looped handles

Characteristics

Form
Vertical rim, edge cracked-off and ground smooth, cylindrical neck, narrow horizontal shoulder, straight, six-sided body, flat or concave base. Two looped, dolphin-shaped, handles applied to shoulder and neck.

Colours
Greenish colourless, colourless.

Decoration
Close-set, diagonal, optic-blown ribs on body.

Other features
The body is blown into a hexagonal mould. The rim, neck and handles of these bottles are identical with the cylindrical bottles (see Figure 94); the most diagnostic part is the body.

Range of measurements
Not known. No complete example has been noted in Britain.

Distribution
Not very common.

Date range
Uncertain. Probably in use in late 3rd–third quarter of 4th century AD.

Illustrated example (Figure 95)
Kölnerstrasse, Bonn: Complete bottle (Follmann-Schulz 1988, 49 no 139 taf 15).

Other finds
Barnsley Park villa, Gloucestershire: Body and base fragments, at least two pale greenish bottles, from contexts dated AD275–315 and later (Price 1982a, 183–4 nos 46–7 fig 60).
Beadlam villa, North Yorkshire: Body fragment, greenish colourless; and body fragment, pale green, without diagonal ribbing (Price and Cottam 1996b, 104 nos 27–28 fig 55).
Caister-on-Sea, Norfolk: Body and base fragments, at least two greenish colourless bottles (Price and Cool 1993, 147 nos 127–9 fig 132).
Canterbury, Kent: Greenish colourless body, from context dated AD350–375, at Marlowe Car Park (Shepherd 1995, 1244 no 406 fig 547).
Claydon Pike, Gloucestershire: Four body fragments, greenish colourless.
Colchester, Essex: Body fragment, greenish colourless, 4th century context (Cool and Price 1995, 208 no 2264 fig 11.18).
Dorchester, Dorset: Body fragment, greenish colourless, from Greyhound Yard (Cool and Price 1993, 167 no 159 fig 88).
Lincoln: Body fragments, one or two greenish colourless bottles, from Saltergate.

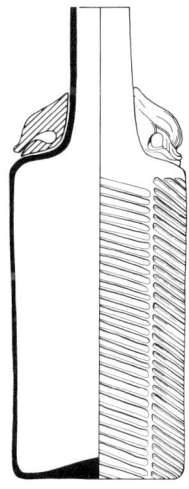

Fig 95 Scale 1:3

London: Body fragment, greenish colourless, from Southwark Street (Shepherd 1995b, 136 fig 41 no 2).
Winterton villa, Lincolnshire: Fragment, colourless, from 3rd century context.
York: Body fragment, greenish colourless, from the Minster site (Price 1995c, 352, 366 no 78 fig 145).

Further reading
For discussion in connection with finds from Colchester, see Cool and Price 1995, 207–8.

Cylindrical bottle with corrugated body
(Frontinus bottle)

Characteristics
Form
Out-turned rim, edge rolled-in, or folded out, up and in, cylindrical neck, horizontal shoulder, vertical side, concave base. One or two reeded or ribbed angular ribbon handles.

Colours
Pale green, yellow/green, greenish/colourless, blue/green.

Decoration
Horizontal corrugations in zones on upper and lower body. Design in low relief on base, usually consisting of concentric circles and letters. Many of these are abbreviations of the name Frontinus, although other names, such as Felix, also occur.

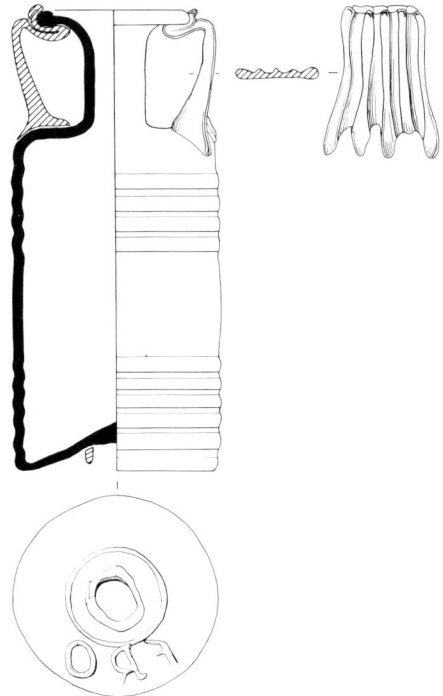

Fig 96   Scale 1:3

Other features

The body and base are blown into a three-part mould. Two vertical mould-seams are present on opposite sides of the body. The undecorated areas of the body are often slightly uneven. A pontil mark is frequently found on the base. The bottles of the 1st–2nd centuries are blue/green, and have folded rims and one reeded handle. Later bottles, which are mostly greenish and yellow/green, have rolled-in rims and one or two ribbed handles. The most diagnostic parts of these bottles are the corrugated body, the undecorated areas of the body with mould-seams and the base.

Range of measurements

Rim diameters *c* 60mm, heights *c* 100–220+mm, body diameters *c* 50–110 mm. Miniature bottles are uncommon.

Distribution

Fairly Common. Sometimes in burials.

Date range

A long-lived, or re-introduced, vessel type. Occasionally found in late 1st–early/2nd century contexts. Most common in the late 3rd–4th century.

Illustrated example (Figure 96, Plate 5.2 and Back cover)
Colchester, Essex: Complete pale yellow/green bottle with two handles, FRO (retrograde) outside small circle on base, from grave 174 dated to second half of 4th century, probably AD 360–80, in Butt Road cemetery (Cool and Price 1995, 206 no 2259 fig 11.17; RIB II,2 no 2419.117)

Other finds
Beadlam villa, North Yorkshire: Body fragments, at least two pale green and greenish colourless bottles (Price and Cottam 1996b, 104 nos 23–6 fig 55).
Birdoswald, Cumbria: Body fragment, blue/green bottle, from context dated *c* AD 290–350 (Price and Cottam 1997a, 353 no 76 fig 249).
Carrawburgh, Coventina's Well, Northumberland: Body fragment, greenish colourless (Allason-Jones & McKay 1985, 39 no 133 and fig).
Chichester, West Sussex: Fragments, blue/green base with letters ..R O.., from Cattle Market (Price and Cool 1989a, 135, 140 no CM56 fig 19.3; RIB II, 2, no 2419.175). Three body fragments, from Chilgrove villa 2 (Down 1979, 163 no 4 fig 56).
Colchester, Essex: Many tiny fragments, probably from colourless Frontinus bottle, in grave 620 dated to later than c AD 320, in Butt Road cemetery, and body fragments from greenish colourless and blue/green bottles, in 4th century contexts (Cool and Price 1995, 204, 206 nos 2260–62 fig 11.17).
Dorchester, Dorset: Fragment, blue/green base with letters ..F R.., from Greyhound Yard (Cool and Price 1993, 164 no 135 fig 87). Base with letters ..R O.. (retrograde), from Colliton Park (RIB II, 2, no 2418.166).
Faversham, Kent: Blue/green bottle, diagonal folded rim, one reeded handle, FELIX FECIT on base (Harden *et al.* 1968, 62 no 79).
London: Blue/green bottle with one handle, FRONT SEXTIN and one circle on base, from burial in Mansell Street in the east cemetery (Barber, Bowsher and Whittaker 1990, 9 pl 4a).
Milton-next-Sittingbourne, Kent: Bottle with two reeded handles, FRONI (also published as IBONI), two concentric circles and pontil mark on base, found outside lead coffin containing pipette-shaped unguent bottle (Payne 1874, 166–8 fig 2; Thorpe 1935, 6 pl 2b; RIB II, 2, no 2419.123).
Silchester, Hampshire: Base fragment with letters FRO (Boon 1974a, 130 fig 36 no 13; RIB II, 2, no 2419.116).
Towcester, Northamptonshire: Body and base fragments, pale green and greenish colourless bottles, including base with letters ..R O.., from contexts dated *c* AD 330–370+ in the Alchester Road Suburb site (Price and Cool 1983, 123–4 nos 57–60, fig 48; RIB II, 2, no 2419.116).
Uley, Gloucestershire: Body fragments, two yellow/green bottles, in very late 4th–early 5th century deposits at the shrine (Price 1993, 215 nos 6–7 fig 159).
Vindolanda, Northumberland: Lower body and base fragment, blue/green bottle (Price 1985c, 213 no 51 fig 78).
Winchester, Hampshire: Body fragments, blue/green and yellow/green bottles.

Further reading
Isings 1957, forms 89, 128. For discussion in connection with finds from Colchester, see Cool and Price 1995, 204–6. Bases with inscriptions are recorded in RIB II, 2.

Table of dated forms

CUPS & BOWLS

A.D.   50   100   150   200   250   300   350   400   450

CAST
Bowl, ribbed
Bowl, convex
Cup, constricted convex
Bowl, cylindrical
Cup, two handles
Bowl, base-ring
Bowl, wide rim and base-ring

MOULD-BLOWN
Bowl, hemispherical
Cup, ovoid
Cup, cylindrical
Beaker, conical

BLOWN
Cup, ribbed and trailed
Cup, stepped rim & stemmed foot
Cup, stepped rim & handle
Cup, convex, wheel-cut/abraded
Beaker, solid base, wheel-cut
Beaker, pushed-in base, wheel-cut
Shallow bowl, tubular rim
Deep bowl, tubular rim
Beaker, ground & facet/relief-cut
Beaker, arcaded
Beaker, concave base, indented
Cup, indented
Cup, domed base, wheel-cut
Beaker, shallow facet-cut

212

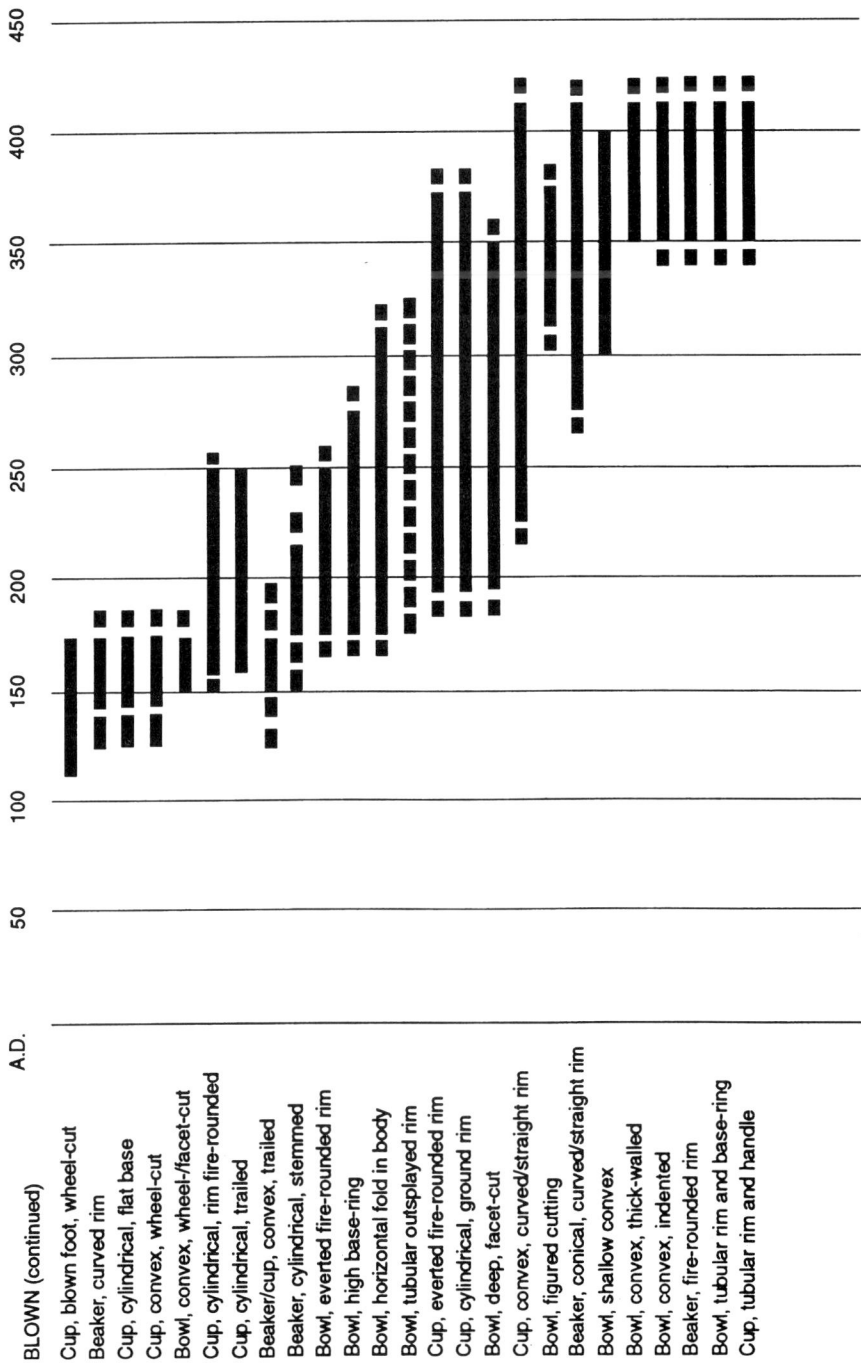

A.D.

BLOWN (continued)

Cup, blown foot, wheel-cut
Beaker, curved rim
Cup, cylindrical, flat base
Cup, convex, wheel-cut
Bowl, convex, wheel-/facet-cut
Cup, cylindrical, rim fire-rounded
Cup, cylindrical, trailed
Beaker/cup, convex, trailed
Beaker, cylindrical, stemmed
Bowl, everted fire-rounded rim
Bowl, high base-ring
Bowl, horizontal fold in body
Bowl, tubular outsplayed rim
Cup, everted fire-rounded rim
Cup, cylindrical, ground rim
Bowl, deep, facet-cut
Cup, convex, curved/straight rim
Bowl, figured cutting
Beaker, conical, curved/straight rim
Bowl, shallow convex
Bowl, convex, thick-walled
Bowl, convex, indented
Beaker, fire-rounded rim
Bowl, tubular rim and base-ring
Cup, tubular rim and handle

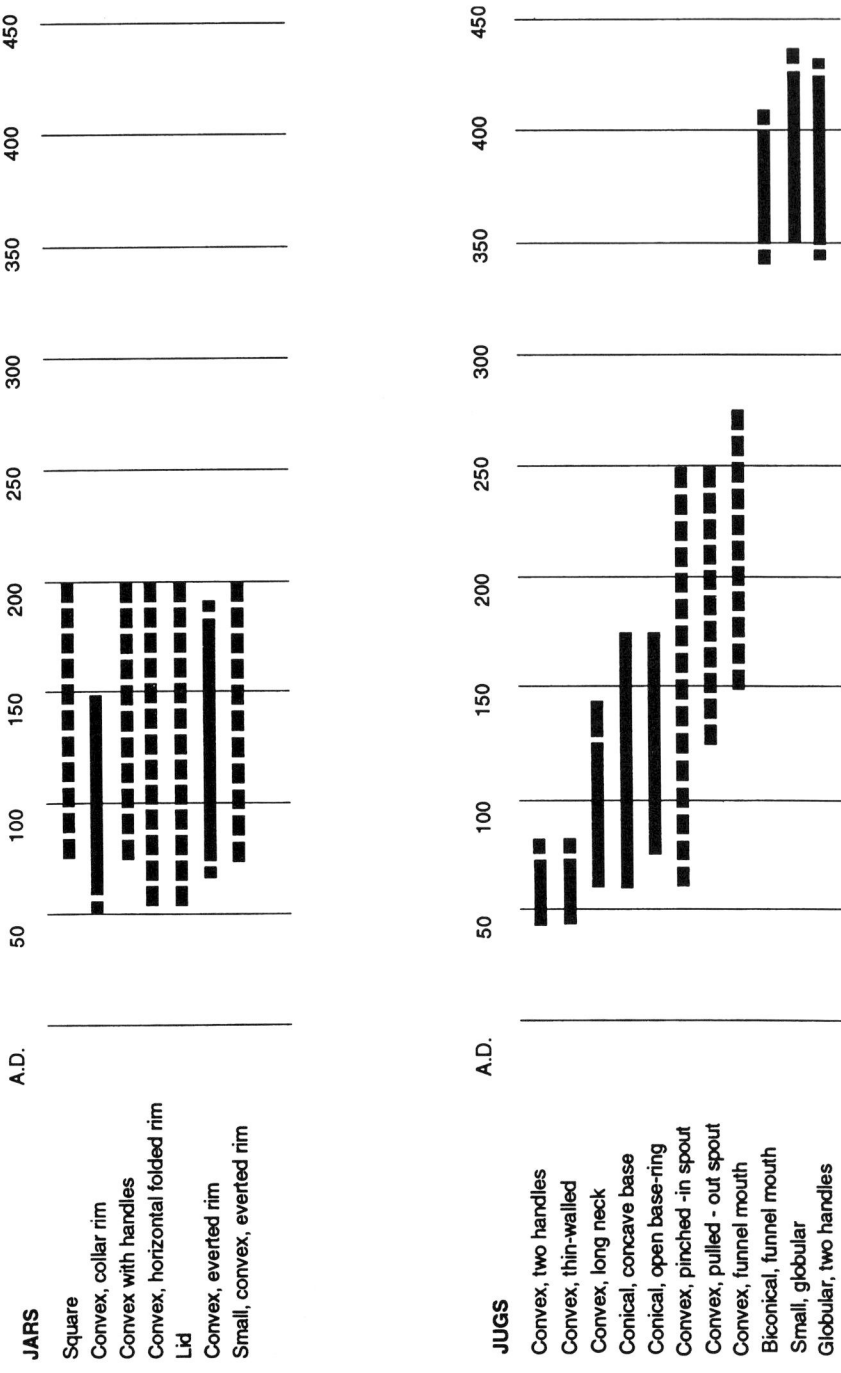

450   400   350   300   250   200   150   100   50   A.D.

JARS

Square
Convex, collar rim
Convex with handles
Convex, horizontal folded rim
Lid
Convex, everted rim
Small, convex, everted rim

450   400   350   300   250   200   150   100   50   A.D.

JUGS

Convex, two handles
Convex, thin-walled
Convex, long neck
Conical, concave base
Conical, open base-ring
Convex, pinched-in spout
Convex, pulled-out spout
Convex, funnel mouth
Biconical, funnel mouth
Small, globular
Globular, two handles

214

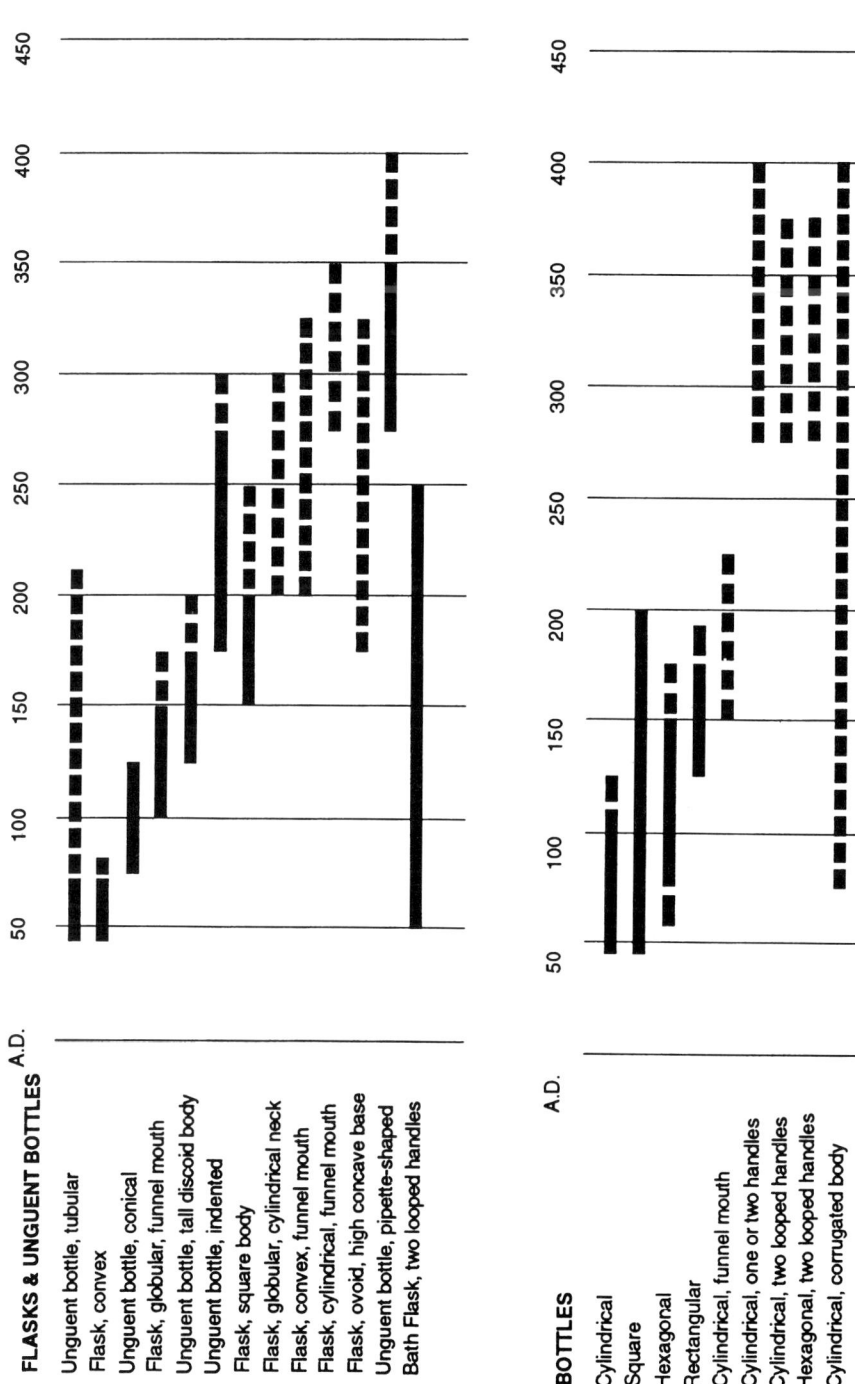

FLASKS & UNGUENT BOTTLES A.D.

Unguent bottle, tubular
Flask, convex
Unguent bottle, conical
Flask, globular, funnel mouth
Unguent bottle, tall discoid body
Unguent bottle, indented
Flask, square body
Flask, globular, cylindrical neck
Flask, convex, funnel mouth
Flask, cylindrical, funnel mouth
Flask, ovoid, high concave base
Unguent bottle, pipette-shaped
Bath Flask, two looped handles

BOTTLES A.D.

Cylindrical
Square
Hexagonal
Rectangular
Cylindrical, funnel mouth
Cylindrical, one or two handles
Cylindrical, two looped handles
Hexagonal, two looped handles
Cylindrical, corrugated body

Map of places mentioned in the text

Alphabetical list of places mentioned in the text

Bibliography

Allason-Jones, L, and McKay, B, 1985 *Coventina's Well: a Shrine on Hadrian's Wall.* Chesters Museum.

Allen, D, 1985 The Roman Glass, in Dool, J, *et al,* Roman Derby: Excavations 1968–1983. *Derbyshire Archaeol J,* **105**, 133–5.

Allen, D, 1986 The Glass Vessels, in Zienkiewicz J D, *The Legionary Fortress Baths at Caerleon, II. The Finds.* Cardiff, 98–116.

Allen, D, 1988 Roman Glass from Corbridge, in Bishop, M C, and Dore, J N, *Corbridge, Excavations of the Roman Fort and Town, 1947–1980. English Heritage Archaeol Rep* no **8**, 287–293.

Allen, D, 1989 The Roman glass, in Blockley, K, *Prestatyn 1984–5. BAR Brit Ser* **210**, 117–24.

Allen, D, 1991 The Glass, in Holbrook N, and Bidwell P T, *Roman Finds from Exeter. Exeter Archaeol Rep* **4**, 220–9.

Allen, D, 1992 The Glass, in Evans, D R, Metcalf, V M, *Roman Gates, Caerleon, Oxbow Monogr* **15**. Oxford, 179–185.

Allen, D, 1993 Roman Glass, in Casey, P J, Davies, J L, and Evans, J, *Excavations at Segontium (Caernarfon) Roman Fort, 1975–1979. CBA Res Rep* **90**, 219–228.

Allen, D, 1994 The glass, in Williams, R J and Zeepvat, R J, *Bancroft, a late Bronze Age/Iron Age settlement, Roman villa and temple-mausoleum. Buckinghamshire Archaeol Soc Monogr ser* **7**, 354–60.

Anon, 1927 Roman Glass with Initials. *Antiq J,* **7**, 65.

Atkinson, D, 1942 *Report on the Excavations at Wroxeter (the Roman City of Viroconium) in the County of Salop 1923–1927).* Birmingham Archaeol Soc.

Avent, R, and Howlett, T, 1980 Excavations at Roman Long Melford, 1970–1972, *Proc Suffolk Inst Archaeol and Hist,* **34**, 229–249.

Baddeley, W St C, 1904 The Painswick or Ifold Villa. *Trans of the Bristol and Gloucestershire Archaeol Soc,* **27**, 156–71.

Barber, B, Bowsher, D, and Whittaker, K, 1990 Recent Excavations of a Cemetery of Londinium. *Britannia* **21**, 1–12.

Biek, L, and Bayley, J, 1979 Glass and other Vitreous Materials. *World Archaeol,* **2 (1)** 1–25.

Bird, J, Graham, A H, Sheldon, H and Townend, P, (eds), 1978 *Southwark Excavations 1972–74. London & Middlesex Archaeol Soc and Surrey Archaeol Soc Joint Publ* No **1**.

Birley, E, 1937/8 Excavations at Birrens, 1936–1937. *Proc Soc Antiq Scotl,* **72**, 275–347.

Boon, G C, 1961 Roman Antiquities at Welshpool. *Antiq J,* **41**, 13–31.

Boon G C, 1967 Roman Glass in Wales. *Annales du 4e Congrès des "Journées Internationales du Verre" (Venice-Ravenna) 1967,* 93–102.

Boon, G C, 1972 *Isca – the Roman legionary Fortress at Caerleon,* National Museum of Wales.

Boon G C, 1972/3 Roman Glass from Caerwent, 1855–1925, *Monmouthshire Antiq,* **3**, ii, 111–123.

Boon, G C, 1974a *Silchester, the Roman Town of Calleva.* Newton Abbot & London.

Boon, G C, 1974b Caernarvon – Segontium. *Amgueddfa Bulletin of the Nat Mus of Wales*, **18**, 26–42.

Brailsford, J W, 1958 *Guide to the Antiquities of Roman Britain*. British Museum

Brown, P D C, 1968 Recent Museum Acquisitions. The Newport Pagnell Beaker (Ashmolean Museum, Oxford). *Burlington Mag*, **110**, 405.

Buckland, P C, 1986 *Roman South Yorkshire: A Source Book*. Department of Archaeology and Prehistory, University of Sheffield.

Buckman, P C, and Newmarsh, C H, 1850 *Illustrations of the remains of Roman Art in Cirencester, the site of Ancient Corinium*. London.

Bushe-Fox, J P, 1913 *Excavations on the Site of the Roman Town at Wroxeter, Shropshire 1912. Rep Res Comm Soc of Antiq of London*, **1**.

Bushe-Fox, J P, 1914 *Second Report on the Excavations on the Site of the Roman Town at Wroxeter, Shropshire 1913. Rep Res Comm Soc Antiq of London*, **2**.

Bushe-Fox, J P, 1916 *Third Report on the Excavations on the Site of the Roman Town at Wroxeter, Shropshire, 1914. Rep Res Comm Soc Antiq London*, **4**.

Bushe-Fox, J P, 1926 *First Report on the Excavation of the Roman Fort at Richborough, Kent. Rep Res Comm Soc Antiq London*, **6**.

Bushe-Fox, J P, 1928 *Second Report on the Excavation of the Roman Fort at Richborough, Kent. Rep Res Comm Soc Antiq London*, **7**.

Bushe-Fox, J P, 1932 *Third Report on the Excavations of the Roman Fort at Richborough, Kent. Rep Res Comm Soc Antiq London*, **10**.

Bushe-Fox, J P, 1949 *Fourth Report on the Excavations of the Roman Fort at Richborough, Kent. Rep Res Comm Soc Antiq London*, **16**.

Carter, J, 1796 Account of Sepulchral Monuments discovered at Lincoln. *Archaeologia*, **12**, 108–113.

Charlesworth, D, 1959a Roman Glass in the Tullie House Museum. *Trans Cumberland and Westmorland Antiq and Archaeol Soc, 2nd ser*, **59**, 32–40.

Charlesworth 1959b The Glass, in Daniels, C M, The Roman Bath-house at Red House, Beaufront, Nr. Corbridge. *Archaeol Aeliana*, 4th ser, **37**, 164–66.

Charlesworth, D, 1959c Roman Glass in Northern Britain. *Archaeol Aeliana*, 4th series, **37**, 33–58.

Charlesworth, D, 1966 Roman Square Bottles. *J Glass Stud*, **8**, 26–40.

Charlesworth, D, 1971a A Group of Vessels from the Commandant's House, Housesteads. *J Glass Studies*, **13**, 34–37.

Charlesworth, D, 1971b The Glass, in Rennie, D M, Excavations in the Parsonage Field, Cirencester, 1958. *Trans Bristol and Gloucestershire Archaeol Soc*, **90**, 84–8.

Charlesworth, D, 1972 The Glass, in Frere, S S, *Verulamium Excavations I*. Rep Res Comm Soc Antiq London, **28**, 196–215.

Charlesworth, D, 1974a The Glass, in Frere, S S, and St Joseph, J K, The Roman Fortress at Longthorpe. *Britannia* **5**, 88–90.

Charlesworth, D, 1974b The Roman Glass, in Down, A, *Chichester Excavations*, **2**. Chichester, 133–7.

Charlesworth, D, 1974c Glass Vessels, in Hassall M, and Rhodes J, Excavations at the New Market Hall, Gloucester 1966/7. *Trans Bristol and Gloucestershire Archaeol Soc*, **93**, 75–6.

Charlesworth, D, 1974/76a The glass from Northchurch Villa, in Neal 1974/76, 31–3.

Charlesworth, D, 1974/6b The glass bowl from the Roman building at Hemel Hempstead Station, in Neal 1974/76, 117.

Charlesworth, D, 1974/6c The glass from the cist graves at Box Lane Chapel, Boxmoor, in Neal 1974/76, 102.

Charlesworth, D, 1975a A Roman Cut Glass Plate from Wroxeter. *Antiq J*, 55, 404–6.

Charlesworth, D, 1975b The Commandant's House, Housesteads. *Archaeol Aeliana*, 5th series, 3, 17–42.

Charlesworth, D, 1975c The Glass, in Hobley, B, 'The Lunt' Roman fort and Training School for Roman Cavalry. *Trans Birmingham and Warwickshire Archaeol Soc*, 87, 38–40.

Charlesworth, D, 1976a Glass, in Stead, I M, *Excavations at Winterton Roman Villa and Other Roman Sites in North Lincolnshire, 1958–1967. Department Environment Archaeol Rep*, 9, 244–50.

Charlesworth, D, 1976b Glass Vessels, in MacGregor, A, *Finds from a Roman Sewer System and an Adjacent Building in Church Street. The Archaeology of York*, 17(1); 15–18. CBA for York Archaeol Trust.

Charlesworth, D, 1978a The Roman Glass, in Down, A, *Chichester Excavations*, **III**. Chichester Excavations Committee, 267–273

Charlesworth, D, 1978b The Glass Vessels, in MacGregor A, *Roman Finds from Skeldergate and Bishophill. The Archaeology of York*, 17 (2), 54–7. CBA for York Archaeol Trust.

Charlesworth, D, 1978c Roman Glass, in Collis, J, *Winchester Excavations, 1949–1960*. Winchester City Museum, 85.

Charlesworth, D, 1978–80 Glass, in MacIvor, I, Thomas, M C, Breeze, D J, Excavations on the Antonine Wall Fort of Rough Castle, Stirlingshire 1957–61. *Proc Soc Antiq Scotl*, 110, 268–9.

Charlesworth, D, 1979a Glass, in Bidwell, P T, *The Legionary Bath-house and Basilica and Forum at Exeter. Exeter Archaeol Rep* 1, 222–231.

Charlesworth, D, 1979b Glass, Beads and Armlets, in Potter, T W, *Romans in North West England. Cumberland and Westmorland Antiq and Archaeol Soc Res Ser*, 1, 230–234.

Charlesworth, D, 1979c Glass, in Hanson, W S, Daniels, C M, Dore, J N, and Gillam, J P, The Agricolan supply-base at Red House, Corbridge. *Archaeol Aeliana* 5th ser, 7, 58–61.

Charlesworth, D. 1980 Glass, in Stead, I M, *Rudston Roman Villa*. Yorkshire Archaeological Society, 84.

Charlesworth, D, 1981a Glass from the Burials in Partridge C, *Skeleton Green, A Late Iron Age and Romano-British Site*. Britannia Monogr Ser no 2, 268–71.

Charlesworth, D, 1981b The Roman Glass, in Down, A, *Chichester Excavations*, **5**. Phillimore, Chichester, 293–8.

Charlesworth, D, 1982 The Glass, in Wacher, J and McWhirr, A, *Early Roman Occupation at Cirencester. Cirencester Excavations* I, 106–107.

Charlesworth, D, 1984a The Glass, in Frere S S, *Verulamium Excavations III. Oxford University Committee for Archaeol Monogr* 1, 145–173.

Charlesworth, D, 1984b The Glass, in Frere, S S, Excavations at Dorchester-on-Thames 1962. *Archaeol J*, 141, 152–5.

Charlesworth, D, 1985a The Glass, in Niblett, R, *Sheepen: an Early Roman Industrial site at Camulodunum. CBA Res Rep* 57, MF 1:A5-A9, 3:F1-F11.

Charlesworth, D, 1985b Glass, in Draper, J, *Excavations by Mr H P Cooper on the Roman Site at Hill Farm, Gestingthorpe. East Anglian Archaeol Rep*, 25, 64–6.

Charlesworth D 1994 Glass. In Greenfield, E, *et al*, The excavation of a 4th-century villa and bath-house at Great Staughton, Cambs, 1958 and 1959. *Proc Cambridge Antiq Soc*, **83**, 101–3.

Charlesworth, D, and Price, J, 1987a The Roman and Saxon Glass, in Frere S S, Bennett, P, Rady, J, and Stow, S, *Canterbury Excavations: Intra- and Extra Mural Sites, 1949–55 and 1980–84. The Archaeology of Canterbury*, **8**, 220–31.

Charlesworth, D, and Price, J, 1992 The Glass Finds from the 1958 excavations, in Heywood, B, and Marvell, A G, Excavations at Neath, *Bull Board of Celtic Stud*, **29**, 196–99.

Christison, D, Buchanan, M, and Anderson, J, 1902/3 Excavations of Castlecary Fort on the Antonine Vallum. *Proc Soc Antiq Scotl*, **37**, 271–346.

Clifford, E M, 1933 The Roman Villa, Hucclecote, near Gloucester. *Trans Bristol and Gloucestershire Archaeol Soc*, **55**, 322–76.

Colchester Museum, 1869 *Catalogue of the Antiquities in the Colchester Museum* (2nd edition).

Cool, H E M, 1990 The Problem of 3rd Century Drinking Vessels in Britain, *Annales du 11e Congrès de l'Association Internationale pour l'Histoire du Verre* (Basel, 1988), 167–175.

Cool, H E M, 1992 The Vessel Glass, in Caruana, I, Carlisle, Excavation of a Section of the Annexe Ditch of the First Flavian Fort. *Britannia*, **23**, 63–8.

Cool, H E M, 1993 The Glass and Frit, in Hands, A R, *The Romano-British Roadside Settlement at Wilcote, Oxfordshire. I, Excavations 1990–92. BAR, British Series*, **232**, 158–163.

Cool, H E M, 1995a Glass Vessels from 9 Blake Street, in Cool, H E M, Lloyd-Morgan, G, and Hooley, A D, *Finds from the Fortress. The Archaeology of York. The Small Finds*, **17** (10), 1559–88. CBA for York Archaeol Trust.

Cool, H E M, 1995b Glass vessels of the fourth and early fifth century in Roman Britain, in Foy 1995, 11–23.

Cool, H E M, and Henderson, J, 1993 An Unusual Fourth-Century Bowl from Dorchester, Dorset, England. *J Glass Studies*, **35**, 145–149.

Cool, H E M, and Price, J, 1987a The Glass, in Meates, G W, *The Lullingstone Roman Villa, Volume II – The Wall Paintings and Finds,* 110–142.

Cool, H E M, and Price, J, 1987b The Roman Glass, in Ellis, P, Sea Mills, Bristol: the 1965–1968 Excavations in the Roman Town of Abonae. *Trans Bristol and Gloucestershire Archaeol Soc*, **105**, 92–9.

Cool, H E M, and Price, J, 1988 Glass, in Darling, M J and Jones, M J, Early Settlement in Lincoln. *Britannia*, **19**, 42–3.

Cool, H E M, and Price, J, 1989 The Glass Vessels, in Britnall J, Caersws Vicus, Powys, *Excavations at the Old Primary School, 1985–86. BAR, British Series*, **205**, 31–43.

Cool, H E M, and Price, J, 1991 The Roman Vessel and Window Glass, in McCarthy M, *Roman Waterlogged Remains at Castle Street, Carlisle. Cumberland and Westmorland Antiq and Archaeol Soc Res Ser*, **5**, 165–176.

Cool, H E M, and Price, J, 1993 Roman Glass, in Woodward, P J, Davies, S M, and Graham, A H, *Excavations at the Old Methodist Chapel and Greyhound Yard, Dorchester. Dorset Nat Hist and Archaeol Soc Monogr Ser*, **12**, 150–167.

Cool H E M, and Price, J, 1993/4 The Glass Vessels, in Booth, P, A Roman Burial near Welford-on-Avon, Warwickshire. *Trans Birmingham and Warwickshire Archaeol Soc*, **98**, 45–7.

Cool, H E M and Price, J 1995 *Roman Vessel Glass from Excavations in Colchester, 1971–85. Colchester Archaeol Rep* **8**.

Cool, H E M and Price, J, 1998 The vessel glass, in Cool, H E M and Philo, C, eds, *Roman Castleford, excavations 1974–85. Volume I – the small finds*. Yorkshire Archaeology 4, 141–81.

Cummings, K, 1980 *The Technique of Glass Forming*. Batsford.

Cunliffe, B, 1988 *Mount Batten, Plymouth, A Prehistoric and Roman Port. Oxford Univ Com for Archaeol, Monogr* **26**.

Curle, J, 1911 *A Roman Frontier Post and its People: the Fort of Newstead in the Parish of Melrose*. Glasgow.

Curle, J 1931–32 An inventory of objects of Roman and provincial Roman origin found on sites in Scotland not definitely associated with Roman constructions. *Proc Soc Antiq Scot*, **66**, 277–397.

Davies, D G, and Saunders, C, 1986 *Verulamium*. Heritage, Tourism and Publicity Sub-Committee, St Albans.

Dore, M P, 1927/8 The Cemeteries of Roman Leicester. *Trans of the Leicestershire Archaeol Soc*, **15**, 34–57.

Down, A, 1979 *The Roman Villas at Chilgrove and Upmarden. Chichester Excavations*, **4**. Chichester Civic Society Excavations Committee.

Down, A, and Rule, M, 1971 *Chichester Excavations 1*. Chichester Civic Society Excavations Committee.

Dryden, H 1840/46 Roman and Romano-British remains at and near Shefford, Co Beds. *Publ of the Cambridge Antiq Soc* **1**, 1–24.

Dudley, C, 1981 A re-appraisal of the evidence for a Roman villa in Springfield Road, Brighton, following further discoveries on the site, in Kelly, E and Dudley, C, Two Romano-British Burials, *Sussex Archaeological Collections*, **119**, 65–88.

Ecroyd Smith, H, 1852 *Reliquiae Isurianae: the Remains of the Roman Isurium (now Aldborough, near Boroughbridge, Yorkshire)*. London.

Ellis, A, 1874 Discovery of Roman remains at Barrow-on-Soar. Trans of the Leicestershire Architec and Archaeol Soc, **3**, 222–6.

Fitzwilliam 1978 *Glass at the Fitzwilliam Museum*. Cambridge University Press

Follmann-Schulz, A-B, 1988 *Die römischen Gläser aus Bonn. Beihefte der Bonner Jahrbucher*, **46**. Bonn.

Fox, C, 1923 *The Archaeology of the Cambridge Region*. Cambridge University Press

Foy, D, ed., 1995 *Le Verre de l'Antiquité Tardive et du Haut Moyen Age. Typologie-Chronologie-Diffusion. Association Française pour l'Archéologie du Verre*. Musée Archéologique Departmentale du Val d'Oise.

Foy, D and Sennequier, G, 1989 *A Travers le Verre, du Moyen Age à la Renaissance*. Rouen.

Fremersdorf, F, 1959 *Römische Gläser mit Fadenauflage in Köln (Schlangen-fadenglaser und Verwandtes). Die Denkmaler des römischen Köln*, **VI**. Köln.

Fremersdorf, F, 1967 *Die römischen Gläser mit Schliff, Bemalung und Goldauflegen aus Köln. Die Denkmaler des römischen Köln* **VIII**. Koln.

Frend, W H C, 1968 A Roman Farm Settlement at Godmanchester. *Procs of the Cambridge Antiq Soc*, **61**, 19–43.

Gage, J, 1834 A plan of barrows called the Bartlow Hills, in the parish of Ashdon, in Essex, with an account of Roman sepulchral relics recently discovered in the Lesser Barrows. *Archaeologia*, **25**, 1–23.

Gage, J, 1836 Recent discovery of Roman sepulchural relics in one of the greater barrows at Bartlow, in the parish of Ashdon, in Essex. *Archaeologia* **26**, 300–17.

Gage, J, 1840 An account of further discoveries of Roman sepulchral relics at the Bartlow Hills. *Archaeologia*, **28**, 1–6.

Gage, J, 1842 An account of the final excavations made at the Bartlow Hills. *Archaeologia*, **29**, 1–4.

Girton, J F, 1838 Roman antiquities found at Hemel Hempstead. *Archaeologia* **27**, 434–5.

Goldney, F B, 1899/1901 Antiquities of the Roman period found near Canterbury. *Proc Soc Antiq London*, 2nd ser, **18**, 279–80.

Grose, D F, 1991 Early Imperial Roman Cast Glass: the translucent coloured and colourless fine wares, in Newby, M, and Painter, K.

Grose, D F, 1997 Glass vessels and objects, in Hostetter, E, and Howe, T N, eds, *The Romano-British villa at Castle Copse, Great Bedwyn*. Indiana Univ Press, 298–305.

Gudenrath, W, 1991 Techniques of Glassmaking and Decoration, in Tait, H, *Five Thousand Years of Glass*. British Museum, London, 213–241.

Guildhall Museum, 1908 *Catalogue of the collection of London antiquities in the Guildhall Museum (2nd edition)*. London.

Haevernick, T E, 1981 *Beitrage zur Glasforschung. Die wichtigsten Aufsatze von 1938 bis 1981*. Mainz, von Zabern.

Harcourt, L V, 1846 Vessels of Glass and Earthenware and Ornaments discovered near Chilgrove in Sussex. *Archaeologia*, **31**, 312–7.

Harden, D B, 1936 The Glass, in Radford, C A R, The Roman Villa at Ditchley, Oxfordshire. *Oxoniensia*, **1**, 62–4

Harden, D B 1939 Romano-British Remains, B.Roads; C.Settlement Sites; D.Industries, in *Oxfordshire, 1. The Victoria History of the Counties of England*, 271–305.

Harden, D B, 1945 Glass, in O'Neil, H E, The Roman Villa at Park Street, near St. Albans, Hertfordshire: Report on the Excavations of 1943–45. *Archaeol J*, **102**, 68–72.

Harden, D B, 1947 The Glass, in Hawkes, C F C, and Hull, M R, *Camulodunum, First Report on the Excavations at Colchester 1930–1939. Rep Res Com Soc Antiq London*, **14**, 287–307.

Harden, D B, 1949 Glass, in Webster, G, The Legionary Fortress at Lincoln. *J Roman Stud*, **39**, 77.

Harden, D B, 1951 Saxon Glass from Sussex. *Sussex County Mag*, **25**, 260–68.

Harden, D B, 1952 Glass, in Fox, A, *Roman Exeter*, 93.

Harden, D B, 1956 Glass vessels in Britain, AD 400–100, in Harden, D B (ed) *Dark Age Britain*. London, 132–67.

Harden, D B, 1958a Glass, in Hull, M R, *Roman Colchester. Rep Res Com Soc Antiq London*, 20, 157–8.

Harden, D B, 1958b Four Roman glasses from Hauxton Mill Cambridge, 1870, in Liversidge, J, Roman Discoveries from Hauxton. *Proc Cambridge Antiq Soc*, **51**, 12–16.

Harden, D B, 1960a The Wint Hill hunting bowl and related glasses. *J Glass Stud*, **2**, 44–81.

Harden, D B, 1960b Glass, in Webster, G, The discovery of a Roman fort at Waddon Hill, Stoke Abbott, 1959. *Proc Dorset Nat Hist and Archaeol Soc*, **82**, 95

Harden, D B, 1961 Glass, in Clifford, E M, *Bagendon: A Belgic Oppidum*, 199–201.

Harden, D B, 1962 Glass in Roman York, in *Eburacum, An Inventory of the Historical Monuments in the City of York, 1. Royal Comm on the Hist Monuments of Eng Inventories*. H M S O, 136–41.

Harden, D B, 1967 The Glass Jug, in Biddle M, Two Flavian Burials from Winchester. *Antiq J*, **47**, 238–40.

Harden, D B, 1968a Glass, in Brodribb A C C, Hands, A R, and Walker D R, *Excavations at Shakenoak Farm near Wilcote, Oxfordshire*, **1**. Privately printed, 74–81.

Harden, D B, 1968b Roman Glass from Huntingdon and Rapsley, Surrey. *Antiq J*, **48**, 308.

Harden, D B, 1968c Glass, in Wenham, L P, *The Romano-British Cemetery at Trentholme Drive, York. Department Environment Archaeol Rep*, **5**, 92–3.

Harden D B 1969 Ancient Glass, II: Roman. *Archaeol J* **126**; 44–77.

Harden, D B, 1971 Glass, in Brodribb A C C, Hands, A R, and Walker D R, *Excavations at Shakenoak Farm near Wilcote, Oxfordshire*, **2**. Privately printed, 98–108.

Harden, D B, 1973 Glass, in Brodribb A C C, Hands, A R, and Walker D R, *Excavations at Shakenoak Farm near Wilcote, Oxfordshire*, **4**. Privately printed, 98–107.

Harden, D B, 1975 The Glass, in Cunliffe B, *Excavations at Porchester Castle I, Roman. Rep Res Comm Soc Antiq London*, **32**, 368–74.

Harden, D B, 1977 Report on the Glass Bowl, in Partridge, C, Excavations and Fieldwork at Braughing, 1968–73. *Hertfordshire Archaeol*, **5**, 102.

Harden, D B, 1978a Glass 'Sports cup' from Topping's and Sun wharves, in Bird *et al* (eds) 1978, 605–7.

Harden, D B, 1978b Glass, in Brodribb, A C C, Hands, A R, and Walker D R, *Excavations at Shakenoak Farm near Wilcote, Oxfordshire*, **5**. Privately printed, 88–94.

Harden, D B, 1979a Glass Vessels, in Clarke G, *The Roman Cemetery at Lankhills. Winchester Stud, 3: Pre-Roman and Roman Winchester, Part 2*. Oxford, 209–220.

Harden, D B, 1979b Glass, in Webster, G, Final Report on the Excavations of the Roman Fort at Waddon Hill, Stoke Abbott, 1963–69. *Proc Dorset Nat Hist and Archaeol Soc*, **101**, 87–8.

Harden, D B, 1979c Glass, in Boddington, A, Excavations at 48–50 Cannon Street, City of London, 1975. *Trans London & Middlesex Archaeol Soc*, **30**, 20–22.

Harden, D B, 1982 New Light on Mold-Blown Glass Sports Cups of the First Century AD bearing both Chariot Races in Bigae and Gladiatorial Combats. *J Glass Stud*, **24**, 30–43.

Harden, D B, 1983 The Glass Hoard, in Johnson S, *Burgh Castle, Excavation by Charles Green 1958–1961,.East Anglia Archaeol Rep*, **20**, 78–89.

Harden, D B, and Green, C, 1978 A Late Roman Grave-Group from the Minories, Aldgate, in Bird, J, Chapman, H and Clark, J, (eds) *Collectanea Londiniensia*, 163–175.

Harden, D B, and Price, J, 1971 The Glass, in Cunliffe B W, *Excavations at Fishbourne 1961–1969. Vol 2, The Finds. Rep Res Comm Soc Antiq London*, **27**, 317–368.

Harden *et al* 1968, Harden, D B, Painter K, Pinder-Wilson R and Tait, H. *Masterpieces of Glass*. British Museum.

Harden *et al* 1987, Harden, D B, Hellenkemper, H, Painter, K and Whitehouse, D, *Glass of the Caesars*. Milan, Olivetti.

Haverfield F and Taylor M V 1908 Romano-British Shropshire, in *Shropshire, I. The Victoria History of the Counties of England*, 205–78.

Hazzledine Warren, S, 1915 The Opening of the Romano-British Barrow on Mersea Island. *Trans Essex Archaeol Soc new ser*, **13**, 116–39.

Henderson, J, 1985 The Raw Materials of Early Glass Production, *Oxford J Archaeol*, **4** (3), 267–91.

Henslow, J S, 1843 *An account of the Roman antiquities found at Rougham near Bury St Edmunds on 15th September 1843*. Bury St Edmunds, Gedge and Barker.

Hochuli-Gysel, A, 1993 Römisches Glas aus dem Südwesten von Frankreich. *Annales du 12e Congrès de l'Association Internationale pour l'Histoire du Verre* (Vienna 1991), 79–88.

Hull, M R 1930A Roman stone coffin found at Rainham. *The Colchester and Essex Museums Annual Report for* 1929, 28–9.

Hull, M R, 1958 *Roman Colchester. Rep Res Comm Soc Antiq London,* **20**.

Hull, M R, 1963 *The Roman Potters' Kilns of Colchester. Rep Res Comm Soc Antiq London,* **21**.

Hunter, J.R. and Jackson, C.M., 1993 Glass, in Rodgers, NSH, *Anglian and other finds from Fishergate. The Archaeology of York. The Small Finds,* 17(9), 1331–44.

Isings, C, 1957 *Roman Glass from Dated Finds,* Groningen.

Isings, C, 1980 Glass from the Canabae Legionis at Nijmegen, *Berichten van de Rijkdienstvoor het Oudheidkundig Bodemonderzoek,* **30**, 281–346.

Johnston D.E. 1974 The Roman settlement at Sandy, Bedfordshire. *Bedfordshire Archaeol J,* **9**, 35–54.

Jones, C E E, 1986 Roman Glass, in Whytehead, R, The Excavation of an Area Within a Roman Cemetery at West Tenter Street, London E1. *Trans London and Middlesex Archaeol Soc,* **37**, 86–8.

Kennett, D H, 1970 The Shefford Burial. *Bedfordshire Mag,* **12**, 201–3.

Kempe, A J, 1836 Sepulchural remains found at Litlington, near Royston, Cambridgeshire. *Archaeologia* **26**, 368–76.

Kern, J H C, 1963 *Römische Modioli des 1 Jahrhunderts n.Chr Mnemosyne* **16**, 400–5.

Kindersley, G M, 1922 Roman Remains at Welwyn. *Antiq J,* **2**, 22–6.

Koster, A, and Whitehouse, D, 1989 Early Roman Cage Cups, *J Glass Stud,* **31**, 25–33.

Lee, J, 1862 *Isca Silurum, an illustrated catalogue of the Museum of Antiquities at Caerleon.* London.

Lightfoot, C, 1988 Report on the Fragment of Cameo Glass, in Hinton, P, ed., *Excavations in Southwark 1973–6, Lambeth 1973–9. London and Middlesex Archaeol Soc and Surrey Archaeol Soc Joint Rep* **3**, 374–8.

Liversidge, J, 1977 Roman Burials in the Cambridge Area. *Proc Cambridge Antiq Soc,* **67**, 11–38.

Low, C W, 1907/9 An Account of the Discovery of Roman Remains at Old Newton. *Proc Suffolk Institute of Archaeol and Nat Hist,* **13**, 255–59.

Lysons, S 1792 Roman antiquities discovered in the county of Gloucester. *Archaeologia* **10**, 131–6.

Maxwell, G, 1974 Objects of Glass 1974, in Rae, A & V, The Roman Fort at Cramond, Edinburgh. Excavations 1954–1966. *Britannia* **5**, 177–9.

May, T, 1930 *Catalogue of the Roman Pottery in the Colchester and Essex Museum.* Cambridge.

Monckton, A, 1979 Romano-British Site at Lower Runhams, Lenham. *Kent Archaeol Rev,* **55**, 118–121.

Montagu-Benton, G, 1926 Roman Burial Group Discovered at West Mersea. *Trans Essex Archaeol Soc, new ser,* **17**, 128–30.

Nash-Williams, V E, 1929 The Roman Legionary Fortress at Caerleon in Monmouthshire. Report on the Excavations carried out in 1926. *Archaeol Cambrensis* **84**, 237–307.

Naumann-Steckner, F, 1991 Depictions of Glass in Roman Wall Paintings, in Newby, M, and Painter, K, (eds), *Roman Glass: Two Centuries of Art and Invention. Soc Antiq London, Occ Papers*, **13**, 86–98.

Neal, D S, 1974/76 Northchurch, Boxmoor and Hemel Hempstead Station: The Excavation of three Roman Buildings in the Bulborne Valley. *Hertfordshire Archaeol* **4**, 1–135.

Neal, D S, Wardle A, Hunn, J, 1990 *The Excavation of the Iron Age, Roman and Medieval Site at Gorhambury, St Albans. Engl Heritage Archaeol Rep*, **14**.

Neville, R C, 1855 Notices of certain shafts containing remains of the Roman period at the Roman station at Chesterford, Essex. *Archaeol J*, **12**, 109–25.

Newby, M and Painter, K (eds) *Roman Glass: Two Centuries of Art and Invention. Soc Antiq London, Occ Papers*, **13**, 1–18.

Newstead, R, 1914 The Roman Cemetery in the Infirmary Field, Chester. *Annals of Archaeol and Anthrop*, **6**, 121–167.

Niblett, R and Reeves, P, 1990 A Wealthy Early Roman Cremation from Verulamium. *Antiq J*, **70**, 441–446.

Oliver, A, 1984 Early Roman Faceted Glass. *J Glass Studies*, **26**, 35–63.

Page, W and Keate Miss, 1907 Romano-British Leicestershire, in *Leicestershire, 1. Victoria History of the Counties of England*, 179–219.

Payne, G, 1874 Roman Coffins of Lead from Bex Hill, Milton-next -Sittingbourne. *Archaeol Cantiana*, 9, 164–173.

Payne, G, 1886 Romano-British interments dscovered at Bayford-next-Sittingbourne, Kent. *Archaeol Cantiana*, **16**, 1–8.

Payne, G, 1893 *Collectanea Cantiana, or Archaeological Researches in the Neighbourhood of Sittingbourne and Other Parts of Kent*. London.

Petch, J A, 1954 The Roman Defences of Roman Manchester. *Trans Lancashire and Cheshire Archaeol Soc*, **62**, 177–95.

Price, J, 1974 The Glass, in Jones G D B and Grealey, S, *Roman Manchester*, 131–4.

Price, J, 1975 The Glass Vessels from the Cremation Groups, in Johnson, A E, Excavations at Bourton Gardens, Thornborough 1972–3. *Rec Buckinghamshire*, **20**, 18–22.

Price, J, 1976a Glass, in Strong, D, and Brown, D, *Roman Crafts*. London, 110–125

Price, J, 1976b Glass, in Jarrett, M G, *Maryport, Cumbria: A Roman Fort and its Garrison. Cumberland and Westmorland Antiq and Archaeol Soc, extra ser*, **22**, 49–54.

Price, J, 1977 The Roman Glass, in Gentry A, Ivens J, and McClean H, Excavations at Lincoln Road, London Borough of Enfield, November 1974-March 1976. *Trans of the London and Middlesex Archaeol Soc*, **28**, 154–161.

Price, J, 1978 The Glass Flask, in Collis, J, *Winchester Excavations, 2, 1949–1960*. Winchester City Museum, 102.

Price, J, 1979 The Glass, in Gracie, H S, and Price, E G, Frocester Court Roman Villa, 2nd Report 1968–77, The Courtyard, *Trans Bristol and Gloucestershire Archaeol Soc*, **97**, 37–46.

Price, J, 1980a The Roman Glass, in Lambrick, G, Excavations in Park Street, Towcester, 1963–8, *Northamptonshire Archaeol* **15**, 63–68.

Price, J, 1980b Roman Glass from 1 Westgate Street, Gloucester, in Heighway C, and Garrod P, Excavations at nos 1 and 30 Westgate Street, Gloucester: The Roman Levels. *Britannia*, 11, 110–4.

Price, J, 1981 The glass, in Jarrett, M G, and Wrathmell, S, *Whitton: an Iron Age and Roman farmstead in South Glamorgan*. Cardiff, University of Wales Press, 149–62.

Price, J, 1982a The Glass, in Webster, G and Smith, L, The Excavation of a Romano-British Rural Establishment at Barnsley Park, Gloucestershire, 1961–1979, Part II, *c* AD 3–60–400+. *Trans Bristol and Gloucestershire Archaeol Soc*, **100**, 174–185.

Price, J, 1982b The Roman Glass, in Leach, P, *Ilchester Volume 1, Excavations 1974–5;* 227–232.

Price, J, 1982c The Glass Jar, in Booth, P, A Romano-British Burial from Mancetter. *Trans Birmingham and Warwickshire Archaeol Soc*, **92**, 134.

Price, J, 1984 The Roman Glass Fragments, in Ellis, P, *Catsgore 1979, Further Excavation of the Romano-British Village. Western Archaeol Trust Monogr*, 7, 30–32.

Price, J, 1985a The Roman Glass, in Pitts L F, and St Joseph J K, *Inchtuthil the Roman Legionary Fortress. Britannia Monogr Ser*, **6**; 303–12.

Price, J, 1985b Two pieces of polychrome mosaic glass tableware from Roman Britain. *Antiq J*, **65**, 468–70.

Price, J, 1985c The Glass, in Bidwell P, T, *The Roman Fort of Vindolanda, English Heritage Archaeol Rep*, **1**, 206–14.

Price, J, 1986a Vessels of Glass, in Miles D, ed, *Archaeology at Barton Court Farm Abingdon, Oxon. CBA Res Rep* 50, MF 6: A7–A14.

Price, J, 1986b Glass Jug, in Stead, I M, and Rigby, V, *Baldock: The Excavation of a Roman and Pre- Roman Settlement 1968–72. Britannia Monogr Ser*, **7**, 61–3.

Price, J, 1987a Glass from Felmongers, Harlow in Essex. A Dated Deposit of Vessel Glass found in an Antonine Pit. *Annales du 10e Congres de l'Association Internationale pour l'Histoire du Verre (Madrid 1985)*, 185–206.

Price J 1987b Late Hellenistic and early Imperial cast glass in Spain. *Annales du 10e Congrès de l'Association Internationale pour l'Histoire du Verre (Madrid 1985)*, 61–80.

Price, J, 1987c The Roman Glass, in Frere, S S, Brandon Camp, Herefordshire. *Britannia*, **18**, 71–76.

Price, J, 1987d Glass, in Mynard, D C, (ed), *Roman Milton Keynes, Excavations and Fieldwork 1971–82. Buckinghamshire Archaeol Soc Monogr Ser*, **1**, 147–57.

Price, J, 1987e The Roman vessel glass. In Woodward, P J, The excavation of a Late Iron Age settlement and Romano-British industrial site at Ower, Dorset. *Romano-British Industries in Purbeck. Dorset Nat Hist and Archaeol Soc Monogr* no **6**, 102–4.

Price, J, 1989a Glass, in Stead I M and Rigby V, *Verulamium, the King Harry Lane Site. Engl Heritage Archaeol Rep*, **12**, 40–50.

Price, J, 1989b The Glass, in O'Leary, T J, *Pentre Farm, Flint 1976–81. BAR British Series*, **207**; 77–86.

Price, J, 1989 The Roman Glass, in Frere S S, and Wilkes J J, *Strageath, Excavations within the Roman Fort 1973–86. Britannia Monogr Series*, **9**, 192–203.

Price, J, 1990a Roman Vessel and Window Glass, in McCarthy M R, *A Roman, Anglian and Medieval Site at Blackfriars Street, Carlisle. Cumberland and Westmorland Antiq and Archaeol Soc Res Ser*, **4**, 163–79.

Price J 1990b The glass. In Wrathmell S & Nicholson A eds, *Dalton Parlours. Iron Age settlement and Roman villa. Yorkshire Archaeol* **3**, 99–105.

Price, J, 1991a Glass, in Wilmott, T, *Excavations in the Middle Walbrook Valley, City of London, 1927–60.* London and Middlesex Archaeol Soc Special Paper **13**, 153–167.

Price, J, 1991b Decorated Mould-Blown Glass Tablewares in the First Century AD in Newby, M, and Painter, K.

Price J 1993a The Romano-British glass, in Blockley K, Ashmore F and P J, Excavations on the Roman fort at Abergavenny Orchard Site, 1972–73. *Archaeol J* **150**, 215–20.

Price, J, 1993b Vessel Glass, in Woodward, A, and Leach, P, *The Uley Shrines, Excavation of a Ritual Complex on West Hill, Uley, Gloucestershire: 1977–9*. Engl Heritage Archaeol Rep, **17**, 210–5.

Price, J, 1994 Glass – Roman, in Zeepvat, R J, Roberts, J S, and King, N A, *Caldecotte, Milton Keynes, excavations and fieldwork 1966–91*. Buckinghamshire Archaeol Soc Monogr Series **9**, 133–6.

Price, J, 1995a Glass Vessels, in Manning, W H, Price, J and Webster, J, *Report on the Excavations at Usk 1965–1976. The Roman Small Finds*. Cardiff, University of Wales Press, 139–191.

Price, J, 1995b Roman Glass, in Phillips, D, and Heywood, B, *Excavations at York Minster, Vol 1: From Roman Fortress to Norman Cathedral*. Royal Commission on the Historical Monuments of England. London, 346–71.

Price, J 1995c Glass Tableware with Wheel-cut Engraved and Abraded Decoration in Britain in the Fourth Century AD in Foy 1995, 25–33.

Price, J, 1995d The Roman Glass, in Casey, P J, and Hoffmann, B, Excavations at Alstone Cottage, Caerleon, 1970. *Britannia*, **26**, 80–8.

Price, J, 1995e The Canterbury-London Group of Chariot-Race Cups, in Blockley, K, Blockley, M, Blockley, P, Frere, S, and Stow, S, *Excavations in the Marlowe Car Park and surrounding areas. The Archaeology of Canterbury, 5. Canterbury Archaeological Trust*, 1220–27.

Price, J, 1996a A ribbed bowl from a late Iron Age burial at Hertford Heath, Hertfordshire. *Annales du 13e Congres de l'Association Internationale pour l'Historire du Verre (Amsterdam 1995)*, 47–54.

Price, J, 1996b Glass, in Jackson, R P J and Potter, T W, *Excavations at Stonea, Cambridgeshire, 1980–85*. British Museum Press, 379–409.

Price, J, and Cool, H E M, 1983 Glass from the Excavations of 1974–76, in Brown A E and Woodfield C, Excavations at Towcester, Northamptonshire: The Alchester Road Suburb. *Northamptonshire Archaeol*, **18**, 115–124.

Price, J, and Cool, H E M, 1985 Glass, in Hurst H R, *Kingsholm. Gloucester Archaeol Reps*, 1, 41–54.

Price, J, and Cool, H E M, 1989a Report on the Roman Glass found at the Cattlemarket, County Hall and East Pallant House sites, Chichester, in Down, A, *Chichester Excavations, 6*. Chichester Excavatons Comm, 132–42.

Price, J, and Cool, H E M, 1991 The Evidence for the Production of Glass in Roman Britain, in Foy, D, and Sennequier, G, (eds), *Ateliers de Verriers de l'Antiquité a la Periode Pre-industrielle. Actes du 4ème Recontres de l'Association Francaise pour l'Archéologie du Verre*. Rouen, 23–9.

Price, J, and Cool, H E M, 1993 The Vessel Glass, in Darling, M J with Gurney, D, *Caister-on-Sea Excavations by Charles Green, 1951–55. East Anglian Archaeol Rep*, **60**, 141–52.

Price J, and Cottam S, 1994 Glass, in Cracknell, S, and Mahaney, C, (eds), *Roman Alcester Vol I, Southern Extramural Area 1964–1966 Excavations. Part 2, Finds and discussion. CBA Res Rep*, **97**, 224–229.

Price J and Cottam S, 1995 Late Roman glass bowls from Beadlam villa, North Yorkshire. In Vyner B ed, *Moorland Monuments: Studies in the Archaeology of North-East Yorkshire in honour of Raymond Hayes and Don Spratt. CBA Res Rep*, **101**, 235–42.

Price, J and Cottam, S, 1996a The Roman glass from Fishbourne, 1983 and 1985–6, in Cunliffe, B, Down, A, and Rudkin, D *Excavations at Fishbourne 1969–1988, Chichester excavations*, **9**, 166–88.

Price, J and Cottam, S, 1996b The glass, in Neal, D S, *Excavations on the Roman villa at Beadlam, Yorkshire. Yorkshire Archaeol Rep 2*. Yorkshire Archaeol Soc, 93–108.

Price, J and Cottam, S, 1997a Roman glass, in Wilmott, T, *Birdoswald. Excavations of a Roman fort on Hadrian's Wall and its successor settlements: 1987–92. Engl Heritage Archaeol Rep* **14**, 341–55.

Price, J and Cottam, S, 1997b Roman glass, in Wenham, L P and Heywood, B. *The 1968 to 1970 excavations in the vicus at Malton, North Yorkshire. Yorkshire Archaeol Rep 2*. Yorkshire Archaeol Soc, 118–131.

Price, J and Cottam, S, 1998 Vessel glass, in Leach, P, *Great Witcombe Roman villa, Gloucestershire. A report on excavations by Ernest Greenfield 1960–1973*. BAR British Series 266, 73–81.

Price, J E, 1888 *Contents of the Private Museum of Anglo-Roman Antiquities Collected by Mr George Joslin at Colchester, Essex*. Colchester.

Rashleigh, P, 1803 Account of a further discovery of antiquities at Southfleet in Kent. *Archeologia* **14**, 221–3.

RCHM London 1928 *Roman London. An Inventory of the Historical Monuments in London*, **3**. Royal Comm Hist Monuments Engl. HMSO.

Renfrew, C, nd, *Bourton-on-the-Water Roman settlement. An area near Bourton Bridge, near Bourton-on-the-Water, Gloucestershire*. Privately printed.

RIB II, 2 Collingwood, R G & Wright, R P, *The Roman Inscriptions of Britain*. Frere S S & Tomlin R S O (eds), 1991 *Volume II: Instrumentum Domesticum Fascicule 2: weights, gold vessel, silver vessell, bronze vessls, lead vessels, pewter vessels, shale vessels, glass vessels, spoons*. Stroud, Alan Sutton.

Richmond, I A, and Gillam, J P, 1952 Further exploration of the Antonine Fort at Corbridge. *Archaeol Aeliana*, 4th series, **30**, 239–266.

Ritterling, E, 1912/13 *Das Fruhrömische Lager bei Hofheim im Taunus*. Wiesbaden.

Roach Smith, C, 1846 Roman vessel glass discovered near Shefford, Bedfordshire. *Archaeologia*, **31**, 488.

Roach Smith, C, 1850 *The Antiquities of Richborough, Reculver and Lymne*.

Roach Smith, C, 1868 *Collectanea Antiqua*, 6. Privately printed.

Robertson, A S, 1975 *Birrens (Blatobulgium)*. Edinburgh.

Robertson, Canon S, 1883 Traces of Roman occupation in and near Maidstone. *Archaeol Cantiana*, **15**, 68–88.

Rodwell, W, 1976 The glass, in Drury, P J, Braintree: excavations and research, 1971–76. *Essex Archaeol and Hist*, **8**, 37–8.

Rütti, B, 1991 *Die römischen Gläser aus Augst und Kaiseraugst. Forschungen in Augst, Band 13*. Augst.

Saunders, A D, 1961 Excavations at Park Street, 1954–57. *Archaeol J*, **118**, 100–35.

Scarth, H M, 1864 *Aquae Sulis, or Notices of Roman Bath*. London and Bath.

Schwab, I, 1974 Glass, in Sheldon, H, Excavations at Toppings' and Sun Wharves, Southwark, 1970–1972. *Trans London and Middlesex Archaeol Soc*, **25**, 103–7.

Shepherd, J, 1985 Roman Glass, in Cunliffe, B and Davenport, P, *The Temple of Sulis Minerva at Bath. Volume 1 (1): The site. Oxford University Comm Archaeol, Monogr* 7, 161–4.

Shepherd, J, 1986 The Vessel and Window Glass, in McWhirr A, *Houses in Roman Cirencester. Cirencester Excavations* 3, 117–121.

Shepherd, J, 1995a The glass vessels, in Blockley, K, Blockley, M, Blockley, P, Frere, S S, and Stow, S, *Excavations in the Marlowe car park and surrounding areas. The Archaeology of Canterbury, V. Canterbury Archaeological Trust*, 1227–60.

Shepherd, J, 1995b The Glass, in Cowan C, A possible mansio in Roman Southwark. Excavations at 15–23 Southwark Street, 1980–86. *Proc London and Middlesex Archaeol Soc*, **43** (1992), 120–36.

Shepherd, J, 1996 The glass, in Milne, G and Wardle, A, Early Roman development at Leadenhall Court, London, and related research. *Trans London and Middlesex Archaeol Soc*, **44** (1993), 99–114.

Shepherd, J D, and Heyworth, M, 1991 Le Travail du Verre dans Londres Romain (Londinium); un Etat de la Question. In Foy, D, and Sennequier, G (eds), *Ateliers de Verriers de L'antiquité à la Periode Pre-industrielle. Actes des 4èmes Rencontres de l'Association Francaise pour l'Archéologie du Verre*. Rouen, 13–22.

Skilbeck, C O, 1923 Notes on the Discovery of a Roman Burial at Radnage, Buckinghamshire. *Antiq J*, **3**, 334–337.

Sumner H 1924 *Excavations at East Grimstead, Wiltshire*. London.

Tatton-Brown V 1987 Glass vessels from Cranmer House, London Road. in Frere SS, Bennett P, Rady J and Stow S, *Canterbury Excavations. Intra- and Extra-Mural Sites, 1949–55 and 1980–84. The Archaeol Canterbury*, **8**, 280–2.

Thorpe, W A, 1933–4 A Glass Jug of Roman Date From Turriff, *Proc Soc of Antiq Scotl*, **68**, 439–44.

Thorpe, W A, 1935 *English Glass*. London.

Tomalin, D J, 1987 *Roman Wight: A Guide Catalogue to 'The Island of Vectis, very near to Britannia'*.

Townend, P, and Hinton, P, 1978a Glass from 1–7 St Thomas Street, in Bird *et al* (eds), 1978, 387–9.

Townend, P, and Hinton, P, 1978b Glass from 201–211 Borough High Street, in Bird *et al* (eds), 1978, 151–3.

Townend, P, and Hinton, P, 1978c Glass from 93–95 Borough High Street, in Bird *et al* (eds), 1978, 462.

Toynbee, J M C, 1962 *Art in Roman Britain*. Phaidon Press.

van Lith, S M E, 1991 First Century Cantheroi with a Stemmed Foot: their distribution and social significance, in Newby, M, and Painter, K.

von Saldern, A, 1991 Roman Glass with Decoration in High-Relief, in Newby, M, and Painter, K.

Westell, W P, 1931 A Romano-British Cemetery at Baldock, Herts. *Archaeol J*, **88**, 247–301.

Wheeler, R E M, 1930 *London in Roman Times*. London Museum Catalogue No 3

Wheeler R E M, and Wheeler, T V, 1936 *Verulamium: A Belgic and Two Roman Cities. Rep Res Comm Soc Antiq London*, **11**.

Whiting, W, 1926 The Roman Cemeteries at Ospringe: Description of the Finds Concluded. *Archaeologia Cantiana*, **38**, 123–51.

Whiting *et al*, 1931 Whiting, W, Hawley, W and May, T, *Report on the Excavation of the Roman Cemetery at Ospringe, Kent. Rep Res Comm Soc Antiq London*, **8**.

Wickham, H, 1874 Roman Remains from Luton, Chatham. *Archaeologia Cantiana*, **9**, 174–5.

Wilson, R D, 1969 Roman Britain in 1968, I. Sites Explored. *J Roman Studies*, **59**, 198–234.

Woodruff, C H, 1902 Romano-British Interments at Lower Walmer. *Archaeologia Cantiana*, **25**, 1–10.

Yadin, Y, 1963 *The Finds from the Bar-Kokhba Period in the Cave of Letters.* Jerusalem.

Yates, J, 1849 Account of a Roman sepulchre at Geldestone, *Norfolk. Archaeol J*, **6**, 109–13.

Zienkiewicz, J D, 1992 Roman Glass Vessels from Caerleon: Excavations at the Legionary Museum Site, 1983–5. *Monmouthshire Antiq*, **8**, 1–9.

Index to Part I   *by Susan Vaughan*

Page numbers in italics indicate illustrations

233